SOURCES IN WESTERN CIVILIZATION

Rome

Sources in Western Civilization

GENERAL EDITOR, *Herbert H. Rowen*
RUTGERS UNIVERSITY

ROME

EDITED BY

William G. Sinnigen

HUNTER COLLEGE OF THE CITY UNIVERSITY OF NEW YORK

THE FREE PRESS, NEW YORK

Collier-Macmillan Limited, London

CONTENTS

SOURCES IN WESTERN CIVILIZATION

Rome

Introduction

I. THE MONARCHY (*ca.* 753–509 B.C.)

Rome was founded, probably about the middle of the eighth century B.C., by shepherds and farmers of essentially Latin extraction. Their settlement on the Palatine was one among several hilltop villages clustered near the Tiber some fifteen miles from its mouth. Although the site was not without disadvantages, it was easily protected, strategically located, and favorable to development by an energetic population.

The society and government of this primitive settlement, like that of other Indo-European peoples, was strongly patriarchal and conservative. This pattern was to remain characteristic of the Romans during much of their history. Theirs was a no-nonsense world of obedience to authority, of perseverance, and of keeping faith in unsettled times when it made sense to do so. Roman ideals were epitomized and transmitted by the most important division of their society, the patriarchal clan (*gens*), which at first performed the social, religious, and economic functions that were only gradually assumed later by the state. The clans were divided in turn into families, over each of which presided with absolute authority a *paterfamilias,* whose word was law even to his adult sons and who performed the sacred rites of the household. The clans assumed the role of patrons of a motley class of dependents or clients, which they protected in return for military and other services. The client system was an extremely important feature of Roman society and, in various forms, was to play an essential role throughout Roman history. Another basic and ever-widening division in the citizenry appeared at an early date, although its origins are obscure. This was the cleavage between the aristocrats or patricians, who increasingly insisted on their economic, social, and political predominance, and a heterogeneous group of commoners or plebeians, composed not merely of peasants and clients but also of prosperous and even prominent citizens.

The power of the clan elders was reflected in the position of the king of this petty settlement, whose office was elective rather than dynastic and whose power was circumscribed in various ways. Although technically the king was supreme warlord, judge, and priest, his authority was limited by the clan organization and by the characteristically Roman habit of taking advice before action. Roman kings turned for advice to a council of elders or senate, allegedly 300 men strong, which probably represented the collective opinion of the patrician clans. Since the success of the state ultimately depended upon the cooperation of the armsbearing citizenry of all classes, the king and his council found it expedient to inform the people of important decisions and therefore convoked on occasion a gathering called the Curiate Assembly. This organization had no power to legislate, yet in the idea of assembly lay the seed for future development along democratic lines.

Little is known definitely about the history of this monarchic city-state. It seems probable that political union of the various hilltop villages under one king had occurred by about 600 B.C. The increasing maturity of Roman life in the early sixth century is reflected in the creation of a market place located in what later became the Forum. It is also reflected in military reorganization by the king, Servius Tullius — if this actually happened at that time. According to one of the selections from Livy [1]*, this ruler organized the citizenry into "centuries" of 100 men and allotted different military duties to each class in the state on the basis of wealth.

These events took place against a background of constant intercourse — both peaceful and warlike — between the Romans and the other peoples of central and southern Italy. These included Italic hill tribes, kindred Latin city-states in the plain of Latium, Greek colonies on the shores of southern Italy, and the Etruscans to the north. There is early evidence of the cultural influence of the Greek colonies on Rome, and Etruscan influence was particularly important during the monarchic period. The Etruscans, who were probably immigrants from western Asia Minor, were firmly settled in Tuscany at the time of Rome's founding. They developed a civilization far superior to anything native to north-central Italy; and by virtue of their powers of organization and their technical skill, they were able during various periods of their history to expand as far south as the Bay of Naples and as far north as the Po Valley. Etruscan kings ruled Rome during part of the sixth century, but we must be wary of ascribing a sudden effulgence of Roman power to Etruscan domination. The

* Bracketed numbers refer to selections in text.

Etruscans left Rome essentially as they had found it, still a petty
city-state. Nevertheless, the Romans owed to the Etruscans lasting
features of their cultural life, especially engineering and architectural
techniques, regalia of office, and religious practices such as divination.

The Monarchy laid the foundations for future greatness, but it was
not destined to endure as Rome's form of government. The circumstances surrounding its demise and even the date of its fall are uncertain, but it seems probable that the kingship came to an end with
the expulsion of the Etruscan King Tarquin the Proud shortly before 500 B.C. Drawing on parallels in the corresponding phase of
Greek historical development, we may assume that the patricians,
chafing under high-handed foreign monarchs who did not respect
their prestige (*dignitas*) or their advice, led a movement that wrested
control of the state from the king. Forever afterward the very word
"king" (*rex*) was anathema to the Roman upper classes.

2. THE EARLY REPUBLIC (*ca.* 509–265 B.C.)

Generally speaking, the patrician class was the immediate and
sole beneficiary of the political revolution that created the Republic.
By the early fifth century it was in absolute control of the principal
offices of the state, including the consulship, a dual, annual, and
elected magistracy that replaced the defunct king in wielding supreme civil and military power, the *imperium*. The patricians, realizing the desirability of unified command in time of emergency, provided that the power of the consuls could be superseded by that of a
dictator for a term of six months. Patricians likewise monopolized
the priestly functions formerly wielded by the king, and in an age
when religion, taboo, and as yet unwritten law were all but identical,
they were able to interpret custom and "find" laws in their own interest. The senate, which was composed entirely of patricians, remained as the supreme consultative body in the state.

Like the Monarchy, the aristocratic commonwealth still found itself obliged to refer to the population at large on important matters.
The armed citizens of all classes, organized in centuries, were convoked as the Centuriate Assembly, which replaced the Curiate and
became the chief legislative body in the state, electing the consuls
and acting as a court of appeals. It was far from being a democratic
organization, however, for the patricians held it in effective control,
the plebeians were grossly under-represented, and the consuls, who
presided over its sessions, rarely permitted the election of candidates
or the passage of laws harmful to their own class. Furthermore, any

laws it passed had to be ratified by the senate before coming into effect.

Under patrician control the plebeian class could hope for little improvement of its social and economic conditions by the normal political means available to it. Prominent plebeians resented their exclusion from office and membership in the senate, which was the only means for attaining prestige. Poorer plebeians were threatened with bankruptcy by the constant military demands made on them by the state, and indebtedness to patricians ruined them when the judges interpreted in favor of their own class the harsh, unwritten laws permitting debt slavery. A selection from Livy shows how tension increased during the fifth century until the "striking" plebeians seceded from Rome and, meeting outside the city as the Tribal Council (so-called from a basic division of Rome's population into tribes), refused to return until the patricians granted certain concessions, including recognition of their council and of their leaders, the tribunes, as the protectors of plebeian interests. The patricians, whose power ultimately rested on plebeian cooperation in fighting Rome's wars, were obliged to give way. The plebeians continued, however, to struggle for further liberalization of the constitution. The patricians resisted bitterly, but the specter of "strikes" wrung important concessions from them over a period of two centuries.

Landmarks in this development were the promulgation of Rome's first written laws, the Twelve Tables (*ca.* 450); the Sextio-Licinian Laws (367), which may have guaranteed plebeian tenure of at least one consulship each year; and the Hortensian Law (287), which decreed that plebiscites passed by the tribes were valid whether or not subsequently approved by the senate. The Tribal Council thereupon became a full-fledged public assembly and competed with the Centuriate as Rome's primary legislative organ. Colonization and improved debtor legislation alleviated the worst forms of economic distress, and gradually prominent plebeians who were elected to the new offices created in the expanding state were admitted into the senate. These new offices included the military tribunes with consular power, who intermittently replaced the consuls as chief executives during the period 444–367 B.C.; the censors, who assigned citizens to the various military centuries and eventually had the power to expel members from the senate; the quaestors, who were consular assistants in the administration of criminal law; the aediles, who supervised public works and markets; and the praetors, who possessed *imperium* and were junior colleagues of the consuls in charge of civil law. Plebeians likewise reached the rank of promagistrate, which was evolved in the fourth century. The promagistracy was essentially a prolongation of consular and praetorian *imperium* over Rome's armies, and later over her provinces.

Rome's constitutional development during the period was directly related to her steady expansion through Italy. Only the barest outline may be given here: almost continuous warfare in cooperation with the Latin League against marauding Italic hill tribes; conquest of Etruscan Veii at Rome's very doorstep about 400 B.C.; the nearly catastrophic Celtic invasion of 390; the revolt of the Latins against Rome's hegemony, their defeat, and their attachment to the Republic on a federal basis in 338; and, finally, Roman intervention in south Italy at the request of Greek cities to protect them against barbaric highlanders. This intervention eventually involved Rome in her first war with a non-Italian power, Pyrrhus of Epirus (281). By 265 B.C. Rome achieved political control over the Italian peninsula by virtue of her discipline, her organization, and her political common sense.

It is difficult to characterize this phase of Rome's development as being exclusively imperialistic. Roman expansion often provided land for her growing population, but population pressure was easily accommodated, and Rome seems not to have been overly eager to annex territory. Without wishing to idealize the Romans, who professed to believe that the wars they waged were inevitably just and purely defensive, we can say that they consciously — though not disinterestedly — championed the cause of civilized populations in Italy. A selection from Livy shows that their involvements made them realize that political entanglements followed military interventions and that they rose to these occasions by creating a remarkably sane and eminently flexible system of federation, which guaranteed stability not only to themselves but also to the many other people of the peninsula.

3. ROME'S RISE TO MEDITERRANEAN LEADERSHIP (265–133 B.C.)

The third century was dominated by Rome's two great wars with Carthage, a powerful Phoenician colony controlled by traders and plantation owners. The non-commercially-minded Romans maintained good relations with Carthage until shortly before the First Punic War (264–241), but conflict resulted when Rome, fearing that a threatened Punic conquest of Messina in Sicily might be a prelude to an attack on mainland Italy, came to the aid of that city and thereby collided with Carthage. The First Punic War made the Romans an important naval power for the first time and gave them after their eventual final victory their first overseas provinces, in Sicily, Sardinia, and Corsica.

The selections from Polybius [2] show how the following decades witnessed a resurgent Carthage recouping her losses by an energetic program of military expansion in Spain under Hamilcar Barca and his son, Hannibal, leaders of the Carthaginians who wanted revenge upon Rome. The Romans attempted to limit Carthaginian expansion by treaty, but Hannibal's attack on one of Rome's Spanish allies in 219 led to war. The Second Punic War (218–201) was the most momentous that Rome ever fought, not only because it decided definitely the question of who would dominate the western Mediterranean, but also because of its internal repercussions on the state.

Hannibal's strategy was to strike at Rome's heartland and to destroy the confederation of states that was the basis of Roman strength. Descending on Italy via the Alps, he inflicted a series of terrible defeats on the Romans. Rome gradually realized that Hannibal could be defeated only by waging a war of attrition in Italy while maintaining offensives on other fronts, in Sicily, Spain, and finally Africa. Having failed to break Rome's Italian alliances, Hannibal was forced to evacuate Italy in order to defend Carthage itself against attack by the popular and able Publius Cornelius Scipio (Africanus). Scipio's victory at Zama in 202 B.C. ended the war. Carthage ceded her Spanish territories to Rome and became a client state, with only technical independence. This relationship, and the very existence of Carthage, came to an end with her revolt and subsequent destruction in the Third Punic War two generations later (149–146).

It seems extraordinary that Rome should have embarked on yet another series of wars, this time in the Greek East, immediately after the end of the Second Punic War. To understand the reasons for her actions, one must note political conditions in the Hellenistic world in the third century, following the break-up of Alexander's empire. A complex state system had emerged in this highly civilized, cosmopolitan world, consisting of three first-rank powers — Macedonia, the Seleucid Empire, and Ptolemaic Egypt — and several consequential but generally less powerful states — the Achaean and Aetolian Federal Leagues, Athens, Rhodes, and Pergamum. Wars were frequent as the larger states sought to maintain a precarious balance of power and the smaller struggled to preserve their independence. Except for brief periods, Rome's relations with the Greek East had been disinterested.

By 200 B.C., however, Rome was drawn into Greek politics. Her military prowess and her apparent lack of imperialistic designs made her appear to the smaller Hellenistic states as a suitable protector of their threatened interests. A series of developments not unlike those that had brought about Rome's rise in Italy and in the western Mediterranean resulted. Smaller Greek states appealed to Rome for help, generally against Macedonia or the Seleucids, suggesting that unless these great powers were humbled, they would eventually pose a direct threat to Italy. Although this was probably not the case, the Romans, after their recent traumatic experience of the Punic invasion, were persuaded that the Greek suggestion was true. Realization of the commercial advantages of imperialism was also gradually dawning on thoughtful Romans in the early second century, even though economic motivations for involvement in the East were initially far less important than political ones.

In the long course of the wars fought during the period 200–146 B.C., Rome eventually discovered that her entanglements in Greek affairs could lead only to the direct annexation of the areas concerned if there was to be lasting peace. At first, however, she withdrew her expeditionary forces following her victories in Greece and in Asia Minor, and early in the second century (196) she even proclaimed "freedom" for Greece. Unfortunately, freedom did not mean the same things to the Hellenes as to their protectors. The Greek states, even those that requested Roman help, felt free to pursue their own aggrandizement. But Rome thought of herself as a patron and of the Greeks as clients, which meant that the Greeks were to pursue only such foreign policies as were congruent with Roman interests. Misunderstandings produced tensions and eventually rebellions against what the Greeks regarded as intolerable Roman interference in their affairs. The exasperated Romans crushed a series of revolts with increasing ruthlessness and finally annexed their first Eastern province in 148 B.C. Thereafter the increasingly few states that remained independent, including Egypt, did so only on Rome's sufferance.

4. INTERNAL DEVELOPMENTS (265–133 B.C.)

Within Italy this was a period of surprising political tranquility. It was marked by two interrelated trends: increasing failure of the mass of Roman citizens, now scattered in colonies throughout Italy, to exercise their political responsibilities, and the complete ascendancy of the senate over the popular assemblies. Although technically democratic, Rome was in fact governed by an "interlocking directorate" composed of a few patrician and plebeian families, an oligarchy that developed when officeholding ceased to be a prerogative of aristocratic birth. Although this oligarchy was split by family alliances and factions, it was united in its determination to exclude new men from high office and to prevent any single statesman from dominating public life.

A significant development during this period was the rise of an important commercial class. Rome's increasingly sophisticated economic interests demanded enterprising men to direct her trade, build her public works, manage her war contracts, and collect her taxes. Since senators were excluded from commerce and industry by custom and law, only the "middle" or equestrian class could provide such men. The importance of this class increased markedly as the second century progressed; ultimately (122 B.C.) equestrians became tax-farmers (*publicani*), collecting revenue from Rome's expanding network of provinces. Although excluded from the oligarchy and basically non-political, the equestrians were inevitably drawn into politics whenever the senate threatened to infringe on their economic prerogatives.

Possibly the most important social and economic development of the age was the gradual decay of the yeoman class on whom the Republic had depended for its legionaries. Its security was in large measure destroyed by the cataclysm of Hannibalic invasion and by subsequent military events, the Second Punic War in particular having devastated and depopulated large areas of Italy. Farmers called away to fight for years on end returned to find their homesteads and fields neglected. Even if they were not mobilized again to fight other wars in the East, they found it difficult to re-establish themselves. Gradually they sold or abandoned their holdings and drifted to the cities, which in the long run offered them limited opportunities for employment and where they eventually became an indigent and demoralized proletariat.

The senate realized the existence of this problem and occasionally attempted resettlement programs. The yeomanry did not disappear completely, nor did agricultural free labor entirely give way to slave gangs, but circumstances were working against any real form. The senators themselves were eager to increase their holdings by buying up farms at bargain prices and by undertaking the cultivation of waste or public land. They could do so profitably by exploiting the mounting flood of war-provided slave labor, which was becoming a decisive factor in the economy, and by converting their estates from cereal agriculture to sheep-herding and the cultivation of the vine and the olive. Large ranches and plantations (*latifundia*) were formed, under the ownership of absentee landlords. Selections from the handbook written by Cato the Censor to instruct the gentleman farmer illustrate the growing interest in scientific agriculture [3].

Rome emerged from cultural backwardness as a result of Greek influence in the third and second centuries. This influence increased as Rome's political involvement extended beyond Sicily to the Greek East and became both close and permanent. Romans such as Scipio and his friends, who experienced the intellectual and artistic amenities of Greek life at first hand, encouraged their imitation at Rome. A minority of archconservatives such as Cato fulminated against the indiscriminate acceptance of Greek ways as being un-Roman, but were little heeded by an increasingly sophisticated society.

Roman literature began modestly in this period with translations of Homeric verse into Latin by Livius Andronicus (*ca.* 284–204), followed by Latin epics composed on Homeric models by Ennius (239–169). Tragedies and comedies, also inspired by Greek works, were produced. The most important comedies were the plays of Plautus (254–184) and Terence (195–159), which rely heavily on the plots and situations of Greek New Comedy. With Fabius Pictor (*ca.* 200) the writing of Roman history began in its characteristically annalistic form. Some historians sought chiefly to justify or to explain Rome's rise to greatness; the most important of these was the Greek Polybius [2], who wrote at Rome under Scipionic patronage. Also introduced at this period were the two great Hellenistic philosophies, Epicureanism and Stoicism. The former was often misunderstood as an invitation to high living, and Romans were much better suited to the practice of Stoicism, which appealed to their sense of duty and became an important and positive force in intelligent society. The Hellenistic world also contributed to Rome's religious development, for Oriental cults, with their exotic rituals, were increasingly attractive to those whose own pantheon appeared cold and formal in comparison.

5. CHALLENGES TO OLIGARCHY (133–79 B.C.)

As the second century progressed, Rome's brilliant successes abroad tended to obscure the fact that all was not right in the Re-

public. Traditional standards of political morality were being corrupted by the ruthless exploitation of vast human and material
resources in the provinces. Of greater immediate importance were
the growing inability of the state to find enough yeoman legionaries
to fight its wars and a noticeable decline in military discipline and
morale. Only drastic reform could rebuild the yeoman class and
Rome's military manpower. In the decade following 133 B.C. the
cause of reform was embraced by two brothers from the liberal wing
of the senatorial oligarchy, the plebeian tribunes Tiberius and Gaius
Gracchus, who set in motion a chain of events that eventually destroyed senatorial control of government and brought about one-man
rule.

The selection from Appian [4] shows the range and nature of the
reforms of the Gracchi. They did not seek violent overthrow of the
existing social order, and their proposal for redistribution of land,
even if it had been fully carried out, would have left the bulk of
senatorial estates intact. Nevertheless, the senate short-sightedly opposed basic land reform. The oligarchy also feared the methods of
the Gracchi, who went so far as to circumvent senatorial authority by
appeals to the Tribal Assembly and by alliance with the equestrians.
Fearing any loss of its power and that the Gracchi were bringing
about mob rule, the senate eventually sanctioned the use of violence to destroy them. The Gracchan program, which really treated
the symptoms rather than the causes of economic and social distress,
became a dead letter within little more than a generation.

The causes of the upheaval that ensued were primarily social and
economic, but political aspects soon became paramount. The frequent
revolutions that followed during the century after the Gracchi were
essentially a struggle between two factions, the *optimates* and the
populares. The *optimates* represented the bulk of the senate and
stood for continued oligarchic control of the state and the least possible reform, while the *populares* were ambitious senators who
sought personal political aggrandizement by defying their fellow
oligarchs and by championing the cause of the discontented elements
in the state, including on one or another occasion the proletariat,
Rome's Italian allies, the equestrians, and eventually the army. The
age of the Gracchi was followed by a series of crises, essentially
political challenges by individuals against rule by a reactionary governing elite. The senate met these challenges ineptly, and, since the
popular assemblies were by now quite unrepresentative and demoralized, real leadership fell into the hands of whoever could gain
control of the commonwealth by force.

The next important challenge to the oligarchy came from Gaius Marius, a political upstart who, in contrast to the senate's ineptitude, waged successful war against Jugurtha of Numidia and Germanic barbarians in Gaul. His success brought him unprecedented and continuous tenure as consul for five years (104–100 B.C.), and his military reforms set a dangerous precedent for ambitious generals in the future. Ignoring the usual methods of levy, he enrolled the proletariat in his armies, and his troops felt that it was he, rather than the senate, to whom they owed their separation benefits in the form of land grants. He thus discovered the principle of client armies, which subsequent generals like Sulla used to advance their own careers.

A decade of turmoil followed Marius' emergence on the political scene and culminated in the so-called Social War (90–88 B.C.), a successful revolution by Rome's Italian allies for attainment of complete Roman citizenship. It was during the Social War and another war fought in the East against Mithradates, King of Pontus, that the optimate Sulla, Marius' arch enemy, attained prominence and became dictator (82–80). Sulla sought to introduce basic reforms to protect the power of the senate against ambitious generals, but they proved short-lived. Indeed, the very methods Sulla used to gain control — military revolution, pitiless proscription of his opponents, and dictatorship — contradicted his professed belief that the senate could rule effectively.

6. THE ERA OF DYNASTS (79–27 B.C.)

The twenty years following Sulla's death were dominated by Pompey, one of the late dictator's henchmen, who was as ambitious for personal power and prestige as any other politician of his age, though at crucial moments he could not bring himself to defy the senate. Historically, Pompey's career was most important because he was voted powers to eliminate piracy and to destroy Mithradates. These powers, especially the proconsular *imperium,* which amounted to an extraordinary command over most of the Mediterranean basin (67–62 B.C.), were subsequently wielded by ambitious men like Caesar and were the prototype of the powers Augustus was granted when he created the Principate.

Mention must be made of the leading and occasionally decisive political role played by the orator Cicero. A "new man" but a staunch optimate, he advocated a united front of the propertied classes, both senatorial and equestrian, to stabilize the government on the occasion of Catiline's conspiracy in 63 B.C. Cicero delighted in playing the role of political mentor to leading statesmen like Pompey, but his political outlook was basically unrealistic.

Less scrupulous and more gifted than Pompey was his fellow-general and politician, Julius Caesar. Scion of an ancient patrician house, Caesar owed his success to singleness of purpose, ruthlessness tempered by a genuine clemency, and astonishing ability in many fields. He held his first consulship in 59 B.C. as the least important member of a triumvirate in which Pompey and Crassus, the richest man in Rome, were senior members. A decade later, following his brilliant conquest of Gaul, he contended with Pompey and the optimates for control of the Republic. After his victory in a bitter civil war (49–45), he turned his attention to reforming the state. As the selections from Suetonius show [6], Caesar energetically mobilized his dictatorial powers to reform the government in a direct and radical manner. But he was unable to persuade the senatorial oligarchy of the need for one-man rule and was assassinated. Whether Caesar's ultimate aims included monarchy on a Hellenistic model is debatable. In fact, if not in name, however, he had been King of Rome.

After Caesar's death in 44 B.C. the chief contenders for the leadership of the Caesarian party were Mark Antony, the dictator's foremost henchman, and Octavian, his teen-aged grandnephew, personal heir, and adopted son. After complicated maneuvers in which they occasionally cooperated with the ruling oligarchy, both men realized that their respective ambitions could be served only by an antisenatorial coalition. The result was the Second Triumvirate (43), which included Lepidus, a third Caesarian party leader. Another civil war followed, in which Caesar's assassins were eliminated (42), while the triumvirs savagely destroyed their remaining opponents by proscription. Lepidus was relegated to political oblivion, and Antony sought military glory in the East, while Octavian accepted the task of governing Italy and the West, although he was hated by the senatorial and equestrian classes, which had borne the brunt of proscriptions and land confiscations.

The decade following the Second Triumvirate was crucial, for the latent rivalry between Antony and Octavian became a struggle for empire. Octavian achieved the apparently impossible by restoring effective government and reconciling the propertied classes in Italy to his authority; Antony, on the other hand, made the fatal error of allying himself politically and personally with Cleopatra, the Greek queen of Egypt. Octavian thereupon mobilized public opinion in Italy against Antony by denouncing his rival as the tool of a foreign monarch. Octavian's victory in the ensuing civil war (31) and the suicide of Antony and Cleopatra left him without any serious political rival.

The society of the Late Republic was diverse and colorful. Below the small ruling class, the mass of humanity in such cities as Rome eked out a living at subsistence level, maintained in part by means of state relief. The situation in rural Italy was disturbed by confiscation of land to reward leaders of contending factions with princely *latifundia* and to settle thousands of veterans on smaller holdings. Many of these veterans became part of the municipal gentry of the various towns, where they maintained a much better sense of public spirit than existed in the capital. Economic conditions outside Italy varied widely. Venal conduct of Roman governors, illustrated by the selections from the *Verrine Orations* of Cicero [5], the passage of Roman armies, and outbreaks of piracy frequently disrupted the normal pursuits of agriculture, trade, and industry.

Roman culture reacted positively to the exciting tensions of political upheaval. Although the development of tragedy and comedy was abortive, the era was notable for first-rate poetry and prose. Only a few of the most outstanding artistic works and personalities can be mentioned here. The emotionally charged, bittersweet love poems of Catullus mirror vividly the life of Rome's "café society." The selections from Lucretius' *On the Nature of the Universe* [8, *a*], a work unique in Roman literature, reflect the ideals of a deeply sensitive adherent of Epicureanism. As might be expected, the age produced a flood of historical or quasi-historical writing of a politically partisan nature, outstanding among which were the works of Sallust and the brilliantly lucid memoirs of Caesar himself. Rome's creativity at this time was epitomized by the life and works of one man, Cicero. In his voluminous correspondence and in his many orations, Latin prose attained its most perfect expression. His philosophical works, while eclectic and less original, reveal his basically Stoic inclinations.

7. REFORMS OF AUGUSTUS (27 B.C.–A.D. 14)

The rule of Octavian, who was known as Augustus after 27 B.C., was epochal for the development of Rome — and indeed for all later Western civilization. During the years following Caesar's assassination he developed from an adroit politician into a statesman of the highest order, successfully meeting the challenges of revolution and remaking his world. His political testament [7] shows how he succeeded where Caesar had failed by concealing his essentially monarchic position and by appealing to respected precedents and constitutional traditions to make it appear that he was "restoring" the Republic. Few of his informed contemporaries were fooled, and few cared. After so many years of turmoil, the Roman world accepted stability under an enlightened ruler who professed to respect the social, economic, and political sensibilities of the classes that mattered.

Augustus, profiting by his experience of factional strife, realized that he could allow no political party or vested interest beside his own. He neutralized the bewildering medley of family alliances and pressure groups that made up the oligarchy, became the chief political patron of the commonwealth, and made all Romans his clients in one way or another. He did not destroy the traditional organs of Republican government. The assemblies and senate still met, senators continued to run for high office and to attain consulships and *dignitas,* and there was — initially at least — even some room for free speech. Augustus eschewed dictatorial powers and pretensions and professed to be no more than *princeps,* Rome's first citizen in a thoroughly Republican sense, but the truth was that initiative had passed from the oligarchy to one man and that the whole system functioned under the potentially autocratic though benevolent control of an emperor.

Following his acts of settlement in 27 and 23 B.C., Augustus based his government on senior proconsular *imperium* over garrisoned provinces and on his tribunician authority, by means of which he could effectively control legislation. Later he became *pontifex maximus,* chief priest of the state cult. Through control of the garrisoned provinces, which were governed by his legates, Augustus became the sole patron of Roman legionaries and prevented the rise of any potential rivals. The senatorial provinces, which were governed by ex-consuls and ex-praetors, could also be controlled by the emperor. Any real division of government between emperor and senate was more apparent than real, since the emperor's *imperium* exceeded that of any senator and since imperial *auctoritas,* the authority traditionally wielded by Rome's elder statesmen, could hardly be questioned by a senatorial officeholder. Furthermore, as a politician who understood the use of propaganda and psychology, Augustus fostered the mystique of imperial power by encouraging his own worship, along with that of the goddess Roma, in the provinces. Although in Rome and Italy he could not appear as a living divinity, even there he fostered cults to his genius or motivating force.

Perhaps the most revolutionary of his reforms was the broadening of the base of the social and political elite to include the equestrian classes of Italy, which for the first time became able to rise in society and the state. The support of the equestrians was essential to the government. Augustus used equestrian civil servants to counteract senatorial disloyalty, especially in the financial administration and in sensitive military posts such as the newly created prefectures of Egypt and the praetorian guard, and patronized their advancement to the senate. The equestrian class was in turn open to rejuvenation from below, because now the lower classes, having attained a measure of social mobility through army service, could eventually achieve equestrian rank. Society became more dynamic than during the Republic, as talented or ambitious men advanced in imperial service.

Augustus reorganized the Roman army as a professional standing force and simultaneously reduced the number of legions, realizing that an excessively large army was a drain on the Empire's human and natural resources and was unnecessary and dangerous once the civil wars had come to an end. Roman citizenship was still required for legionary service, but a noncitizen force of auxiliary troops was maintained; the auxiliaries were approximately equal in number to the legionaries and could themselves expect Roman citizenship upon their discharge. This new army, a remarkably effective fighting machine, was used by Augustus as the instrument of a markedly imperialistic foreign policy for much of his reign. Ultimately, however, he abandoned expansionism and sought to create defensive frontiers behind which Roman civilization could be consolidated peacefully. He himself was not an outstanding general and preferred to let such trusted subordinates as Agrippa and Tiberius undertake his campaigns. Augustus' ultimate defensive policy was successful, and at the end of his reign the frontiers rested on such natural boundaries as the Rhine and Danube or were insulated by client states that acted as buffers against possible barbarian invasion. His only notable failure was his attempt to reach the Elbe, which ended in a disastrous defeat at the hands of the Germans in A.D. 9.

Augustus also sought to change the moral tone of Roman society, which had strayed far from the puritanical ideals of an earlier day. He fostered old-fashioned religious cults and attempted to change upper-class morals by legislation. Large families were encouraged, childlessness became a disability for aspiring officeholders, and adultery was made an offense punishable by the state. Such measures were doomed to failure; the disgrace of the emperor's own daughter, the adulteress Julia, showed that it was impossible to change habits of life either by personal example or by fiat.

The political reforms instituted by Augustus, however useful they proved over the next two centuries, were marred by two basic weaknesses. Both derived from the contradiction between Augustus' constitutional status as a Roman magistrate whose tenure derived from the senate and people and his *de facto* status as emperor, ultimately dependent on control of the armed forces to maintain his position. The Principate depended normally upon continuity of imperial person and policy for its success, yet it might become urgently necessary to depose a worthless emperor. But magistrates could not normally be deposed during their tenure of office, and the position of emperor was in effect lifelong as well. Augustus himself wrestled with the problem of succession, and his solution was to make the imperial office hereditary within his own family. No solution was ever found to the problem of deposing an emperor without recourse to violence. It is no wonder that Rome was ruled by a succession of short dynasties, whose domination was punctuated — at least in the first century A.D. — by frequent plots, intrigues, and assassinations.

8. THE EARLY PRINCIPATE (A.D. 14–180)

No more than a bare outline of subsequent political events can be attempted here. During the period A.D. 14–68 Augustus was succeeded by the emperors of the Julio-Claudian house, his descendants by blood or by adoption. These included the morose but capable Tiberius, the mad Caligula, the pedantic and bureaucratically minded Claudius, and Nero, part fiend, part whimsical Epicurean. This dynasty came to an end in the revolutionary year 68–69, when, as Tacitus put it, the secret of empire was revealed — that an emperor could be made elsewhere than in Rome. In quick succession the field armies put three candidates on the throne, until Vespasian established the Flavian dynasty, which lasted through the reigns of his sons, Titus and Domitian, ending with the latter's assassination in A.D. 96. The center of government was stained with bloodshed, but the provinces were little affected by imperial caprice or tyranny. As the selection [9] from Tacitus shows, violence had been mainly directed against those nearest the emperors, especially the senators, among whom arose a bitter and sullen opposition to the Principate.

A politically tranquil period of astonishing length followed during the years A.D. 96–180, when emperors and senate were reconciled. This was the age of the "good emperors," a series of highminded rulers who fortunately had no sons and so could overcome dynastic problems by adopting as their successors capable or promising men. Thus the well-meaning but weak Nerva was succeeded by the brilliant general Trajan, under whom the Empire reached its greatest territorial extent. He was succeeded by his adopted son Hadrian, perhaps the most intriguing personality to occupy the throne — a man of the world, a consolidator of Empire, and a superb executive. The peaceful reign of Antoninus Pius, which followed, was a calm before the storm of barbarian invasion and plague that broke under Marcus Aurelius, a Stoic prince who met unflinchingly the calamities of his reign.

These events were the political background to an economic expansion in the Mediterranean world unparalleled before modern times. Imperial government for the most part adopted a laissez-faire attitude toward agriculture, industry, and commerce, except for the production and distribution of a few essential or strategic commodities, especially the grain supply for the city of Rome. Doctrinaire economic programs in the modern sense were all but unknown, and the economy depended primarily on almost unbroken peace for its continued development. Within the Empire widespread trade by sea and land developed. Mass production evolved in certain industries, notably Italian pottery and Egyptian glass, and these products found their way to markets hundreds and even thousands of miles distant from the centers of production. As illustrated by selections from *The Red Sea Guide Book* [11], international trade, especially with the Near and Far East, also expanded. Although expansion of trade and industry is perhaps the phenomenon most interesting to the modern observer, it must be remembered that the bulk of Rome's income was always derived from agriculture. The most important development in agriculture was the gradual substitution of tenant farmers (*coloni*) for slaves on the estates. Many slaves were manumitted and the wars by which they were procured became infrequent.

If we had — as we do not — the statistics to illustrate the development of Rome's economy during the Early Principate, we should probably be able to trace a graph ascending rapidly in the first century and leveling off early in the second. There were many factors definitely limiting economic expansion. The Empire never created wealth in depth or a vast body of consumers except for the barest necessities of life. Most of humanity, whether peasants or city-dwellers, continued to live at subsistence level. Trade and commerce mainly benefited only a small minority. Technology failed to develop, in part because of the inhibiting effects of cheap or servile labor; industrial mass production was the exception rather than the rule. Even then, it "exported itself" and became localized, since transportation costs were high and there were no patent laws protecting industrial inventions and production techniques. The economic supremacy of Italy in the western Mediterranean declined when its markets in Gaul and elsewhere disappeared as these areas increased their own agriculture and trade. Agricultural production, technically limited like industry, expanded only as Rome's exploitable territory expanded and stagnated when the Empire ceased to grow.

But these were latent rather than actual problems in a relatively flourishing age. The outstanding social by-product of Mediterranean prosperity was the development of a numerically small but significant middle class in almost all of Rome's privincial cities. Rome fostered urban life wherever possible by granting city charters and by permitting local administration by town councils. The councilors (decurions), municipal gentry whose wealth was derived mainly from estates, gave willingly and lavishly of their time and money not only to govern their cities but also to embellish them with the material amenities of civilized life.

9. APPRAISAL OF THE EARLY PRINCIPATE

It is easy to describe the Principate in glowing terms. Some modern interpretations are not unlike those of contemporary, second-century observers such as Aelius Aristides, excerpts from whose glowing *Roman Panegyric* are included in the selections. At its best the Empire won the loyalty of the articulate classes [12]. The grant of citizenship was increasingly widespread and the provincial elite was gradually absorbed into the equestrian and senatorial classes. By the second century even emperors, although "Roman" to the core, came from the provinces. Imperial government, inspired by humane and Stoic principles, won respect through its greatest and most lasting contribution, its law, whose development was to culminate in the work of a series of notable jurists in the early third century.

There is another side to the story, however. Corruption and repression, although better controlled by a salaried civil service than under the Republic, never disappeared from public life. Although it seems unfair to criticize the Romans because they never created a "free" or "democratic" society in the modern sense, it is true that imperial government, under good and bad emperors alike, moved inexorably toward ultimate despotism. The public assemblies were already withering away under Augustus and Tiberius. Of greater importance was the senate's gradual surrender of its residual responsibilities to the expanding imperial civil service, which was fostered especially by such able emperors as Claudius and Hadrian.

The Principate was a period of outstanding cultural productivity, although decline set in later in the age. Augustus' reign in particular saw an outburst of creativity; its greatness was not diminished because it was deliberately fostered by the emperor and Maecenas, his propaganda minister, to advertise the ideals of the regime. Several selections indicate the character of this artistic Golden Age: the *Aeneid* of Vergil, designed to stimulate respect for the traditional Roman virtues of piety and faith; the poetry of Horace, which celebrated rural life and the Augustan Peace; and of Ovid, whose sensuous love poetry clashed with the puritanical ideals of the emperor and helped earn his banishment [8]. Livy's monumental prose history [1] served, like the *Aeneid*, to glorify Rome's past, her ideals, and her destined mission in the world. Plastic art, epitomized by the solemn beauty of the Altar of Peace, was equally inspired by official ideals.

The Augustan Golden Age was followed by a century in which literary production, while still excellent, was no longer epochal. This was the so-called Silver Age, the age of the satire and epigram, perhaps the most typically Roman genres, illustrated by the works of Petronius, Martial, and Juvenal. A selection [8, *e*] from the last-named shows the nature of such writing. Important for our reconstruction of events in the first century are the surviving works of Rome's greatest historian, the brilliant Tacitus [9]; his high standards of accuracy are blended with a bitter if understandable prejudice against the imperial system. Less worthy both as a stylist and as an interpreter of events is the gossipy bureaucrat Suetonius, whose *Lives of the Caesars* [6] reveals an essentially journalistic and superficial approach to historical biography. Stoicism remained the most vigorous philosophy and produced notable literature in the works of Seneca, a minister of state under Nero, and the lowly freedman Epictetus. Of such works none reveals more vividly what Stoicism could mean as a way of life than the poignant *Meditations* of Marcus

Aurelius [13], who came closest in all of antiquity to realizing the ideal of the philosopher prince.

Paradoxically, Roman culture became less productive and original just as the Empire reached its culmination. To ascribe intellectual stagnation to the straitening effects of autocracy is to run the risk of oversimplification. Meritorious works of literary art were produced even under bad emperors, and in some characteristically Roman fields, such as engineering, architecture, and law, decline did not appear until the Empire had gone far down the road to despotism. Cultural and artistic ennui was evidenced in the second century A.D. by a growing dilettantism, by a conscious archaism in both the plastic arts and literature, and by an increasing striving for rhetorical effect at the expense of substance. The rise of the rhetoricians depended in large measure on prevalent educational theory, as illustrated by the passages quoted from Quintilian [10].

10. A CENTURY OF CRISIS (A.D. 180–285)

Marcus Aurelius was succeeded by an unworthy son, Commodus, whose assassination in 192 initiated a period of upheaval not unlike that of A.D. 68–69. This revolution brought to power a new dynasty, the Severan (A.D. 193–235), with African and Eastern affiliations and ideals. More than any other Roman dynasty the Severans frankly based their rule on military force and exalted themselves as autocrats. The dynasty was noted for its brilliant jurists and for extending Roman citizenship to practically all free-born males in the Empire in A.D. 212. But it could not arrest developments both within and outside the Empire that led to fifty years of chaos following 235. This catastrophic period marked the end of classical antiquity and produced a radical reorganization of government and society.

The reasons for this great crisis of the third century were economic, military, and political, and the trends leading to the crisis were operative even beneath the surface of the superficially tranquil and prosperous second century. Prosperity was a delicate thing, precariously maintained. Signs of trouble had appeared even under the good emperors, when excessively prodigal municipalities teetered on the verge of bankruptcy. Although the gross income of the Empire failed to expand after the early second century, bureaucracy and the army continued to grow and became more costly. Imperial government was trying to do too much with available resources. Over the long run it was living beyond its means. With increasing frequency Rome's subjects were forced to draw upon capital to pay their taxes. Just as these symptoms of economic weakness began to appear under Marcus Aurelius, the Empire was swept by plague, seriously reducing its productive population, and by the first shock of barbarian invasions.

Unrelenting pressure by the Persians in the East and by the Germans, especially the Goths, to the north culminated during A.D. 235–285 in a series of invasions that ravaged nearly every province. The Roman legions were unequal to stemming the barbarian tide for two reasons. First, as a final result of Augustan military policy, the army had become a frontier garrison force unsupported by large mobile reserves. Frontiers were frequently denuded of protection when troops had to be shifted to threatened areas, and thus defense was impossible when the Empire was penetrated in depth. Second, the legions represented a special interest of their own. Recruitment had gradually become provincialized during the Principate; by the third century the soldiery often represented the least Romanized elements of the frontier population, out of touch with the more civilized hinterland. The revolutionary experiences of A.D. 68–69 and 193 were repeated almost exactly: civil war erupted as field armies and the praetorian guard proclaimed their generals as emperors. The civilian population, peasants and city dwellers alike, suffered doubly during the chaos, since Roman armies now looted and destroyed scarcely less than the invading barbarians.

The breakdown of law and order was almost complete. What little effective central government existed tried to meet skyrocketing expenses by taxes and requisitions from depopulated and wasted provinces. The government sought desperately to keep things going, but the only means it could choose were economically primitive. The coinage was debased, and disastrous inflation followed. The Empire began to revert to a "natural" economy, in which business and fiscal transactions were made in kind rather than in worthless coin. The government countered by regimenting the agricultural and commercial classes, especially the decurions, in order to compel them to produce, collect, and distribute necessary revenue and to perform any other services deemed essential by the state. The gradual introduction of these compulsory services, accompanied not infrequently by brutality on the part of government agents, is illustrated in selections [15, a and b].

In that unhappy age men turned for consolation to other-worldly philosophies such as the mystical Neoplatonism of Plotinus or to one of the many mystery religions spreading from the Near East, such as Mithraism, a cult whose soldierly ideals appealed especially to the legionaries. Of much greater significance was the spread of Christianity. By and large the Christians had been left alone by the authorities during the first two centuries A.D., even though Christianity was regarded by most intelligent Romans as immoral and even subversive. The various charges brought against the sect were answered eloquently in the *Apology* of Tertullian [14].

The very existence of the Christian Church was soon threatened. In an era when emperors insisted on their quasi-divine status and sought tangible evidence of their subjects' support, they instituted what was in effect a loyalty oath in the form of open sacrifice to Rome's gods and to the imperial "genius" (guardian spirit). The Christians refused to comply; they denied Rome's pagan gods and insisted they could pray *for* the emperor but never *to* him. Sporadic but vicious persecution ensued throughout the Empire (A.D. 249 and 257), some defections resulted, but Christian resistance was solidified and made even more militant.

II. THE LATE EMPIRE (A.D. 285–395)

The Roman World was saved from utter collapse by the comprehensive reforms begun by Diocletian (285–305) and completed by Constantine (312–337). Like Augustus before them, they met the crisis by institutionalizing various precedents established during a preceding period of upheaval. Most of their measures were temporarily successful. They saved Rome and her civilization, but they were unable to restore her prosperity. They also created, however, an Empire that bore little resemblance to the Principate. If they inaugurated the last phase of Roman history, they ushered in the medieval world as well.

In order to bolster the imperial authority they felt obliged to surround themselves with oriental pomp and to exalt themselves through religion. Diocletian claimed to be the elect of Jove and Constantine, after his conversion to Christianity, assumed sacred status. Diocletian attempted to make imperial authority all-pervasive by nominating a colleague of equal power to rule with him, and to solve the perennial problem of orderly succession by appointing two successors-designate to work with and eventually to replace the two senior *Augusti*. This so-called Tetrarchic system was a failure, but his reform of the army establishment, completed by Constantine, was successful. In organization, armament, and tactics the new army bore little resemblance to the force created by Augustus.

Although in principle Roman subjects remained subject to military service, in practice the reforming emperors faced an acute shortage of Romans available for duty in the army. Like their immediate predecessors, Diocletian and Constantine had to depend increasingly on the enlistment of barbarians. A new and powerful mobile reserve was created to support the troops stationed along the frontiers, and the total strength of the army was increased. Applying the principle of "divide and rule," the reforming emperors separated military and civil jurisdiction almost everywhere in the Empire, broke the provinces into smaller units, expanded the bureaucracy at all levels, and instituted a complicated system of administrative checks and balances designed to prevent the accumulation of power by possible rivals. The emperor, surrounded by his privy council of high court officials, was the supreme autocrat and the sole source of law. The ancient senate continued to exist at Rome, although the emperors seldom resided there any more, and about A.D. 340 another senate was created at Constantinople. Both bodies were important only as municipal councils and as forums for the expression of senatorial opinion.

As a result of the reforms, revolution and barbarian invasion were suppressed, and the provinces revived somewhat with the return of peace. The success of the reforms was not lasting, however, since the emperors were unable to tap new sources of social and economic strength to keep the corrupt, inefficient, and expensive machine of government running. The writings of Ammianus Marcellinus [17] illustrate the corruption of fourth-century life in Rome and in the provinces and show that it would have been difficult to re-establish society on a healthier basis.

To find revenue imperial government could only apply principles of compulsion and regimentation inherited from the third century. Rigidly defined hereditary castes, each with a definite rank in society, were legalized. Tenant farmers were bound to the land, becoming serfs. The commercial urban classes were organized into hereditary guilds, which were required to transport and distribute essential foodstuffs for the cities. The once flourishing municipal councilors, now also a caste, groaned under fiscal demands made on them by the central government and, at least in the West, headed toward bankruptcy and extinction. Entrance by the lower and middle classes into the more privileged orders, such as the church, army, and bureaucracy, was prohibited. Enforcement of such regulations was inefficient, and there was in fact greater social mobility than the law allowed. Only the senators, profiting by their great estates and capital, their monopoly of the great civil offices, and their privileged legal status, were able to maintain and even improve their standard of living. Of great importance was the patronage (*patrocinium*) extended by senatorial land barons over weaker landholders, who became their clients and tenants in return for protection against imperial and municipal fiscal agents. The senatorial class, especially in the West, became a state within a state and successfully defied the prerogatives of the central government.

The reforms of Diocletian and Constantine may rightly be described as conservative, since they merely represented the culmination of tendencies which already existed. Two truly unprecedented and revolutionary changes were made by Constantine: the foundation of a new Eastern capital, Constantinople, which became a great center of civilization during the next millennium, and the legalization of Christianity, the most vigorous and vital force in that grim age. The Christians had been subject to persecution during and after Diocletian's reign. Upon Constantine's personal conversion in 312, described by Eusebius [16], the Christians immediately became a legally recognized minority sect enjoying increasing privileges and favors from the imperial court. Their numbers increased rapidly, and during the reign of Theodosius I (379–395) Christianity became the state religion. The old Roman aristocracy and the apostate emperor Julian (361–363) fought a stubborn rear-guard action to preserve pagan practices, but paganism was finally defeated by the end of the fourth century. Affairs of Church and state now intermeshed as imperial government sought to use Christianity as a unifying force.

But the Church itself was convulsed by religious controversy that fed on the spread of monasticism in the East and on the political rivalry of the great apostolic bishops contending for leadership. The Arian and Monophysitic heresies of the fourth and fifth centuries, even though they concerned arguments of an extremely metaphysical character, the nature of the Trinity and of Christ himself, engendered intense interest among all classes and necessitated both government intervention and convocation of the first ecumenical councils for their resolution.

Culturally the Late Empire was a period of swift transition in which classical standards of art and literature gave way to values and canons more acceptable to Christianity. The plastic arts betrayed an increasing abstraction and disinterest in technical competence. Architecture, at least in so far as it pertained to public works, remained vigorous and even developed new techniques. The basilica floor plan was adapted to Christian churches, becoming the basic pattern of church design for long thereafter. The rhetorical trend in literature culminated in a verbose and turgid style, epitomized by the language of law and by the panegyrical literature in which the age abounded. Traditional classical interests were maintained by such pagan rhetoricians as the orator Libanius of Antioch and by the circle affiliated with the Roman senator Symmachus, but their works were generally spiritless and antiquarian. Poetry languished, save for the better work of artists like Ausonius and Claudian. Although the emperors consciously fostered education, at least for the governing elite, they were powerless to arrest the changes in artistic standards and ideals.

Only within the Church was there a ferment of intellectual vitality evoked by its new and increasingly dominant role in society, by controversy over dogma, and by the challenge posed by the gradual disintegration of the Empire itself. This was the age of the great Church fathers, Athanasius, Ambrose, Chrysostom, Jerome, and Augustine, whose sermons, correspondence, and works on dogma explained the ideals of a new world dedicated to salvation in the hereafter. Although treatment of their work is properly part of the intellectual history of the Middle Ages, it should be noted that many of the Church fathers received a classical education, started life as lawyers or administrators, and were intimately acquainted with Rome's heritage. In spite of their ascetic ideals they could not completely deny the culture of classical Rome. For some churchmen life was inconceivable without the Empire, which appeared to be the divinely instituted political instrument for propagation of the true faith.

Politically the Empire held together until A.D. 395. Fourth-century emperors were by and large vigorous, able, and even heroic men deserving of a better age. They struggled unsuccessfully, though with the best of intentions, to eliminate bureaucratic corruption and senatorial special privilege. They were more successful in holding the barbarians at bay, at least until 376, when for the first time an entire barbarian nation, the Visigoths, were allowed within the imperial boundaries as allies serving in the Roman army. It was not long before the Visigoths revolted against mistreatment by imperial officials, and in 378 they annihilated a Roman army and a Roman emperor at Adrianople.

12. COLLAPSE OF THE WEST (A.D. 395–476)

The situation became even graver in 395, when the Eastern and Western provinces were divided between two emperors, one in Constantinople and the other in Italy, who governed independently within an only theoretically united Empire. For reasons both complex and obscure, East and West thereafter experienced very different fates. While imperial rule disappeared completely in the West as a result of renewed Germanic invasion, the East survived the fifth century with its frontiers and institutions buffeted but intact. The East apparently had greater survival power, in part at least because it could draw on an internal supply of military manpower in the Balkans and Asia Minor, but also because it was relatively more healthy economically and because the central government successfully defended its prerogatives against feudalizing landlords and generalissimos. But its strength must not be overemphasized. On occasion it was forced to divert attacks and buy time by a wily and cunning diplomacy.

In the West revenues evaporated as cities declined and senatorial estates continued to expand. The political power of the central government melted away as it relied increasingly on barbarian mercenaries and their generals, who, as "king-makers," really ruled the state. Beginning in 406, the imperial government at Milan or Ravenna was powerless to prevent the permanent large-scale settlement of Franks, Burgundians, Visigoths, and Vandals in Gaul, Spain, and Africa. Nor could it prevent the ultimate indignity, the sack of Rome in 410 and again in 455. Within two generations most of the West slipped under the control of German princes, who, however, maintained the fiction that they were governing as agents of shadow emperors residing in Italy. The deposition of the last West Roman Emperor by the barbarian king, Odoacer, in 476 meant that Italy at last shared the full fate of her Western provinces. In spite of the survival of the Empire in the East, the date A.D. 476 is a convenient terminal date for Roman history.

The thousand years of this history cover the rise and fall of a dynamic people whose sober accomplishments in bringing law, order, and long periods of stability to the Western World were a tremendous contribution to civilization. Even in decline, Rome was a civilizing catalyst, refining rude barbarians who wished not so much to destroy as to enjoy the amenities of her life. For long centuries afterward Rome continued to stand for them, as it does for us, as a symbol of security in a chaotic world.

1

Early Rome

THE FOLLOWING selections from Livy of Padua (59 B.C.–A.D. 17) were
for the Romans accepted versions of three important moments in their
early history: the promulgation of a constitution based upon distinctions
of wealth by King Servius Tullius (sixth century B.C.); discontent leading
to the first plebeian secession and recognition of the tribuni plebis (ca.
494 or 471 B.C.); and Rome's settlement of the Latin War (338 B.C.).
The Livian tradition often projects back on a remote past the institutions
and motivations of a very different epoch. Thus the "Servian" Constitution described below is essentially the highly developed Centuriate Assembly of a much later date, and the circumstantial details in all three
selections, especially the speeches, are certainly apocryphal. Nevertheless,
even for the earliest periods, Livy contains a substantial core of truth,
and if the historian must tread cautiously, using archaeological information wherever possible as a check on the litereray sources, he must still
treat Livy with a healthy but not excessive skepticism.

Livy, History of Rome, I, 42–44;
II, 23–24, 27–33; VIII, 13–14

The "Servian" Constitution]

i

42] SERVIUS[1] consolidated his power quite as much by his private as by his public measures. To guard against the children of
Tarquin[2] treating him as those of Ancus had treated Tarquin, he
married his two daughters to the scions of the royal house, Lucius
and Arruns Tarquin. Human counsels could not arrest the inevitable
course of destiny, nor could Servius prevent the jealousy aroused by
his ascending the throne from making his family the scene of disloyalty and hatred.

From Livy, HISTORY OF ROME, translated by Rev. Canon W. M. Roberts
(New York and London 1912, Everyman's Library Edition), vol. i . . .
ii. Reprinted by permission of E. P. Dutton & Co., Inc. and J. M. Dent
& Sons, Ltd.

The truce with the Veientines had now expired, and the resumption of war with them and other Etruscan cities came most opportunely to help in maintaining tranquillity at home. In this war the courage and good fortune of Tullius were conspicuous, and he returned to Rome, after defeating an immense force of the enemy, feeling quite secure on the throne, and assured of the goodwill of both patricians and commons.

Then he set himself to by far the greatest of all works in times of peace. Just as Numa[3] had been the author of religious laws and institutions, so posterity extols Servius as the founder of those divisions and classes in the State by which a clear distinction is drawn between the various grades of dignity and fortune. He instituted the census, a most beneficial institution in what was to be a great empire, in order that by its means the various duties of peace and war might be assigned, not as heretofore, indiscriminately, but in proportion to the amount of property each man possessed. From it he drew up the classes and centuries and the following distribution of them, adapted for either peace or war.

43] Those whose property amounted to, or exceeded 100,000 lbs. weight of copper were formed into eighty centuries, forty of juniors and forty of seniors.[4] These were called the First Class. The seniors were to defend the City, the juniors to serve in the field. The armour which they were to provide themselves with comprised helmet, round shield, greaves, and coat of mail, all of brass; these were to protect the person. Their offensive weapons were spear and sword. To this class were joined two centuries of carpenters whose duty it was to work the engines of war; they were without arms. The Second Class consisted of those whose property amounted to between 75,000 and 100,000 lbs. weight of copper; they were formed, seniors and juniors together, into twenty centuries. Their regulation arms were the same as those of the First Class, except that they had an oblong wooden shield instead of the round brazen one and no coat of mail. The Third Class he formed of those whose property fell as low as 50,000 lbs.; these also consisted of twenty centuries, similarly divided into seniors and juniors. The only difference in the armour was that they did not wear greaves. In the Fourth Class were those whose property did not fall below 25,000 lbs. They also formed twenty centuries; their only arms were a spear and a javelin. The Fifth Class was larger, it formed thirty centuries. They carried slings and stones, and they included the supernumeraries, the horn-blowers, and the trumpeters, who formed three centuries. This Fifth Class was assessed at

11,000 lbs. The rest of the population whose property fell below this were formed into one century and were exempt from military service.

After thus regulating the equipment and distribution of the infantry, he re-arranged the cavalry. He enrolled from amongst the principal men of the State twelve centuries. In the same way he made six other centuries (though only three had been formed by Romulus) under the same names under which the first had been inaugurated. For the purchase of the horse, 10,000 lbs. were assigned them from the public treasury; whilst for its keep certain widows were assessed to pay 2000 lbs. each, annually. The burden of all these expenses was shifted from the poor on to the rich.

Then additional privileges were conferred. The former kings had maintained the constitution as handed down by Romulus, viz., manhood suffrage in which all alike possessed the same weight and enjoyed the same rights. Servius introduced a graduation; so that whilst no one was ostensibly deprived of his vote, all the voting power was in the hands of the principal men of the State. The knights[5] were first summoned to record their vote, then the eighty centuries of the infantry of the First Class; if their votes were divided, which seldom happened, it was arranged for the Second Class to be summoned; very seldom did the voting extend to the lowest Class. Nor need it occasion any surprise, that the arrangement which now exists since the completion of the thirty-five tribes, their number being doubled by the centuries of juniors and seniors, does not agree with the total as instituted by Servius Tullius. For, after dividing the City with its districts and the hills which were inhabited into four parts, he called these divisions "tribes," I think from the tribute they paid, for he also introduced the practice of collecting it at an equal rate according to the assessment. These tribes had nothing to do with the distribution and number of the centuries.

44] The work of the census was accelerated by an enactment in which Servius denounced imprisonment and even capital punishment against those who evaded assessment. On its completion he issued an order that all the citizens of Rome, knights and infantry alike, should appear in the Campus Martius, each in their centuries. After the whole army had been drawn up there, he purified it by the triple sacrifice of a swine, a sheep, and an ox. This was called "a closed lustrum," because with it the census was completed. Eighty thousand citizens are said to have been included in that census. Fabius Pictor, the oldest of our historians, states that this was the number of those who could bear arms.

Class conflict]

ii

23] But a war with the Volscians[6] was imminent and the State was torn with internal dissensions; the patricians and the plebeians were bitterly hostile to one another, owing mainly to the desperate condition of the debtors. They loudly complained that whilst fighting in the field for liberty and empire they were oppressed and enslaved by their fellow-citizens at home; their freedom was more secure in war than in peace, safer amongst the enemy than amongst their own people. The discontent, which was becoming of itself continually more embittered, was still further inflamed by the signal misfortunes of one individual.

An old man, bearing visible proofs of all the evils he had suffered, suddenly appeared in the Forum. His clothing was covered with filth, his personal appearance was made still more loathsome by a corpse-like pallor and emaciation, his unkempt beard and hair made him look like a savage. In spite of this disfigurement he was recognized by the pitying bystanders; they said that he had been a centurion, and mentioned other military distinctions he possessed. He bared his breast and showed the scars which witnessed to many fights in which he had borne an honourable part. The crowd had now almost grown to the dimensions of an Assembly of the people. He was asked, "Whence came that garb, whence that disfigurement?" He stated that whilst serving in the Sabine war he had not only lost the produce of his land through the depredations of the enemy, but his farm had been burnt, all his property plundered, his cattle driven away, the war-tax demanded when he was least able to pay it, and he had got into debt. This debt had been vastly increased through usury and had stripped him first of his father's and grandfather's farm, then of his other property, and at last like a pestilence had reached his person. He had been carried off by his creditor, not into slavery only, but into an underground workshop, a living death. Then he showed his back scored with recent marks of the lash.

On seeing and hearing all this a great outcry arose; the excitement was not confined to the Forum, it spread everywhere throughout the City. Men who were in bondage for debt and those who had been released rushed from all sides into the public streets and invoked "the

protection of the Quirites."[7] Every one was eager to join the mal-
contents, numerous bodies ran shouting through all the streets to the
Forum. Those of the senators who happened to be in the Forum and
fell in with the mob were in great danger of their lives. Open violence would have been resorted to, had not the consuls, P. Servilius
and Ap. Claudius,[8] promptly intervened to quell the outbreak. The
crowd surged round them, showed their chains and other marks of
degradation. These, they said, were their rewards for having served
their country; they tauntingly reminded the consuls of the various
campaigns in which they had fought, and peremptorily demanded
rather than petitioned that the senate should be called together. Then
they closed round the Senate-house, determined to be themselves the
arbiters and directors of public policy.

A very small number of senators, who happened to be available,
were got together by the consuls, the rest were afraid to go even to
the Forum, much more to the Senate-house. No business could be
transacted owing to the requisite number not being present. The
people began to think that they were being played with and put off,
that the absent senators were not kept away by accident or by fear,
but in order to prevent any redress of their grievances, and that the
consuls themselves were shuffling and laughing at their misery. Matters were reaching the point at which not even the majesty of the
consuls could keep the enraged people in check, when the absentees,
uncertain whether they ran the greater risk by staying away or coming, at last entered the Senate-house. The House was now full, and a
division of opinion showed itself not only amongst the senators but
even between the two consuls. Appius, a man of passionate tempera-
ment, was of opinion that the matter ought to be settled by a display
of authority on the part of the consuls; if one or two were brought
up for trial, the rest would calm down. Servilius, more inclined to
gentle measures, thought that when men's passions are aroused it
was safer and easier to bend them than to break them.

24] In the middle of these disturbances, fresh alarm was created by
some Latin horsemen who galloped in with the disquieting tidings
that a Volscian army was on the march to attack the City. This intelligence affected the patricians and the plebeians very differently;
to such an extent had civic discord rent the State in twain. The plebeians were exultant, they said that the gods were preparing to avenge
the tyranny of the patricians; they encouraged each other to evade
enrolment, for it was better for all to die together than to perish
one by one. "Let the patricians take up arms, let the patricians serve

as common soldiers, that those who get the spoils of war may share its perils." The senate, on the other hand, filled with gloomy apprehensions by the twofold danger from their fellow-citizens and from their enemy, implored the consul Servilius, who was more sympathetic towards the people, to extricate the State from the perils that beset it on all sides.

He dismissed the senate and went into the Assembly of the plebs. There he pointed out how anxious the senate were to consult the interests of the plebs, but their deliberations respecting what was certainly the largest part, though still only a part, of the State had been cut short by fears for the safety of the State as a whole. The enemy were almost at their gates, nothing could be allowed to take precedence of the war, but even if the attack were postponed, it would not be honourable on the part of the plebeians to refuse to take up arms for their country till they had been paid for doing so, nor would it be compatible with the self-respect of the senate to be actuated by fear rather than by good-will in devising measures for the relief of their distressed fellow-citizens. He convinced the Assembly of his sincerity by issuing an edict that none should keep a Roman citizen in chains or duress whereby he would be prevented from enrolling for military service, none should distrain or sell the goods of a soldier as long as he was in camp, or detain his children or grandchildren.

On the promulgation of this edict those debtors who were present at once gave in their names for enrolment, and crowds of persons running in all quarters of the City from the houses where they were confined, as their creditors had no longer the right to detain them, gathered together in the Forum to take the military oath. These formed a considerable force, and none were more conspicuous for courage and activity in the Volscian war.

The consul led his troops against the enemy and encamped a short distance from them. . . .[9]

*　　*　　*

27] After the defeat of the Auruncans, the Romans, who had, within a few days, fought so many successful wars, were expecting the fulfilment of the promises which the consul had made on the authority of the senate. Appius, partly from his innate love of tyranny and partly to undermine the confidence felt in his colleague, gave the harshest sentences he could when debtors were brought before him. One after another those who had before pledged their persons as security were now handed over to their creditors, and others were compelled to give such security.

A soldier to whom this happened appealed to the colleague of Appius. A crowd gathered round Servilius, they reminded him of his promises, upbraided him with their services in war and the scars they had received, and demanded that he should either get an ordinance passed by the senate, or, as consul, protect his people; as commander, his soldiers. The consul sympathised with them, but under the circumstances he was compelled to temporise; the opposite policy was so recklessly insisted on not only by his colleague but by the entire party of the nobility. By taking a middle course he did not escape the odium of the plebs nor did he win the favour of the patricians. These regarded him as a weak popularity-hunting consul, the plebeians considered him false, and it soon became apparent that he was as much detested as Appius. . . .

At length the consuls, detested as they were by the plebs, went out of office — Servilius equally hated by both orders, Appius in wonderful favour with the patricians.

28] Then A. Verginius and T. Vetusius took office.[10] As the plebeians were doubtful as to what sort of consuls they would have, and were anxious to avoid any precipitate and ill-considered action which might result from hastily adopted resolutions in the Forum, they began to hold meetings at night, some on the Esquiline and others on the Aventine. The consuls considered that state of things to be fraught with danger, as it really was, and made a formal report to the senate. But any orderly discussion of their report was out of the question, owing to the excitement and clamour with which the senators received it, and the indignation they felt at the consuls throwing upon them the odium of measures which they ought to have carried on their own authority as consuls. "Surely," it was said, "if there were really magistrates in the State, there would have been no meetings in Rome beyond the public Assembly; now the State was broken up into a thousand senates and assemblies, since some consuls were being held on the Esquiline and others on the Aventine. Why, one man like Appius Claudius, who was worth more than a consul, would have dispersed these gatherings in a moment." When the consuls, after being thus censured, asked what they wished them to do, as they were prepared to act with all the energy and determination that the senate desired, a decree was passed that the levy should be raised as speedily as possible, for the plebs was waxing wanton through idleness. . . .

29] Having had quite enough of trying to coerce the plebs on the one hand and persuading the senate to adopt a milder course on the other, the consuls at last said: "Senators, that you may not say you have not been forewarned, we tell you that a very serious disturbance is at hand. We demand that those who are the loudest in charging us with cowardice shall support us whilst we conduct the levy. We will act as the most resolute may wish, since such is your pleasure." They returned to the tribunal and purposely ordered one of those who were in view to be called up by name. As he stood silent, and a number of men had closed round him to prevent his being seized, the consuls sent a lictor to him. The lictor was pushed away, and those senators who were with the consuls exclaimed that it was an outrageous insult and rushed down from the tribunal to assist the lictor. The hostility of the crowd was diverted from the lictor, who had simply been prevented from making the arrest, to the senators. The interposition of the consuls finally allayed the conflict. There had, however, been no stones thrown or weapons used, it had resulted in more noise and angry words than personal injury.

The senate was summoned and assembled in disorder; its proceedings were still more disorderly. Those who had been roughly handled demanded an inquiry, and all the more violent members supported the demand by shouting and uproar quite as much as by their votes. When at last the excitement had subsided, the consuls censured them for showing as little calm judgment in the senate as there was in the Forum. Then the debate proceeded in order. Three different policies were advocated. P. Valerius did not think the general question ought to be raised; he thought they ought only to consider the case of those who, in reliance on the promise of the consul P. Servilius, had served in the Volscian, Auruncan, and Sabine wars. Titus Larcius considered that the time had passed for rewarding only men who had served, the whole plebs was overwhelmed with debt, the evil could not be arrested unless there was a measure for universal relief. Any attempt to differentiate between the various classes would only kindle fresh discord instead of allaying it. Appius Claudius, harsh by nature, and now maddened by the hatred of the plebs on the one hand and the praises of the senate on the other, asserted that these riotous gatherings were not the result of misery but of licence, the plebeians were actuated by wantonness more than by anger. This was the mischief which had sprung from the right of appeal, for the consuls could only threaten without the power to execute their threats as long as a criminal was allowed to appeal to his fellow-criminals. "Come," said he, "let us create a Dictator from whom there is no appeal, then this madness which is setting everything on fire will soon die down. Let me see any one strike a lictor then, when he knows that his back and even his life are in the sole power of the man whose authority he attacks."

30] To many the sentiments which Appius uttered seemed cruel and monstrous, as they really were. On the other hand, the proposals of Verginius and Larcius would set a dangerous precedent, that of Larcius at all events, as it would destroy all credit. The advice given by Verginius was regarded as the most moderate, being a middle course between the other two. But through the strength of his party, and the consideration of personal interests which always have injured and always will injure public policy, Appius won the day. He was very nearly being himself appointed Dictator, an appointment which would more than anything have alienated the plebs, and that too at a most critical time when the Volscians, the Æqui, and the Sabines were all in arms together. The consuls and the older patricians, however, took care that a magistracy clothed with such tremendous powers should be entrusted to a man of moderate temper. They created M. Valerius, the son of Volesus, Dictator. Though the plebeians recognised that it was against them that a Dictator had been created, still, as they held their right of appeal under a law which his brother had passed, they did not fear any harsh or tyrannical treatment from that family. Their hopes were confirmed by an edict issued by the Dictator, very similar to the one made by Servilius. That edict had been ineffective, but they thought that more confidence could be placed in the person and power of the Dictator, so, dropping all opposition, they gave in their names for enrolment. Ten legions, were formed, a larger army than had ever before been assembled. Three of them were assigned to each of the consuls, the Dictator took command of four. . . .[11]

31] . . . Whilst these three wars were thus brought to a successful issue, the course which domestic affairs were taking continued to be a source of anxiety to both the patricians and the plebeians. The money-lenders possessed such influence and had taken such skilful precautions that they rendered the commons and even the Dictator himself powerless. After the consul Vetusius had returned, Valerius introduced, as the very first business of the senate, the treatment of the men who had been marching to victory, and moved a resolution as to what decision they ought to come to with regard to the debtors. His motion was negatived, on which he said, "I am not acceptable as an advocate of concord. Depend upon it, you will very soon wish that the Roman plebs had champions like me. As far as I am concerned, I will no longer encourage my fellow-citizens in vain hopes nor will I be Dictator in vain. Internal dissensions and foreign wars have made this office necessary to the commonwealth; peace has now been secured abroad, at home it is made impossible. I would rather be involved in the revolution as a private citizen than as Dictator." So saying, he left the House and resigned his dictatorship. The reason was quite clear to the plebs; he had resigned office because he was indignant at the way they were treated. The non-fulfilment of his pledge was not due to him, they considered that he had practically kept his word, and on his way home they followed him with approving cheers.

32] The senate now began to feel apprehensive lest on the disbandment of the army there should be a recurrence of the secret conclaves and conspiracies. Although the Dictator had actually conducted the enrolment, the soldiers had sworn obedience to the consuls. Regarding them as still bound by their oath, the senate ordered the legions to be marched out of the City on the pretext that war had been recommenced by the Æqui. This step brought the revolution to a head. It is said that the first idea was to put the consuls to death that the men might be discharged from their oath; then, on learning that no religious obligation could be dissolved by a crime, they decided, at the instigation of a certain Sicinius, to ignore the consuls and withdraw to the Sacred Mount, which lay on the other side of the Anio, three miles from the City. This is a more generally accepted tradition than the one adopted by Piso that the secession was made to the Aventine, There, without any commander, in a regularly entrenched camp, taking nothing with them but the necessaries of life, they quietly maintained themselves for some days, neither receiving nor giving any provocation.[12]

A great panic seized the City, mutual distrust led to a state of universal suspense. Those plebeians who had been left by their comrades in the City feared violence from the patricians; the patricians feared the plebeians who still remained in the City, and could not make up their minds whether they would rather have them go or stay. "How long," it was asked, "would the multitude who had seceded remain quiet? What would happen if a foreign war broke out in the meantime?" They felt that all their hopes rested on concord amongst the citizens, and that this must be restored at any cost.

The senate decided, therefore, to send as their spokesman Menenius Agrippa, an eloquent man, and acceptable to the plebs as being himself of plebeian origin.[13] He was admitted into the camp, and it is reported that he simply told them the following fable in primitive and uncouth fashion. "In the days when all the parts of the human body were not as now agreeing together, but each member took its own course and spoke its own speech, the other members, indignant at seeing that everything acquired by their care and labour and ministry went to the belly, whilst it, undisturbed in the middle of them all, did nothing but enjoy the pleasures provided for it, entered into a conspiracy; the hands were not to bring food to the mouth, the mouth was not to accept it when offered, the teeth were not to masticate it. Whilst, in their resentment, they were anxious to coerce the belly by starving it, the members themselves wasted away, and the whole body was reduced to the last stage of exhaustion. Then it became evident that the belly rendered no idle service, and the nourishment it received was no greater than that which it bestowed by returning to all parts of the body this blood by which we live and are strong, equally distributed into the veins, after being matured by the digestion of the food." By using this comparison, and showing how the internal disaffection amongst the parts of the body resembled the animosity of the plebeians against the patricians, he succeeded in winning over his audience.

33] Negotiations were then entered upon for a reconciliation. An agreement was arrived at, the terms being that the plebs should have its own magistrates, whose persons were to be inviolable, and who should have the right of affording protection against the consuls. And further, no patrician should be allowed to hold that office. Two "tribunes of the plebs" were elected, C. Licinius and L. Albinus. These chose three colleagues. It is generally agreed that Sicinius, the instigator of the secession, was amongst them, but who the other two were is not settled. Some say that only two tribunes were created on the Sacred Hill, and that it was there that the *lex sacrata*[14] was passed.

Rome and the Latins]

viii

13] The consuls for the next year were L. Furius Camillus and C. Maenius.[15] In order to bring more discredit upon Æmilius for his neglect of his military duties the previous year, the senate insisted that no expenditure of arms and men must be spared in order to reduce and destroy Pedum. The new consuls were peremptorily ordered to lay aside everything else and march at once. The state of affairs in Latium was such that they would neither maintain peace nor undertake war. For war their resources were utterly inadequate, and they were smarting too keenly under the loss of their territory to think of peace. They decided, therefore, on a middle course, namely, to confine themselves to their towns, and if they were informed of any town being attacked, to send assistance to it from the whole of Latium. The people of Tibur and Praeneste, who were the nearest, reached Pedum, but the troops from Aricium, Lanuvium, and Veliternae, in conjunction with the Volscians of Antium, were suddenly attacked and routed by Maenius at the river Astura. Camillus engaged the Tiburtines who were much the strongest force, and, though with greater difficulty, achieved a similar success. During the battle the townsmen made a sudden sortie, but Camillus, directing a part of his army against them, not only drove them back within their walls, but stormed and captured the town, after routing the troops sent to their assistance, all in one day. After this successful attack on one city, they decided to make a greater and bolder effort, and to lead their victorious army on to the complete subjugation of Latium. They did not rest until, by capturing or accepting the surrender of one city after another, they had effected their purpose. Garrisons were placed in the captured towns, after which they returned to Rome to enjoy a triumph which was by universal consent accorded to them. An additional honor was paid to the two consuls in the erection of their equestrian statues in the Forum, a rare incident in that age.

Before the consular elections for the following year were held, Camillus brought before the senate the question of the future settlement of Latium. "Senators," he said, "our military operations in Latium have by the gracious favour of the gods and the bravery of our troops been brought to a successful close. The hostile armies were cut down at Pedum and the Astura, all the Latin towns and the Volscian Antium have either been stormed or have surrendered and are now held by your garrisons. We are growing weary of their constant renewal of hostilities, it is for you to consult as to the best means of binding them to a perpetual peace. The immortal gods have made you so completely masters of the situation that they have put it into your hands to decide whether there shall be henceforth a Latium or not. So far, then, as the Latins are concerned, you can secure for yourselves a lasting peace by either cruelty or kindness. Do you wish to adopt ruthless measures against a people that have surrendered and been defeated? It is open to you to wipe out the whole Latin nation and create desolation and solitude in that country which has furnished you with a splendid army of allies which you have employed in many great wars. Or do you wish to follow the example of your ancestors and make Rome greater by conferring her citizenship on those whom she has defeated? The materials for her expansion to a glorious height are here at hand. That is assuredly the most firmly-based empire, whose subjects take a delight in rendering it their obedience. But whatever decision you come to, you must make haste about it. You are keeping so many peoples in suspense, with their minds distracted between hope and fear, that you are bound to relieve yourselves as soon as possible from your anxiety about them, and by exercising either punishment or kindness to pre-occupy minds which a state of strained expectancy has deprived of the power of thought. Our task has been to put you in a position to take the whole question into consultation, your task is to decree what is best for yourselves and for the republic."

14] The leaders of the senate applauded the way in which the consul had introduced the motion, but as the circumstances differed in different cases they thought that each case ought to be decided upon its merits, and with the view of facilitating discussion they requested the consul to put the name of each place separately.

Lanuvium received the full citizenship and the restitution of her sacred things, with the proviso that the temple and grove of Juno Sospita should belong in common to the Roman people and the citizens living at Lanuvium. Aricium, Nomentum, and Pedum obtained the same political rights as Lanuvium. Tusculum retained the citizenship which it had had before, and the responsibility for the part it took in the war was removed from the State as a whole and fastened on a few individuals. The Veliternians, who had been Roman citizens from old times, were in consequence of their numerous revolts severely dealt with; their walls were thrown down, their senate deported and ordered to live on the other side of the Tiber; if any of them were caught on this side of the river, he was to be fined 1000 *ases,* and the man who caught him was not to release him from confinement until the money was paid. Colonists were sent on to the land they had possessed, and their numbers made Velitrae look as populous as formerly.

Antium also was assigned to a fresh body of colonists, but the Antiates were permitted to enroll themselves as colonists if they chose; their warships were taken away, and they were forbidden to possess any more; they were admitted to citizenship. Tibur and Praeneste had their domains confiscated, not owing to the part which they, in common with the rest of Latium, had taken in the war, but because, jealous of the Roman power, they had joined arms with the barbarous nation of the Gauls. The rest of the Latin cities were deprived of the rights of intermarriage, free trade, and common councils with each other. Capua, as a reward for the refusal of its aristocracy to join the Latins, were allowed to enjoy the private rights of Roman citizens, as were also Fundi and Formiae, because they had always allowed a free passage through their territory. It was decided that Cumae and Suessula should enjoy the same rights as Capua. Some of the ships of Antium were taken into the Roman docks, others were burnt and their beaks (*rostra*) were fastened on the front of a raised gallery which was constructed at the end of the Forum, and which from this circumstance was called the Rostra.

NOTES

1. Traditional dates for Servius Tullius' kingship, 578–534 B.C.

2. Tarquinius Priscus, the late king, who had been murdered by the sons of his predecessor, Ancus Marcius.

3. Numa Pompilius, Rome's second king.

4. Juniors were aged 17 to 46, seniors were above 46, and service was not obligatory after age 60.

5. The equestrians or cavalry classes.

6. Hill people to the southeast of Latium.

7. Another name for the Roman citizenry.

8. Supposedly consuls in 495 B.C.

9. Livy next describes the defeat by the Romans of their mountain enemies, the Volscians, Sabines, and Aruncans.

10. 494 B.C.

11. There follows an account of more wars against the Aequi, Volscians, and Sabines.

12. The first secession of the plebs and the creation of the plebeian tribunate, dated by Livy in 494 B.C., in reality belongs in the year 471 or even later.

13. This statement cannot be accepted unless one admits that plebeians initially could attain membership in the senate upon the creation of the Republic.

14. A law that put a curse upon offenders, with their families and property.

15. 338 B.C.

2

Rome and Carthage

POLYBIUS (198–117 B.C.) ranks with Herodotus and Thucydides as one of the most distinguished ancient Greek historians. The son of a president of the Achaean League, he came to Rome as a hostage in 167 and quickly won the patronage of the Scipionic circle. Conceiving of history as a pragmatic tool for statesmen, he sought to explain Rome's rise to world dominance during the period 264–145 B.C. His work is important because of his general lack of bias, his critical approach to his sources, and his high standards of accuracy. He was a contemporary or near contemporary of the events he described and knew the Roman elite who themselves or whose immediate ancestors had made the history he wrote. The following selections illustrate his interest in historical causation and provide valuable information regarding the immediate causes of the Second Punic War and previous relations between Rome and Carthage.

Polybius, Histories, III, 9-15, 17, 20-30

iii

9] ... THIS IS a digression from my immediate subject, which is the war between Carthage and Rome. The cause of this war we must reckon to be the exasperation of Hamilcar, surnamed Barcas, the father of Hannibal. The result of the war in Sicily had not broken the spirit of that commander. He regarded himself as unconquered; for the troops at Eryx which he commanded were still sound and undismayed: and though he yielded so far as to make a treaty, it was a concession to the exigencies of the times brought on by the defeat of the Carthaginians at sea. But he never relaxed in his determined purpose of revenge; and, had it not been for the mutiny of the mercenaries at Carthage, he would at once have sought and made another occasion for bringing about a war, as far as he was able to do so: as it was, he was preoccupied by the domestic war, and had to give his attention entirely to that.

From Evelyn S. Shuckburgh, trans., THE HISTORIES OF POLYBIUS (London, 1889), vol. i, pp. 174–181, 183–192.

10] When the Romans, at the conclusion of this mercenary war,[1] proclaimed war with Carthage, the latter at first was inclined to resist at all hazards, because the goodness of her cause gave her hopes of victory, — as I have shown in my former book, without which it would be impossible to understand adequately either this or what is to follow. The Romans, however, would not listen to anything: and the Carthaginians therefore yielded to the force of circumstances; and though feeling bitterly aggrieved, yet being quite unable to do anything, evacuated Sardinia, and consented to pay a sum of twelve hundred talents, in addition to the former idemnity paid them, on condition of avoiding the war at that time. This is the second and the most important cause of the subsequent war. For Hamilcar, having this public grievance in addition to his private feelings of anger, as soon as he had secured his country's safety by reducing the rebellious mercenaries, set at once about securing the Carthaginian power in Iberia with the intention of using it as a base of operations against Rome. So that I record as a third cause of the war the Carthaginian success in Iberia: for it was the confidence inspired by their forces there which encouraged them to embark upon it. It would be easy to adduce other facts to show that Hamilcar, though he had been dead ten years at its commencement, largely contributed to bring about the second Punic war, but what I am about to say will be sufficient to establish the fact.

11] When, after his final defeat by the Romans, Hannibal had at last quitted his country and was staying at the court of Antiochus, the warlike attitude of the Aetolian league induced the Romans to send ambassadors to Antiochus, that they might be informed of the king's intentions.[2] These ambassadors found that Antiochus was inclined to the Aetolian alliance, and was eager for war with Rome; they accordingly paid great court to Hannibal with a view of bringing him into suspicion with the king. And in this they entirely succeeded. As time went on the king became ever more and more suspicious of Hannibal, until at length an opportunity occurred for an explanation of the alienation that had been thus secretly growing up between them. Hannibal then defended himself at great length but without success, until at last he made the following statement: "When my father was about to go on his Iberian expedition[3] I was nine years old: and as he was offering the sacrifice to Zeus I stood near the altar. The sacrifice successfully performed, my father poured the libation and went through the usual ritual. He then bade all the other worshippers stand a little back, and calling me to him asked me affectionately whether I wished to go with him on his expedition. Upon my eagerly assenting, and begging with boyish enthusiasm to be allowed to go, he took me by the right hand and led me up to the altar, and bade me lay my hand upon the victim and swear that I would never be friends with Rome. So long, then, Antiochus, as your policy is one of hostility to Rome, you may feel quite secure of having in me a most thoroughgoing supporter. But if ever you make terms or friendship with her, then you need not wait for any slander to make you distrust me and be on your guard against me; for there is nothing in my power that I would not do against her."

12] Antiochus listened to this story, and being convinced that it was told with genuine feeling and sincerity, gave up all his suspicions. And we, too, must regard this as an unquestionable proof of the animosity of Hamilcar and of the aim of his general policy; which, indeed, is also proved by facts. For he inspired his son-in-law Hasdrubal and his son Hannibal with a bitterness of resentment against Rome which nothing could surpass. Hasdrubal, indeed, was prevented by death from showing the full extent of his purpose; but time gave Hannibal abundant opportunity to manifest the hatred of Rome which he had inherited from his father.

. . . So much for the causes of the war. I will now relate the first actions in it.

13] The Carthaginians were highly incensed by their loss of Sicily, but their resentment was heightened still more, as I have said, by the transaction as to Sardinia, and by the addition recently made to their tribute. Accordingly, when the greater part of Iberia had fallen into their power, they were on the alert to seize any opportunity that presented itself of retaliating upon Rome. At the death of Hasdrubal, to whom they had committed the command in Iberia after the death of Hamilcar,[4] they waited at first to ascertain the feelings of the army; but when news came from thence that the troops had elected Hannibal as commander-in-chief, a popular assembly was at once held, and the choice of the army confirmed by a unanimous vote. As soon as he had taken over the command, Hannibal set out to subdue the tribe of the Olcades; and, having arrived before their most formidable city Althaea, he pitched his camp under its walls; and by a series of energetic and formidable assaults succeeded before long in taking it: by which the rest of the tribe were overawed into submission to Carthage. Having imposed a contribution upon the towns, and thus become possessed of a large sum of money, he went to the New Town[5] to winter. There, by a liberal treatment of the forces under his command, giving them an instalment of their pay at once and promising the rest, he established an excellent feeling towards himself in the army, as well as great hopes for the future.

14] Next summer he set out on another expedition against the Vaccaei, in which he took Salmantica by assault, but only succeeded in storming Arbucala, owing to the size of the town and the number and valour of its inhabitants, after a laborious siege. After this he suddenly found himself in a position of very great danger on his return march: being set upon by the Carpesii, the strongest tribe in those parts, who were joined also by neighbouring tribes, incited principally by refugees of the Olcades, but roused also to great wrath by those who escaped from Salmantica. If the Carthaginians had been compelled to give these people regular battle, there can be no doubt that they would have been defeated: but as it was, Hannibal, with admirable skill and caution, slowly retreated until he had put the Tagus between himself and the enemy; and thus giving battle at the crossing of the stream, supported by it and the elephants, of which he had about forty, he gained, to every one's surprise, a complete success. For when the barbarians attempted to force a crossing at several points of the river at once, the greater number of them were killed as they left the water by the elephants, who marched up and down along the brink of the river and caught them as they were coming out. Many of them also were killed in the river itself by the cavalry, because the horses were better able than the men to stand against the stream, and also because the cavalry were fighting on higher ground than the infantry which they were attacking. At length Hannibal turned the tables on the enemy, and, recrossing the river, attacked and put to flight their whole army, to the number of more than a hundred thousand men. After the defeat of this host, no one south of the Iber rashly ventured to face him except the people of Saguntum. From that town Hannibal tried his best to keep aloof; because, acting on the suggestions and advice of his father Hamilcar, he did not wish to give the Romans an avowed pretext for war until he had thoroughly secured the rest of the country.

15] But the people of Saguntum kept sending ambassadors to Rome,[6] partly because they foresaw what was coming, and trembled for their own existence, and partly that the Romans might be kept fully aware of the growing power of the Carthaginians in Iberia. For a long time the Romans disregarded their words: but now they sent out some commissioners to see what was going on. Just at that

time Hannibal had finished the conquests which he intended for that
season, and was going into winter quarters at the New Town again,
which was in a way the chief glory and capital town of the Carthaginians in Iberia. He found there the embassy from Rome,
granted them an interview, and listened to the message with which
they were charged. It was a strong injunction to him to leave
Saguntum alone, as being under the protection of Rome; and not
to cross the Iber, in accordance with the agreement come to in the
time of Hasdrubal. To this Hannibal answered with all the heat of
youth, inflamed by martial ardour, recent success, and his long-
standing hatred of Rome. He charged the Romans with having a
short time before, when on some political disturbances arising in the
town they had been chosen to act as arbitrators, seized the opportunity to put some of the leading citizens to death; and he declared
that the Carthaginians would not allow the Saguntines to be thus
treacherously dealt with, for it was the traditional policy of Carthage
to protect all persons so wronged. At the same time he sent home for
instructions as to what he was to do "in view of the fact that the
Saguntines were injuring certain of their subject allies." And altogether he was in a state of unreasoning anger and violent exasperation, which prevented him from availing himself of the real
causes for war, and made him take refuge in pretexts which would
not admit of justification, after the manner of men whose passions
master all considerations of equity. How much better it would have
been to demand of Rome the restoration of Sardinia, and the remis-
sion of the tribute, which she had taken an unfair opportunity to
impose on pain of a declaration of war. As it was, he said not a word
of the real cause, but alleged the fictitious one of the matter of
Saguntum; and so got the credit of beginning the war, not only in
defiance of reason, but still more in defiance of justice. The Roman
ambassadors, finding that there must undoubtedly be a war, sailed
to Carthage to enter the same protest before the people there. They
expected, however, that they would have to fight not in Italy, but in
Iberia, and that they would have Saguntum as a base of operations.

*   *   *

17] But Hannibal had started from New Carthage and was leading
his army straight against Saguntum. This city is situated on the seaward foot of the mountain chain on which the frontiers of Iberia and
Celtiberia converge, and is about seven stades[7] from the sea. The
district cultivated by its inhabitants is exceedingly producive, and

has a soil superior to any in all Iberia. Under the walls of this town Hannibal pitched his camp and set energetically to work on the siege, foreseeing many advantages that would accrue if he could take it. Of these the first was that he would thereby disappoint the Romans in their expectation of making Iberia the seat of war: a second was that he would thereby strike a general terror, which would render the already obedient tribes more submissive, and the still independent ones more cautious of offending him: but the greatest advantage of all was that thereby he would be able to push on his advance, without leaving an enemy on his rear. Besides these advantages, he calculated that the possession of this city would secure him abundant supplies for his expedition, and create an enthusiasm in the troops excited by individual acquisitions of booty; while he would conciliate the good will of those who remained at Carthage by the spoils which would be sent home. With these ideas he pressed on the siege with energy: sometimes setting an example to his soldiers by personally sharing in the fatigues of throwing up the siege works; and sometimes cheering on his men and recklessly exposing himself to danger. After a siege extending to the eighth month, in the course of which he endured every kind of suffering and anxiety, he finally succeeded in taking the town. An immense booty in money, slaves, and property fell into his hands, which he disposed of in accordance with his original design. The money he reserved for the needs of his projected expedition; the slaves were distributed according to merit among his men; while the property was at once sent entire to Carthage. The result answered his expectations: the army was rendered more eager for action; the home populace more ready to grant whatever he asked; and he himself was enabled, by the possession of such abundant means, to carry out many measures that were of service to his expedition.

* * *

20] But when news came to Rome of the fall of Saguntum, there was indeed no debate on the question of war, as some historians assert; who even add the speeches delivered on either side. . . .

The truth is that, when the Romans heard of the disaster at Saguntum, they at once elected envoys, whom they despatched in all haste to Carthage with the offer of two alternatives, one of which appeared to the Carthaginians to involve disgrace as well as injury if they accepted it, while the other was the beginning of a great struggle and of great dangers. For one of these alternatives was the surrender of Hannibal and his staff to Rome, the other was war. When the Roman envoys arrived and declared their message to the Senate, the choice proposed to them between these alternatives was listened to by the Carthaginians with indignation. Still they selected the most capable of their number to state their case, which was grounded on the following pleas.

21] Passing over the treaty made with Hasdrubal, as not having ever been made, and, if it had, as not being binding on them because made without their consent (and on this point they quoted the precedent of the Romans themselves, who in the Sicilian war repudiated the terms agreed upon and accepted by Lutatius, as having been made without their consent) — passing over this, they pressed with all the vehemence they could, throughout the discussion, the last treaty made in the Sicilian war;[8] in which they affirmed that there was no clause relating to Iberia, but one expressly providing security for the allies of both parties to the treaty. Now, they pointed out that the Saguntines at that time were not allies of Rome, and therefore were not protected by the clause. To prove their point, they read the treaty more than once aloud. On this occasion the Roman envoys contented themselves with the reply that, while Saguntum was intact, the matter in dispute admitted of pleadings and of discussion on its merits; but that, that city having been treacherously seized, they had only two alternatives, — either to deliver the persons guilty of the act, and thereby make it clear that they had no share in their crime, and that it was done without their consent; or, if they were not willing to do that, and avowed their complicity in it, to take the consequences.

The question of treaties between Rome and Carthage was referred to in general terms in the course of this debate: but I think a more particular examination of it will be useful both to practical statesmen, who require to know the exact truth of the matter, in order to avoid mistakes in any critical deliberation; and to historical students, that they may not be led astray by the ignorance or partisan bias of historians; but may have before them a conspectus, acknowledged to be accurate, of the various compacts which have been made between Rome and Carthage from the earliest times to our own day.

22] The first treaty between Rome and Carthage was made in the year of Lucius Junius Brutus and Marcus Horatius, the first Consuls appointed after the expulsion of the kings, by which men also the temple of Jupiter Capitolinus was consecrated. This was twenty-eight years before the invasion of Greece by Xerxes.[9] Of this treaty

I append a translation, as accurate as I could make it, — for the fact is that the ancient language differs so much from that at present in use, that the best scholars among the Romans themselves have great difficulty in interpreting some points in it, even after much study. The treaty is as follows: —

"There shall be friendship between the Romans and their allies, and the Carthaginians and their allies, on these conditions:

"Neither the Romans nor their allies are to sail beyond the Fair Promontory,[10] unless driven by stress of weather or the fear of enemies. If any one of them be driven ashore he shall not buy or take aught for himself save what is needful for the repair of his ship and the service of the gods, and he shall depart within five days.

"Men landing for traffic shall strike no bargain save in the presence of a herald or town-clerk. Whatever is sold in the presence of these, let the price be secured to the seller on the credit of the state — that is to say, if such sale be in Libya or Sardinia.

"If any Roman comes to the Carthaginian province in Sicily he shall enjoy all rights enjoyed by others. The Carthaginians shall do no injury to the people of Ardea, Antium, Laurentium, Circeii, Tarracina, nor any other people of the Latins that are subject to Rome.

"From those townships even which are not subject to Rome they shall hold their hands; and if they take one shall deliver it unharmed to the Romans. They shall build no fort in Latium; and if they enter the district in arms, they shall not stay a night therein."

23] The "Fair Promontory" here referred to is that which lies immediately to the north of Carthage; south of which the Carthaginians stipulated that the Romans should not sail with ships of war, because, as I imagine, they did not wish them to be acquainted with the coast near Byzacium, or the lesser Syrtis, which places they call Emporia, owing to the productiveness of the district. The treaty then goes on to say that, if any one of them is driven thither by stress of weather or fear of an enemy, and stands in need of anything for the worship of the gods and the repair of his vessel, this and no more he may take; and all those who have come to anchor there must necessarily depart within five days. To Carthage, and all the country on the Carthaginian side of the Fair Promontory in Libya, to Sardinia, and the Carthaginian province of Sicily, the treaty allows the Romans to sail for mercantile purposes; and the Carthaginians engage their public credit that such persons shall enjoy absolute security.

It is clear from this treaty that the Carthaginians speak of Sardinia and Libya as belonging to them entirely; but, on the other hand, make a distinction in the case of Sicily, and only stipulate for that part of it which is subject to Carthage. Similarly, the Romans also only stipulate concerning Latium; the rest of Italy they do not mention, as not being under their authority.

24] After this treaty there was a second,[11] in which we find that the Carthaginians have included the Tyrians and the township of Utica in addition to their former territory; and to the Fair Promontory Mastia and Tarseium are added, as the points east of which the Romans are not to make marauding expeditions or found a city. The treaty is as follows: "There shall be friendship between the Romans and their allies, and the Carthaginians, Tyrians, and township of Utica, on these terms: The Romans shall not maraud, nor traffic, nor found a city east of the Fair Promontory, Mastia, Tarseium. If the Carthaginians take any city in Latium which is not subject to Rome, they may keep the prisoners and the goods, but shall deliver up the town. If the Carthaginians take any folk, between whom and Rome a peace has been made in writing, though they be not subject to them, they shall not bring them into any harbours of the Romans; if such an one be so brought ashore, and any Roman lay claim to him, he shall be released. In like manner shall the Romans be bound towards the Carthaginians.

"If a Roman take water or provisions from any district within the jurisdiction of Carthage, he shall not injure, while so doing, any between whom and Carthage there is peace and friendship. Neither shall a Carthaginian in like case. If any one shall do so, he shall not be punished by private vengeance, but such action shall be a public misdemeanour.

"In Sardinia and Libya no Roman shall traffic nor found a city; he shall do no more than take in provisions and refit his ship. If a storm drive him upon those coasts, he shall depart within five days.

"In the Carthaginian province of Sicily and in Carthage he may transact business and sell whatsoever it is lawful for a citizen to do. In like manner also may a Carthaginian at Rome."

Once more in this treaty we may notice that the Carthaginians emphasize the fact of their entire possession of Libya and Sardinia, and prohibit any attempt of the Romans to land in them at all; and on the other hand, in the case of Sicily, they clearly distinguish their own province in it. So, too, the Romans, in regard to Latium, stipulate that the Carthaginians shall do no wrong to Ardea, Antium,

Circeii, Tarracina, all of which are on the seaboard of Latium, to which alone the treaty refers.

25] A third treaty again was made by Rome at the time of the invasion of Pyrrhus into Sicily;[12] before the Carthaginians undertook the war for the possession of Sicily. This treaty contains the same provisions as the two earlier treaties with these additional clauses: —

"If they make a treaty of alliance with Pyrrhus, the Romans or Carthaginians shall make it on such terms as not to preclude the one giving aid to the other, if that one's territory is attacked.

"If one or the other stand in need of help, the Carthaginians shall supply the ships, whether for transport or war; but each people shall supply the pay for its own men employed on them.

"The Carthaginians shall also give aid by sea to the Romans if need be; but no one shall compel the crews to disembark against their will."

Provision was also made for swearing to these treaties. In the case of the first, the Carthaginians were to swear by the gods of their ancestors, the Romans by Jupiter Lapis, in accordance with an ancient custom; in the case of the last treaty, by Mars and Quirinus. . . .

26] Seeing that such treaties exist and are preserved to this day, engraved on brass in the treasury of the Aediles in the temple of Jupiter Capitolinus, the historian Philinus[13] certainly does give us some reason to be surprised at him. Not at his ignorance of their existence: for even in our own day those Romans and Carthaginians, whose age placed them nearest to the times, and who had the reputation of taking the greatest interest in public affairs, were unaware of it. But what is surprising is, that he should have ventured on a statement exactly opposite: "That there was a treaty between Rome and Carthage, in virtue of which the Romans were bound to keep away from the whole of Sicily, the Carthaginians from the whole of Italy; and that the Romans broke the treaty and their oath when they first crossed over to Sicily." Whereas there does not exist, nor ever has existed, any such written compact at all. . . .

27] At the end of the first Punic war another treaty was made,[14] of which the chief provisions were these: "The Carthaginians shall evacuate Sicily and all islands lying between Italy and Sicily.

"The allies of neither of the parties to the treaty shall be attacked by the other.

"Neither party shall impose any contribution, nor erect any public building, nor enlist soldiers in the dominions of the other, nor make any compact of friendship with the allies of the other.

"The Carthaginians shall within ten years pay to the Romans two-thousand two-hundred talents, and a thousand on the spot; and shall restore all prisoners, without ransom, to the Romans."

Afterwards, at the end of the Mercenary war in Africa,[15] the Romans went so far as to pass a decree for war with Carthage, but eventually made a treaty to the following effect: "The Carthaginians shall evacuate Sardinia, and pay an additional twelve hundred talents."

Finally, in addition to these treaties, came that negotiated with Hasdrubal in Iberia, in which it was stipulated that "the Carthaginians should not cross the Iber with arms."[16]

Such were the mutual obligations established between Rome and Carthage from the earliest times to that of Hannibal.

28] As we find then that the Roman invasion of Sicily was not in contravention of their oaths, so we must acknowledge in the case of the second proclamation of war, in consequence of which the treaty for the evacuation of Sardinia was made, that it is impossible to find any reasonable pretext or ground for the Roman action. The Carthaginians were beyond question compelled by the necessities of their position, contrary to all justice, to evacuate Sardinia, and to pay this enormous sum of money. For as to the allegation of the Romans, that they had during the Mercenary war been guilty of acts of hostility to ships sailing from Rome, — that was barred by their own act in restoring, without ransom, the Carthaginian prisoners, in gratitude for similar conduct on the part of Carthage to Romans who had landed on their shores; a transaction which I have spoken of at length in my previous book.

These facts established, it remains to decide by a thorough investigation to which of the two nations the origin of the Hannibalian war is to be imputed.

29] I have explained the pleas advanced by the Carthaginians; I must now state what is alleged on the contrary by the Romans. For though it is true that in this particular interview, owing to their anger at the fall of Saguntum, they did not use these arguments, yet they were appealed to on many occasions, and by many of their citizens. First, they argued that the treaty of Hasdrubal could not be ignored, as the Carthaginians had the assurance to do: for it did not contain the clause, which that of Lutatius did, making its validity conditional on its ratification by the people of Rome; but Hasdrubal made the agreement absolutely and authoritatively that "the Carthaginians should not cross the Iber in arms."

Next they alleged that the clause in the treaty respecting Sicily, which by their own admission stipulated that "the allies of neither party should be attacked by the other," did not refer to then existing allies only, as the Carthaginians interpreted it; for in that case a clause would have been added, disabling either from making new alliances in addition to those already existing, or excluding allies, taken subsequently to the making of the treaty, from its benefits. But since neither of these provisions was made, it was plain that both the then existing allies, and all those taken subsequently on either side, were entitled to reciprocal security. And this was only reasonable. For it was not likely that they would have made a treaty depriving them of the power, when opportunity offered, of taking on such friends or allies as seemed to their interest; nor, again, if they had taken any such under their protection, was it to be supposed that they would allow them to be injured by any persons whatever. But, in fact, the main thing present in the minds of both parties to the treaty was, that they should mutually agree to abstain from attacking each other's allies, and on no account admit into alliance with themselves the allies of the other: and it was to subsequent allies that this particular clause applied, "Neither shall enlist soldiers, or impose contributions on the provinces or allies of the other; and all shall be alike secure of attack from the other side."

30] These things being so, they argued that it was beyond controversy that Saguntum had accepted the protection of Rome, several years before the time of Hannibal. The strongest proof of this, and one which would not be contested by the Carthaginians themselves, was that, when political disturbances broke out at Saguntum, the people chose the Romans, and not the Carthaginians, as arbitrators to settle the dispute and restore their constitution, although the latter were close at hand and were already established in Iberia.

I conclude, then, that if the destruction of Saguntum is to be regarded as the cause of this war, the Carthaginians must be acknowledged to be in the wrong, both in view of the treaty of Lutatius, which secured immunity from attack for the allies of both parties, and in view of the treaty of Hasdrubal, which disabled the Carthaginians from passing the Iber with arms. If on the other hand the taking Sardinia from them, and imposing the heavy money fine which accompanied it, are to be regarded as the causes, we must certainly acknowledge that the Carthaginians had good reason for undertaking the Hannibalian war: for as they had only yielded to the pressure of circumstances, so they seized a favourable turn in those circumstances to revenge themselves on their injurers.

NOTES

1. 238 B.C.
2. 195 B.C.
3. 238 B.C.
4. Hamilcar died in 229 B.C., Hasdrubal in 221.
5. Modern Cartagena.
6. 220–219 B.C.
7. About two-thirds of a mile.
8. First Punic War.
9. *Ca.* 509–508 B.C., but Polybius may well have mistaken the date of the first of these treaties. In any case, his statement that their language was difficult and archaic cannot apply to the most recent of them.
10. Cape Bon.
11. 348 B.C.
12. 279 B.C.
13. A historian who wrote from a markedly pro-Carthaginian viewpoint.
14. 241 B.C.
15. 238 B.C.
16. 228 B.C.

3

Agriculture in the Second Century B.C.

MARCUS PORCIUS CATO (234–149 B.C.) was one of the few "new men" to attain the highest offices in the first half of the second century B.C. His consulship (195 B.C.) was followed in 184 by his famous censorship. He is best known for his political and cultural conservatism, expressed in his bitter opposition to the liberal Scipio Africanus and his faction and for his intransigent hostility to Carthage before the Third Punic War. In addition to being a statesman and soldier, he was a prolific writer. His rambling treatise On Agriculture, written ca. 175–150, is the earliest extant Latin prose work. A handbook designed to instruct absentee senatorial landlords on the management of estates run on a capitalistic basis and using slave labor, his book gives invaluable insights into the new type of agriculture emerging in the second century B.C. as well as into the folklore of rural society.

Cato the Censor, On Agriculture, "Preface" and sections 1-4, 10-11, 56-60, 70, 98, 134-135, 138-140, 142-144

PREFACE] It is true that it would sometimes be better to seek a fortune in trade if it were not so subject to risk, or again, to lend money at interest, if it were an honorable occupation. But our forefathers held this belief and enacted it into law, that while a thief was compelled to repay double, one who loaned at interest had to repay fourfold. From this one may judge how much worse than a common thief they thought the fellow citizen who lent at interest. And when they were trying to praise a good man they called him a good farmer and a good tiller of the soil, and the one who received

From Ernest Brehaut, trans., CATO THE CENSOR ON FARMING (New York, 1933), pp. 1–11, 20–27, 78–81, 87, 99, 113–115, 118–119, 122–125. Reprinted by permission of the Columbia University Press.

this compliment was considered to have received the highest praise.

Now I esteem the merchant as active and keen to make money, but [consider him], as I have said before, exposed to risk and absolute ruin.

Moreover, it is from among the farmers that the sturdiest men and keenest soldiers come, and the gain they make is the most blameless of all, the most secure, and the least provocative of envy, and the men engaged in this pursuit are least given to disaffection.

Now, to come to my subject, this will serve as a preface to the undertaking I have promised.

1] When you think of buying a farm, make up your mind not to be eager to buy, and not to spare any exertion on your own part in going to see farms, and not to think it enough to go over them once. The oftener you visit it the more a good farm will please you.

Notice carefully how prosperous the neighbors are; in a good district they should be quite prosperous. And see that you go on a farm and look around it in such a way that you can find your way off it. See that it has a good exposure to the heavens or it may be subject to disaster. It should have a good soil and be valuable for its own worth. If possible, let it be at the foot of a mountain, looking toward the south, in a healthful situation, and where there is plenty of labor. It should have a good water supply.

It should be near a thriving town or near the sea or a river where ships go up or a good and well-traveled highway. It should be in a region where owners do not often change, and where those who do sell their farms repent of having sold them. See that it has good buildings. Beware of hastily disregarding the experience of others. It will be better to buy from an owner who is a good farmer and a good builder.

When you come to the farmstead, notice whether there is much equipment for pressing and many storage jars. If there are not, be sure the profit is in proportion. . . . Take care that it is not a farm requiring the least possible equipment and expense. Be sure [on the other hand] that a farm is like a man, that however much it brings in, if it pays much out, not a great deal is left.

If you ask me what sort of farm is best, I will say this: One hundred *jugera*[1] of land consisting of every kind of cultivated field, and in the best situation; [of these] the vineyard is of first importance if the wine is good and the yield is great; the irrigated garden is in the second place, the willow plantation in the third, the olive orchard in the fourth, the meadow in the fifth, the grain land in the sixth, forest trees to furnish foliage in the seventh, the vineyard trained on trees in the eighth, the acorn wood in the ninth.

2] When the head of the household comes to the farmhouse, on the same day, if possible, as soon as he has paid respect to the god of the household, he should make the round of the farm; if not on the same day, at least on the next. When he has learned in what way the farm work has been done and what tasks are finished and what not yet finished, he should next day summon the foreman and inquire how much of the work is done, how much remains, whether the different operations have been completed in good season and whether he can complete what remains, and what is the situation as to wine and grain and all other produce.

After he has been informed on these points he should go into an accounting of the day's works and the days. If the work accomplished is not made clear to him, and the foreman says he has pushed the work hard, but the slaves have not been well, the weather has been bad, the slaves have run away, they have done work on the public account — when he has given these and many other excuses, then bring the foreman back to an accounting of the farm tasks and of the day's works spent on them.

When the weather was rainy, [tell him] what work could have been done in spite of the rain: the storage jars could have been washed and tarred, the farm buildings could have been cleaned out, the grain shifted, the manure carried out and a manure pile made, the seed cleaned, the ropes mended and new ones made; the slaves should have mended their patchwork cloaks and hoods.

On festivals they could have cleaned old ditches, repaired the public road, cut briars, dug the garden, weeded the meadow, made bundles of the small wood cut in pruning, dug out thorns, broken up the spelt into grits and made the place neat. When slaves were sick they should not have been given as large an allowance of food.

When this has been gone over without irritation, [it is necessary] to consider how the remaining tasks are to be finished; to take account of money, of grain, of what has been stored for fodder, of wine and oil, [reckoning] what has been sold, what paid for, what is still to be collected and what remains to be sold; satisfactory guarantees of payment should be accepted. The balance remaining should be arrived at.

If anything is needed for the year's supply it should be bought; if there is a surplus of anything it should be sold. What needs to be put out under contract should be contracted for. The owner should give directions and leave them in writing as to what work he wishes to be done and what he wishes put out on contract.

He should look over the flock. He should hold an auction and, if he gets his price, sell the oil, the wine and the surplus grain; let him sell the old work oxen, the blemished cattle, the blemished sheep, the wool, the skins, the old wagon, the worn-out iron tools, the aged slave, the slave that is diseased, and everything else that he does not need. An owner should be a man who is a seller rather than a buyer.

3] In his early manhood the head of the household should be eager to plant his land. He should think long before building but he should not think about planting, but plant. When you have approached the age of thirty-six years you should build, if you have your land well planted. Build in such a way that the farm buildings will not find fault with the farm nor the farm with the buildings. It is an advantage to the owner to have a well-built farmstead with storerooms for oil and wine and many storage jars, so that it will be agreeable to wait for high prices. It will prove a source of gain and influence and reputation to him. He should have good press equipment so that the work can be done well. When the olives are gathered the oil should be made at once, to prevent its spoiling. Remember that great storms are wont to come every year and shake the olives down. If you gather them up quickly and the presses are ready, there will be no loss from the storm and the oil will be of a greener color and better. If they remain too long on the ground or on the floor they will begin to decay and the oil will be rank. A fresher and better oil can be made from any kind of olive if it is made in time.

For one hundred and twenty *jugera* of olive orchard there ought to be two presses, if the orchard is a good one and is closely planted and well cared for. There should be good olive-pulping mills, one to each press, of different sizes so that if the millstones are worn you can change them from one to the other; for each press, rawhide press ropes, six levers and twelve crosspieces, press-basket ropes of rawhide and two pulley blocks of the Greek style, worked with fiber ropes, the upper pulleys being eight finger-breadths in diameter and the lower, six. You will draw the press beam up faster if you wish to make [simple] rollers; [with the blocks] it will be lifted more slowly but with less labor.

4] The stable for the work oxen should be good and the [summer] pens built in the Faliscan[2] style with lattice work feed racks should also be good. The bars of the lattice work should be a foot apart. If you make them so, the oxen will not toss their fodder out.

Build your farm residence according to your means. In the case of a good farm, if you build well and on a good site, if you dwell comfortably in the country, you will visit it oftener and with greater pleasure; the farm will be the better for it, less mischief will be done and you will get more profit. The face is better than the back of the head. Be a good neighbor. Don't allow your slaves to do mischief. If the neighbors are glad to see you, you will sell your produce more readily, you will put work out on contract more easily, you will hire laborers more easily. If you build, they will help you with day's works, work animals, and building materials. If any need arises — and may it not — they will protect your interests with a good will.

* * *

10] How an olive orchard of two hundred and forty *jugera* should be equipped.

[It should have] a foreman, a foreman's wife, five laborers, three ox drivers, one ass driver, one swineherd, one shepherd, thirteen persons in all; three teams of oxen, three asses equipped with pack saddles to carry out the manure, one ass for mill work, one hundred sheep.

Five oil presses fully equipped including the pulping mills, a bronze cauldron to hold thirty *amphorae*,[3] a cover for the cauldron, three iron hooks, three water pitchers, two funnels, a bronze cauldron to hold five *amphorae*, a cover for it, three hooks, a small vat for water, two *amphorae* for oil, one half-*amphora* measure holding fifty, three skimming ladles, one well bucket, one wash basin, one water pitcher, one slop pail, one small tray, one chamber pot, one watering pot, one ladle, one lamp stand, one *sextarius* measure.[4]

Three wagons of the larger size, six plows with plowshares, three yokes fitted with rawhide ropes, harness for six oxen; one harrow with iron teeth, four wickerwork baskets for manure, three rush baskets for manure, three pack-saddles, three pads for asses.

Implements of iron: eight heavy spades, eight heavy two-pronged hoes, four spades, five shovels, two four-pronged drags, eight scythes for mowing grass, five sickles for harvesting, five billhooks for trimming trees, three axes, three wedges, one mortar for spelt, two fire tongs, one fire shovel, two portable fire pans.

One hundred storage jars for oil, twelve vats, ten storage jars for the wine-press refuse, ten for oil dregs, ten for wine, twenty for grain, one vat for lupins, ten storage jars of the smaller kind, a vat used for washing, one tub for bathing, two vats for water, separate covers for all storage jars large and small.

One mill to be worked by an ass, one hand mill, one Spanish mill, three harnesses for the mill asses, one kneading table, two round plates of bronze, two tables, three long benches, one stool for the chamber, three low stools, four chairs, two large chairs, one bed in the chamber, four beds with woven thongs and three beds; one wooden mortar, one mortar for fuller's work, one loom for cloaks, two mortars, one pestle for beans and one for spelt, one for [cleaning] spelt for seed, one to separate olive pits, one *modius* measure and one half-*modius* measure.[5]

Eight mattresses, eight spreads, sixteen pillows, ten coverlets, three towels, six cloaks made of patchwork for the slaves.

11] How a vineyard of a hundred *jugera* should be equipped.

[It should have] a foreman, a foreman's wife, ten laborers, one ox driver, one ass driver, one man in charge of the willow grove, one swineherd, in all sixteen persons; two oxen, two asses for wagon work, one ass for the mill work.

Three presses fully equipped, storage jars in which five vintages amounting to eight hundred *cullei*[6] can be stored, twenty storage jars for wine-press refuse, twenty for grain, separate coverings for the jars, six fiber-covered half-*amphorae,* four fiber-covered *amphorae,* two funnels, three basketwork strainers, three strainers to dip up the flower, ten jars for [handling] the wine juice.

Two wagons, two plows, one wagon yoke, one yoke for the vineyard, one ass yoke, one round plate of bronze, one harness for the mill ass.

One bronze cauldron to hold one *culleus,* one cover for it, three iron hooks, one bronze cauldron for concentrated wine to hold one *culleus,* two water pitchers, one watering pot, one washbasin, one water pitcher, one slop bucket, one well bucket, one small tray, one skimming ladle, one lampstand, one chamber pot, four beds, one bench, two tables, one kneading table, one chest for clothing, one store closet, six long benches.

One well pulley, one *modius* measure, iron bound, one half-*modius* measure, one vat for washing, one bathtub, one vat for lupins, ten storage jars of the smaller size.

Harness for two oxen, three pads for asses and three packsaddles, three baskets for the wine settlings, three mills worked by asses, one hand mill.

Implements of iron: five sickles for cutting reeds, six bill-hooks for use in cutting foliage, three for the orchards, five axes, four wedges, two plowshares, ten heavy spades, six spades, four shovels, two four-pronged drags, four wickerwork baskets for manure, one rush basket for manure, forty knives for cutting bunches of grapes, ten for butcher's broom, two portable fire pans, two fire tongs, one fire shovel.

Twenty hampers of the kind used in Ameria, forty baskets of the sort used in planting, or forty wooden picking trays, forty wooden shovels, two dugout carriers, four mattresses, four spreads, six pillows, six coverlets, three towels, six patchwork cloaks for the slaves.

* * *

56] Bread rations for the slaves. For those who do the field work, four *modii* of wheat in winter, four and one-half in summer; for the foreman, the foreman's wife, the overseer and the shepherd, three *modii;* for the slaves working in chains, four pounds of bread in winter, five when they begin to dig the vineyard, until there begin to be figs, then go back to four pounds.

57] Wine for the slaves. When the vintage is over, let them drink the after wine for three months. In the fourth month a half-*sextarius* daily, i.e., for the month, two and one-half *congii;* in the fifth, sixth, seventh and eighth months, a *sextarius* daily, i.e., for the month, five *congii;* in the ninth, tenth, eleventh and twelfth months, a *sextarius* and one-half daily, i.e., for the month, an *amphora;* in addition to this, on the Saturnalia and the Compitalia, three and a half *congii* for each man; the total of wine for the year for each man, seven *amphorae.* For the slaves working in chains add more in proportion to the work they are doing. It is not too much if they drink ten *amphorae* of wine apiece in a year.

58] Relishes for the slaves. Preserve as many as possible of the dropped olives. Later, when the olives are ripe, preserve some of those that yield the least oil, and use them sparingly so that they will last as long as possible. After the olives have been eaten, give them fish pickle and vinegar. Give each one per month one *sextarius* of olive oil. A *modius* of salt is enough for each one for a year.

59] Clothing for the slaves. A tunic weighing three and one-half pounds and a cloak in alternate years. Whenever you give a tunic or a cloak to any of them, first get the old one back to make patchwork cloaks of. Good wooden shoes should be given to them every second year.

60] A year's grain feed for the work oxen. For each team, one hundred and twenty *modii* of lupins or two hundred and forty of acorns, five hundred and twenty pounds of hay, *ocinum,* twenty *modii* of beans, thirty of vetches. On this account see that you sow enough vetches to have some for grain. When you sow fodder make many sowings.

* * *

70] Medicine for the work oxen.

If you are afraid of sickness, give them while they are still in good health three grains of salt, three leaves of bay, three shreds of cut leek, three spikes of bulbed leek, three spikes of garlic, three grains of incense, three plants of the Sabine herb, three leaves of rue, three tendrils of the white vine, three small white beans, three live coals, three *sextarii* of wine.

The one who gathers all these, pounds them [in the mortar] and gives the dose, should hold himself upright as he does so. He who gives the dose should be fasting. Give some of this potion to each work ox three days in succession. So divide it that when you give three doses to each you will use it all up, and see that the ox and the one who gives the dose shall both stand upright. Give it from a dish of wood.

* * *

98] To keep moths from touching clothes:

Boil oil dregs down to half and dress with them the bottom of the chest and the outside and the feet and the corners. When it has dried, put the clothes in it. If you do this, moths will do no injury. And if you dress any kind of wooden furniture in the same way it will not decay and when you polish it, it will be brighter. In the same way dress all articles of bronze, but first polish them well. Later on, after you have dressed them, polish when you wish to use. They will be brighter and corrosion will not harm them.

* * *

134] Before you make the harvest you should offer a preliminary sacrifice of a sow pig in the following way. Offer a sow pig to Ceres before you store away these crops: spelt, wheat, barley, beans, rape seed. First address Janus, Jupiter and Juno with incense and wine before you sacrifice the sow pig.

Offer a sacrificial cake to Janus with these words:

"Father Janus, in offering to thee this sacrificial cake I make good prayers that thou will be kind and favorable to me, my children, and my house and household."

Offer an oblation cake to Jupiter and worship him in these words:

"Jupiter, in offering thee this oblation cake I make good prayers that thou be kind and favorable to me, my children, and my house and household, being worshipped with this offering."

Afterward offer wine to Janus thus:

"Father Janus, as I besought thee with good prayers in offering the sacrificial cake, let me honor thee for the same purpose with the sacrificial wine."

And then in these words to Jupiter:

"Jupiter, as thou wert worshipped with the cake, so be worshipped with this sacrificial wine."

Then slaughter the preliminary sow pig. When the internal organs have been taken out, offer a sacrificial cake to Janus and worship him in the same terms as before when you offered the cake. Offer an oblation cake to Jupiter and worship him in the same terms as before. Likewise offer wine to Janus and offer wine to Jupiter in the same terms as it was offered before in the offering of the sacrificial cake and the oblation cake. Then sacrifice the internal organs and wine to Ceres.

135] At Rome [buy] tunics, togas, rough cloaks, patched cloaks, wooden shoes; at Cales and Minturnae, hoods, iron implements, sickles, spades, grubbing hoes, axes, harness, bridle-bits, and small chains; at Venafrum, spades; at Suessa and in Lucania, wagons; threshing sledges at Alba and Rome; storage jars, vats and roof tiles at Venafrum.

Plows of the Roman style will be good for stiff land, of the Campanian style for light soil; yokes of the Roman style will be best; the plow-share that slips over will be the best.

Olive mills at Pompeii and at the walls of Rufrium near Nola; keys and door bars at Rome; water buckets, half-*amphora* oil measures, water pitchers, half-*amphora* measures for wine and other containers made of bronze, at Capua and Nola.

Press baskets of Campanian style are useful [?]; ropes to raise the press beam and every sort of fibre rope at Capua; press baskets of Roman style at Suessa and Casinum, but the best will be at Rome.

If anyone is going to have a press rope made, there are L. Tunnius at Casinum, and C. Mennius, son of Lucius, at Venafrum. It is necessary to furnish for it eight good native hides, freshly dressed and having the least possible amount of salt. They should first be dressed and greased, and then dried. . . .

*   *   *

138] It is permitted to yoke oxen on festivals. This is the work they may do: haul wood, bean vines, grain which [the owner] does not expect to feed. There are no festivals for mules, horses or asses unless they belong to the *familia*.

139] Harvesting leaves in a sacred grove should be done according to the Roman custom in the following manner. Offer a pig as atonement and use this form of words: "Whether thou art god or goddess" — [naming here the divinity] to whom the sacred grove belongs — "as it is right to make thee an offering of a pig as atonement with a view to trimming this sacred grove and with a view to such and such uses" — provided the offering is made in due form, whether I make it or some one else makes it at my direction [is of no importance] — "with this purpose, then, in offering this pig as atonement, I make thee good prayers that thou be of good will and favorable to me, my house and household and my children; for these reasons be thou honored by the sacrifice of this pig as atonement."

140] If you wish to dig up trees, offer a second atonement in the same way, and add this further expression: "With a view to doing a piece of work." As long as the work goes on, make the offering daily in parts. If you miss a day, or a festival of the state or one of the household intervenes, make another atonement.

*   *   *

142] The duties of the foreman.

As to the orders the master has given in regard to all that needs to be done on the farm, and all the purchases that must be made and the supplies that must be made ready, and as to how provisions and clothing should be given to the slaves, I urge him to attend to the same and do them and be obedient to the master's word. More than this, in the matter of how he should manage the housekeeper, and how he should order her, [I urge upon him to see to it] that at the master's arrival the necessary supplies are at hand and are carefully provided.

143] See to it that the housekeeper attends to her duties. If the master has given her to you as a wife, be satisfied with her. See that she fears you; do not let her be too inclined to ease; let her associate with neighboring and other women as little as possible and not welcome them to her home or to visit her. She should not go out anywhere to dinner or be in the habit of walking about. She should not do any act of religion, or commission anyone to do it for her, except by direction of her master or mistress. She should know that the master attends to the observances of religion for the entire household. Let her be clean; let her keep the farmhouse swept and neat; let her have the hearth swept clean every night before she goes to bed. On the kalends, the ides, the nones, and whenever there is a festival, let her put a wreath on the hearth, and on the same days let her worship the Lar of the household with what she has. Let her see to it that she has food cooked for you and the household; that she has many hens and eggs. Let her have dried pears, service berries, figs and raisins; service berries in grape-juice syrup in storage jars, and also pears and grapes and sparrow quinces; grapes [packed in] jars and covered up in the grapeskins or buried in the earth, and fresh hazel nuts in a jar buried in the earth. As for Santian quinces in storage jars and other fruits that are usually stored, and wild fruits, she should store all these away diligently every year. She should know how to make good flour and fine spelt grits.

144] The olive harvest should be put out on contract in this way:

[The contractor] shall gather all the olives rightly according to the will of the owner or the overseer whom he has appointed or the buyer to whom the olive crop has been sold. Let him not pick the olives from the trees or beat the trees except according to the directions of the owner or overseer. If anyone acts contrary to this, no one shall pay for what he has gathered on that day and no payment shall be due.

All the gatherers shall swear in the presence of the master or the overseer that they have not stolen olives during that harvest from L. Manlius' farm, nor has anyone else with their connivance. If anyone of them will not take oath to this effect, no one shall pay for all that he has gathered and payment shall not be due. [The contractor] shall give security to the satisfaction of L. Manlius that the olives will be gathered in a workmanlike way. He shall return the ladders in the condition in which they were given, except if some old ones have been broken. If he does not return them he shall pay what is fair, and the amount shall be deducted according to the decision of a good man. If any loss has been caused to the owner through an act of the contractor, he shall pay for it. The amount shall be deducted according to the decision of a good man.

He shall furnish as many gatherers from the ground as are necessary and pickers from the trees. If he does not do so, deduction shall be made [of the sum] at which men are hired or the work farmed out: so much less will be due. He shall not carry wood or olives from the farm, and if any picker carries them away, for each time two sesterces shall be deducted,[9] and this sum shall not be due. He shall measure all the olives, after they have been freed from trash, with the *modius* for olives.

He shall furnish fifty men working constantly and two-thirds of them shall be pickers from the trees. No partner shall go off to where the picking and pressing of the olives is being farmed out at a higher price except in case he has named a substitute for the work at hand. If anyone acts contrary to these conditions, if the owner or overseer wishes it, all the partners shall take oath. If they do not do so, no one shall pay for gathering and pressing the olives, and nothing shall be due to one who has not taken the oath. . . .

NOTES

1. One *jugerum*, about five-eighths of an acre.
2. Falerii was an Etruscan town.
3. One *amphora*, about 7.225 gallons.
4. One *sextarius*, about 1.2 pints.
5. One *modius*, about 9.62 quarts or 1.2 pecks.
6. One *culleus*, about 144.5 gallons.
7. One *congius*, about 3.6 quarts.

4

The Gracchi

APPIAN OF ALEXANDRIA (ca. A.D. 95–165), an equestrian civil servant, wrote his Roman History about A.D. 150. His work is occasionally rhetorical, and its reliability is uneven, since the sources he used varied widely in accuracy. Parts, especially those covering the latter decades of the second and the beginning of the first century B.C., are nevertheless extremely important, since they provide the principal continuous literary narrative covering the early phases of the Roman Revolution. Generally speaking, his account of the Gracchi is both accurate and balanced; it reveals clearly the social and economic tensions that produced the reform movement and at the same time portrays fairly the points of view of both the optimates and populares. Modern interpretations of the Gracchan reforms tend to be controversial. If Appian is to be believed, they scarcely qualify as social revolutionaries in a twentieth-century sense.

Appian, The Civil Wars I, 1, 7-13; 2, 14-17; 3, 18-26

i

1, 7] THE ROMANS, as they subdued the Italian peoples successively in war, used to seize a part of their lands and build towns there, or enrol colonists of their own to occupy those already existing, and their idea was to use these as outposts; but of the land acquired by war they assigned the cultivated part forthwith to the colonists, or sold or leased it. Since they had no leisure as yet to allot the part which then lay desolated by war (this was generally the greater part), they made proclamation that in the meantime those who were willing to work it might do so for a toll of the yearly crops, a tenth of the grain and a fifth of the fruit. From those who kept flocks was required a toll of the animals, both oxen and small

From Horace White, trans., APPIAN'S ROMAN HISTORY (Cambridge, Mass., 1913), vol. iii, pp. 15–53. Reprinted by permission of Harvard University Press and The Loeb Classical Library.

cattle. They did these things in order to multiply the Italian race, which they considered the most laborious of peoples, so that they might have plenty of allies at home. But the very opposite thing happened; for the rich, getting possession of the greater part of the undistributed lands, and being emboldened by the lapse of time to believe that they would never be dispossessed, absorbing any adjacent strips and their poor neighbours' allotments, partly by purchase under persuasion and partly by force, came to cultivate vast tracts instead of single estates, using slaves as labourers and herdsmen, lest free labourers should be drawn from agriculture into the army. At the same time the ownership of slaves brought them great gain from the multitude of their progeny, who increased because they were exempt from military service. Thus certain powerful men became extremely rich and the race of slaves multiplied throughout the country, while the Italian people dwindled in numbers and strength, being oppressed by penury, taxes, and military service. If they had any respite from these evils they passed their time in idleness, because the land was held by the rich, who employed slaves instead of freemen as cultivators.

8] For these reasons the people became troubled lest they should no longer have sufficient allies of the Italian stock, and lest the government itself should be endangered by such a vast number of slaves. As they did not perceive any remedy, for it was not easy, nor in any way just, to deprive men of so many possessions they had held so long, including their own trees, buildings, and fixtures, a law was at last passed with difficulty at the instance of the tribunes, that nobody should hold more than 500 jugera of this land, or pasture on it more than 100 cattle or 500 sheep.[1] To ensure the observance of this law it was provided also that there should be a certain number of freemen employed on the farms, whose business it should be to watch and report what was going on.

Having thus comprehended all this in a law, they took an oath over and above the law, and fixed penalties for violating it, and it was supposed that the remaining land would soon be divided among the poor in small parcels. But there was not the smallest consideration shown for the law or the oaths. The few who seemed to pay some respect to them conveyed their lands to their relations fraudulently, but the greater part disregarded it altogether, 9] till at length Tiberius Sempronius Gracchus, an illustrious man, eager for glory, a most powerful speaker, and for these reasons well known to all, delivered an eloquent discourse, while serving as tribune,[2] concerning the Italian race, lamenting that a people so valiant in war, and related in blood to the Romans, were declining little by little into pauperism and paucity of numbers without any hope of remedy. He inveighed against the multitude of slaves as useless in war and never faithful to their masters, and adduced the recent calamity brought upon the masters by their slaves in Sicily,[3] where the demands of agriculture had greatly increased the number of the latter; recalling also the war waged against them by the Romans, which was neither easy nor short, but long-protracted and full of vicissitudes and dangers. After speaking thus he again brought forward the law, providing that nobody should hold more than the 500 jugera of the public domain. But he added a provision to the former law, that the sons of the occupiers might each hold one-half of that amount, and that the remainder should be divided among the poor by three elected commissioners, who should be changed annually.

10] This was extremely disturbing to the rich because, on account of the triumvirs, they could no longer disregard the law as they had done before; nor could they buy the allotments of others, because Gracchus had provided against this by forbidding sales. They collected together in groups, and made lamentation, and accused the poor of appropriating the results of their tillage, their vineyards, and their dwellings. Some said that they had paid the price of the land to their neighbours. Were they to lose the money with the land? Others said that the graves of their ancestors were in the ground, which had been alloted to them in the division of their fathers' estates. Others said that their wives' dowries had been expended on the estates, or that the land had been given to their own daughters as dowry. Moneylenders could show loans made on this security. All kinds of wailing and expressions of indignation were heard at once. On the other side were heard the lamentations of the poor — that they were being reduced from competence to extreme penury, and from that to childlessness, because they were unable to rear their offspring. They recounted the military services they had rendered, by which this very land had been acquired, and were angry that they should be robbed of their share of the common property. They reproached the rich for employing slaves, who were always faithless and ill-disposed and for that reason unserviceable in war, instead of freemen, citizens, and soldiers. While these classes were thus lamenting and indulging in mutual accusations, a great number of others, composed of colonists, or inhabitants of the free towns, or persons otherwise interested in the lands and who were under like apprehensions, flocked in and took sides with their respective factions. Emboldened by numbers and exasperated against each other they kindled considerable disturbances, and waited eagerly for the voting on the new law, some intending to prevent its enactment by all means, and others to enact it at all costs. In addition to personal interest the spirit of rivalry spurred both sides in the preparations they were making against each other for the appointed day.

11] What Gracchus had in his mind in proposing the measure was not money, but men. Inspired greatly by the usefulness of the work, and believing that nothing more advantageous or admirable could ever happen to Italy, he took no account of the difficulties surrounding it. When the time for voting came he advanced many other arguments at considerable length and also asked them whether it was not just to let the commons divide the common property; whether a citizen was not worthy of more consideration at all times than a slave; whether a man who served in the army was not more useful than one who did not; and whether one who had a share in the country was not more likely to be devoted to the public interests. He did not dwell long on this comparison between freemen and slaves, which he considered degrading, but proceeded at once to a review of their hopes and fears for the country, saying that the Romans possessed most of their territory by conquest, and that they had hopes of occupying the rest of the habitable world; but now the question of greatest hazard was, whether they should gain the rest by having plenty of brave men, or whether, through their weakness and mutual jealousy, their enemies should take away what they already possessed. After exaggerating the glory and riches on the one side and the danger and fear on the other, he admonished the rich to take heed, and said that for the realization of these hopes they ought to bestow this very land as a free gift, if necessary, on men who would rear children, and not, by contending about small things, overlook larger ones; especially since for any labour they had spent they were receiving ample compensation in the undisputed title to 500 jugera each of free land, in a high state of cultivation, without cost, and half as much more for each son in the case of those who had sons. After saying much more to the same purport and exciting the poor, as well as others who were moved by reason rather than by the desire for gain, he ordered the clerk to read the proposed law.

12] Marcus Octavius, however, another tribune, who had been

induced by those in possession of the lands to interpose his veto (for among the Romans the negative veto always defeats an affirmative proposal), ordered the clerk to keep silence. Thereupon Gracchus reproached him severely and adjourned the comitia to the following day. Then he stationed near himself a sufficient guard, as if to force Octavius against his will, and ordered the clerk with threats to read the proposed law to the multitude. He began to read, but when Octavius again forbade he stopped. Then the tribunes fell to wrangling with each other, and a considerable tumult arose among the people. The leading citizens besought the tribunes to submit their controversy to the Senate for decision. Gracchus seized on the suggestion, believing that the law was acceptable to all well-disposed persons, and hastened to the senate-house. But, as he had only a few followers there and was upbraided by the rich, he ran back to the forum and said that he would take the vote at the comitia of the following day, both on the law and on the official rights of Octavius, to determine whether a tribune who was acting contrary to the people's interest could continue to hold office. And this Gracchus did; for when Octavius, nothing daunted, again interposed, Gracchus proposed to take the vote on him first.

When the first tribe voted to abrogate the magistracy of Octavius, Gracchus turned to him and begged him to desist from his veto. As he would not yield, he took the votes of the other tribes. There were thirty-five tribes at that time. The seventeen that voted first passionately supported the motion. If the eighteenth should do the same it would make a majority. Again did Gracchus, in the sight of the people, urgently importune Octavius in his present extreme danger not to prevent a work which was most righteous and useful to all Italy, and not to frustrate the wishes so earnestly entertained by the people, whose desires he ought rather to share in his character of tribune, and not to risk the loss of his office by public condemnation. After speaking thus he called the gods to witness that he did not willingly do any despite to his colleague. As Octavius was still unyielding he went on taking the vote. Octavius was forthwith reduced to the rank of a private citizen and slunk away unobserved. Quintus Mummius was chosen tribune in his place, and the agrarian law was enacted.

13] The first triumvirs appointed to divide the land were Gracchus himself, the proposer of the law, his brother of the same name, and his father-in-law, Appius Claudius, since the people still feared that the law might fail of execution unless Gracchus should take the

lead with his whole family. Gracchus became immensely popular by
reason of the law and was escorted home by the multitude as though
he were the founder, not of a single city or race, but of all the
nations of Italy. After this the victorius party returned to the fields
from which they had come to attend to this business. The defeated
ones remained in the city and talked the matter over, feeling
aggrieved, and saying that as soon as Gracchus should become a
private citizen he would be sorry that he had done despite to the
sacred and inviolable office of tribune, and had sown in Italy so
many seeds of future strife.

*　　*　　*

2, 14] It was now summer, and the election of tribunes was imminent. As the day for voting approached it was very evident that the
rich had earnestly promoted the election of those most inimical to
Gracchus. The latter, fearing that evil would befall if he should not
be re-elected for the following year,[4] summoned his friends from the
fields to attend the election, but as they were occupied with harvest
he was obliged, when the day fixed for the voting drew near, to have
recourse to the plebeians of the city. So he went around asking each
one separately to elect him tribune for the ensuing year, on account
of the danger he was incurring for them. When the voting took
place the first two tribes pronounced for Gracchus. The rich ob-
jected that it was not lawful for the same man to hold the office
twice in succession. The tribune Rubrius, who had been chosen by
lot to preside over the comitia, was in doubt about it, and Mummius,
who had been chosen in place of Octavius, urged him to hand over
the comitia to his charge. This he did, but the remaining tribunes
contended that the presidency should be decided by lot, saying that
when Rubrius, who had been chosen in that way, resigned, the
casting of lots ought to be done over again by all. As there was much
strife over this question, Gracchus, who was getting the worst of it,
adjourned the voting to the following day. In utter despair he went
about in black, though still in office, and led his son around the
forum and introduced him to each man and committed him to their
charge, as if he himself felt that death, at the hands of his enemies,
were at hand.

15] The poor when they had time to think were moved with deep
sorrow, both on their own account (for they believed that they were
no longer to live in a free estate under equal laws, but would be
reduced to servitude by the rich), and on account of Gracchus him-

self, who was in such fear and torment in their behalf. So they all accompanied him with tears to his house in the evening, and bade him be of good courage for the morrow. Gracchus cheered up, assembled his partisans before daybreak, and communicated to them a signal to be displayed if there were need for fighting. He then took possession of the temple on the Capitoline hill, where the voting was to take place, and occupied the middle of the assembly. As he was obstructed by the other tribunes and by the rich, who would not allow the votes to be taken on this question, he gave the signal. There was a sudden shout from those who knew of it, and violence followed. Some of the partisans of Gracchus took position around him like body-guards. Others, having girded up their cloaks, seized the fasces and staves in the hands of the lictors and broke them in pieces. They drove the rich out of the assembly with such disorder and wounds that the tribunes fled from their places in terror, and the priests closed the doors of the temple. Many ran away pell-mell and scattered wild rumours. Some said that Gracchus had deposed all the other tribunes, and this was believed because none of them could be seen. Others said that he had declared himself tribune for the ensuing year without any election.

16] In these circumstances the Senate assembled at the temple of Fides. It is astonishing to me that they never thought of appointing a dictator in this emergency, although they had often been protected by the government of a single ruler in such times of peril; but a resource which had been found most useful in former times was never even recollected by the people, either then or later. After reaching such decision as they did reach, they marched up to the Capitol, Cornelius Scipio Nasica, the pontifex maximus, leading the way and calling out with a loud voice, "Let those who would save our country follow me." He wound the border of his toga about his head either to induce a greater number to go with him by the singularity of his appearance, or to make for himself, as it were, a helmet as a sign of battle for those who saw it, or in order to conceal himself from the gods on account of what he was about to do. When he arrived at the temple and advanced against the partisans of Gracchus they yielded out of regard for so excellent a citizen, and because they observed the Senators following with him. The latter wresting their clubs out of the hands of the Gracchans themselves, or breaking up benches and other furniture that had been brought for the use of the assembly, began beating them, and pursued them, and drove them over the precipice. In the tumult many of the Gracchans perished, and Gracchus himself, vainly circling round the temple, was slain at the door close by the statues of the kings. All the bodies were thrown by night into the Tiber.

17] So perished on the Capitol, and while still tribune, Gracchus, the son of that Gracchus who was twice consul, and of Cornelia, daughter of that Scipio who robbed Carthage of her supremacy. He lost his life in consequence of a most excellent design too violently pursued; and this abominable crime, the first that was perpetrated in the public assembly, was seldom without parallels thereafter from time to time. On the subject of the murder of Gracchus the city was divided between sorrow and joy. Some mourned for themselves and for him, and deplored the present condition of things, believing that the commonwealth no longer existed, but had been supplanted by force and violence. Other considered that their dearest wishes were accomplished.

* * *

3, 18] These things took place at the time when Aristonicus was contending with the Romans for the government of Asia; but after Gracchus was slain and Appius Claudius died, Fulvius Flaccus and Papirius Carbo were appointed, in conjunction with the younger Gracchus, to divide the land. As the persons in possession neglected to hand in lists of their holdings, a proclamation was issued that informers should furnish testimony against them. Immediately a great number of embarrassing lawsuits sprang up. Wherever a new field adjoining an old one had been bought, or divided among the allies, the whole district had to be carefully inquired into on account of the measurement of this one field, to discover how it had been sold and how divided. Not all owners had preserved their contracts, or their allotment titles, and even those that were found were often ambiguous. When the land was resurveyed some owners were obliged to give up their fruit-trees and farm-buildings in exchange for naked ground. Others were transferred from cultivated to uncultivated lands, or to swamps, or pools. In fact, the land having originally been so much loot, the survey had never been carefully done. As the original proclamation authorized anybody to work the undistributed land who wished to do so, many had been prompted to cultivate the parts immediately adjoining their own, till the line of demarcation between public and private had faded from view. The progress of time also made many changes. Thus the injustice done by the rich, although great, was not easy to ascertain. So there was nothing but a general turn-about, all parties being moved out of their own places and settling down in other people's.

19] The Italian allies who complained of these disturbances,[5] and especially of the lawsuits hastily brought against them, chose Cornelius Scipio, the destroyer of Carthage, to defend them against these grievances. As he had availed himself of their very zealous support in war he was reluctant to disregard their request. So he came into the Senate, and although, out of regard for the plebeians, he did not openly find fault with the law of Gracchus, he expatiated on its difficulties and urged that these causes should not be decided by the triumvirs, because they did not possess the confidence of the litigants, but should be assigned to other courts. As his view seemed reasonable, they yielded to his persuasion, and the consul Tuditanus was appointed to give judgment in these cases. But when he took up the work he saw the difficulties of it, and marched against the Illyrians as a pretext for not acting as judge, and since nobody brought cases for trial before the triumvirs they remained idle. From this cause hatred and indignation arose among the people against Scipio because they saw a man, in whose favour they had often opposed the aristocracy and incurred their enmity, electing him consul twice contrary to law, now taking the side of the Italian allies against themselves. When Scipio's enemies observed this, they cried out that he was determined to abolish the law of Gracchus utterly and for that end was about to inaugurate armed strife and bloodshed.

20] When the people heard these charges they were in a state of alarm until Scipio, after placing near his couch at home one evening a tablet on which to write during the night the speech he intended to deliver before the people, was found dead in his bed without a wound. Whether this was done by Cornelia, the mother of the Gracchi (aided by her daughter, Sempronia, who though married to Scipio was both unloved and unloving because she was deformed and childless), lest the law of Gracchus should be abolished, or whether, as some think, he committed suicide because he saw plainly that he could not accomplish what he had promised, is not known. Some say that slaves under torture testified that unknown persons were introduced through the rear of the house by night who suffocated him, and that those who knew about it hesitated to tell because the people were angry with him still and rejoiced at his death.

So died Scipio, and although he had been of extreme service to the Roman power he was not even honoured with a public funeral; so much does the anger of the present moment outweigh gratitude for the past. And this event, sufficiently important in itself, took place as a mere incident of the sedition of Gracchus.

21] Even after these events those who were in possession of the lands postponed the division on various pretexts for a very long time. Some proposed that all the Italian allies, who made the greatest resistance to it, should be admitted to Roman citizenship so that, out of gratitude for the greater favour, they might no longer quarrel about the land. The Italians were ready to accept this, because they preferred Roman citizenship to possession of the fields. Fulvius Flaccus, who was then both consul and triumvir,[6] exerted himself to the utmost to bring it about, but the senators were angry at the thought of making their subjects equal citizens with themselves.

For this reason the attempt was abandoned, and the populace, who had been so long in the hope of acquiring land, became disheartened. While they were in this mood Gaius Gracchus, who had made himself agreeable to them as a triumvir, offered himself for the tribuneship.[7] He was the younger brother of Tiberius Gracchus, the promoter of the law, and had been quiet for some time after his brother's death, but since many of the senators treated him scornfully he announced himself as a candidate for the office of tribune. Being elected with flying colours he began to lay plots against the Senate, and made the unprecedented suggestion that a monthly distribution of corn should be made to each citizen at the public expense. Thus he quickly got the leadership of the people by one political measure, in which he had the cooperation of Fulvius Flaccus. Directly after that he was chosen tribune for the following year, for in cases where there was not a sufficient number of candidates the law authorized the people to choose further tribunes from the whole body of citizens.

22] Thus Gaius Gracchus was tribune a second time. Having bought the plebeians, as it were, he began, by another like political manœuvre, to court the equestrian order, who hold the middle place between the Senate and the plebeians. He transferred the courts of justice, which had become discredited by reason of bribery, from the senators to the knights, reproaching the former especially with the recent examples of Aurelius Cotta, Salinator, and, third in the list, Manius Aquilius (the subduer of Asia), all notorious bribe-takers, who had been acquitted by the judges, although ambassadors sent to complain of their conduct were still present, going around uttering bitter accusations against them. The Senate was extremely ashamed of these things and yielded to the law, and the people ratified it. In this way were the courts of justice transferred from the Senate to the knights. It is said that soon after the passage of this law Gracchus remarked that he had broken the power of the Senate once for all, and the saying of Gracchus received a deeper and deeper significance by the course of events. For this power of sitting in judgment on all Romans and Italians, including the senators themselves, in all matters as to property, civil rights, and banishment, exalted the knights to be rulers over them, and put senators on the level of subjects. Moreover, as the knights voted in the election to sustain the power of the tribunes, and obtained from them whatever they wanted in return, they became more and more formidable to the senators. So it shortly came about that the political mastery was turned upside down, the power being in the hands of the knights, and the honour only remaining with the Senate. The knights indeed went so far that they not only held power over the senators, but they openly flouted them beyond their right. They also became addicted to bribe-taking, and when they too had tasted these enormous gains, they indulged in them even more basely and immoderately than the senators had done. They suborned accusers against the rich and did away with prosecutions for bribe-taking altogether, partly by agreement among themselves and partly by open violence, so that the practice of this kind of investigation became entirely obsolete. Thus the judiciary law gave rise to another struggle of factions, which lasted a long time and was not less baneful than the former ones.

23] Gracchus also made long roads throughout Italy and thus put a multitude of contractors and artisans under obligations to him and made them ready to do whatever he wished. He proposed the founding of numerous colonies. He also called on the Latin allies to demand the full rights of Roman citizenship, since the Senate could not with decency refuse this privilege to men of the same race. To the other allies, who were not allowed to vote in Roman elections, he sought to give the right of suffrage, in order to have their help in the enactment of laws which he had in contemplation. The Senate was very much alarmed at this, and it ordered the consuls to give the following public notice, "Nobody who does not possess the right of suffrage shall stay in the city or approach within forty stades[9] of it while voting is going on concerning these laws." The Senate also persuaded Livius Drusus, another tribune, to interpose his veto against the laws proposed by Gracchus, but not to tell the people his reasons for doing so; for a tribune was not required to give reasons for his veto. In order to conciliate the people they gave Drusus the privilege of founding twelve colonies, and the plebeians were so much pleased with this that they scoffed at the laws proposed by Gracchus.

24] Having lost the favour of the rabble, Gracchus sailed for Africa in company with Fulvius Flaccus, who, after his consulship, had been chosen tribune for the same reasons as Gracchus himself. It had been decided to send a colony to Africa on account of its reputed fertility, and these men had been expressly chosen the founders of it in order to get them out of the way for a while, so that the Senate might have a respite from demagogism. They marked out the city for the colony on the place where Carthage had formerly stood, disregarding the fact that Scipio, when he destroyed it, had devoted it with solemn imprecations to sheep-pasturage for ever. They assigned 6000 colonists to this place, instead of the smaller number fixed by law, in order further to curry favour with the people thereby. When they returned to Rome they invited the 6000 from the whole of Italy. The functionaries who were still in Africa laying out the city wrote home that wolves had pulled up and scattered the boundary marks made by Gracchus and Fulvius, and the soothsayers considered this an ill omen for the colony. So the Senate summoned the comitia, in which it was proposed to repeal the law concerning this colony. When Gracchus and Fulvius saw their failure in this matter they were furious, and declared that the Senate had lied about the wolves. The boldest of the plebeians joined them, carrying daggers, and proceeded to the Capitol, where the assembly was to be held in reference to the colony.

25] Now the people had come together already, and Fulvius had begun speaking about the business in hand, when Gracchus arrived at the Capitol attended by a body-guard of his partisans. Consciencestricken by what he knew about the extraordinary plans on foot he turned aside from the meeting-place of the assembly, passed into the portico, and walked about waiting to see what would happen. Just then a plebeian named Antyllus, who was sacrificing in the portico, saw him in this disturbed state, laid his hand upon him, either because he had heard or suspected something, or was moved to speak to him for some other reason, and begged him to spare his country. Gracchus, still more disturbed, and startled like one detected in a crime, gave the man a sharp look. Then one of his party, although no signal had been displayed or order given, inferred merely from the angry glance that Gracchus cast upon Antyllus that the time for action had come, and thought that he should do a favour to Gracchus by striking the first blow. So he drew his dagger and slew Antyllus.

A cry was raised, the dead body was seen in the midst of the crowd, and all who were outside fled from the temple in fear of a like fate.

Gracchus went into the assembly desiring to exculpate himself of the deed, but nobody would so much as listen to him. All turned away from him as from one stained with blood. So both he and Flaccus were at their wits' end and, having lost through this hasty act the chance of accomplishing what they wished, they hastened to their homes, and their partisans with them. The rest of the crowd occupied the forum after midnight as though some calamity were impending, and Opimius the consul who was staying in the city, ordered an armed force to gather in the Capitol at daybreak, and sent heralds to convoke the Senate. He took his own station in the temple of Castor and Pollux in the centre of the city and there awaited events. 26] When these arrangements had been made the Senate summoned Gracchus and Flaccus from their homes to the senate-house to defend themselves. But they ran out armed toward the Aventine hill, hoping that if they could seize it first the Senate would agree to some terms with them. As they ran through the city they offered freedom to the slaves, but none listened to them. With such forces as they had, however, they occupied and fortified the temple of Diana, and sent Quintus, the son of Flaccus, to the Senate seeking to come to an arrangement and to live in harmony. The Senate replied that they should lay down their arms, come to the senate-house, and tell them what they wanted, or else send no more messengers. When they sent Quintus a second time the consul Opimius arrested him, as being no longer an ambassador after he had been warned, and at the same time sent his armed men against the Gracchans.

Gracchus fled across the river by the wooden bridge with one slave to a grove, and there, being on the point of arrest, he presented his throat to the slave.[10] Flaccus took refuge in the workshop of an acquaintance. As his pursuers did not know which house he was in they threatened to burn the whole row. The man who had given shelter to the suppliant hesitated to point him out, but directed another man to do so. Flaccus was seized and put to death. The heads of Gracchus and Flaccus were carried to Opimius, and he gave their weight in gold to those who brought them, but the people plundered their houses. Opimius then arrested their fellow conspirators, cast them into prison, and ordered that they should be strangled; but he allowed Quintus, the son of Flaccus, to choose his own mode of death. After this a lustration of the city was performed for the bloodshed, and the Senate ordered the building of a temple to Concord in the forum.

NOTES

1. The reference is to the Sextio-Licinian Laws of *ca.* 367 B.C. which had allegedly limited the size of estates. If they in fact did, the provision had become a dead letter by the time of the Gracchi. One *jugerum* was about five-eighths of an acre.
2. 133 B.C.
3. Slave rebellion of 135 B.C.
4. 132 B.C.
5. 129 B.C.
6. 125 B.C.
7. For the year 123 B.C.
8. For the year 122 B.C.
9. Less than five miles.
10. 121 B.C.

5

Corruption in the Provinces

GAIUS VERRES returned to Rome in 70 B.C. from Sicily, where he had served for three years as praetorian governor. The Sicilian cities immediately charged him with malfeasance before a senatorial court. Cicero prosecuted, while Hortensius, Rome's leading orator, led the defense. Since Verres had powerful friends in the senate, the outcome of the trial was doubtful. Cicero's minute documentation of the scandal, delivered in part as a brilliant courtroom oration, caused Verres to seek a voluntary exile and Hortensius to abandon his brief before the case was concluded. Cicero's reputation as Rome's foremost barrister was thereby established. The following excerpts from the Verrine Orations, although not actually delivered before the court, provide an extreme example of corruption in senatorial administration and show why subsequent imperial rule, with its closer supervision over public servants, undoubtedly improved the political and economic status of Rome's provincials.

Cicero, Verrine Orations, II, 3, 20-23, 27-33, 89-90, 97

ii

3, 20] . . . I CANNOT, indeed, display to you, gentlemen, the full extent and number of his outrages. It would be an endless task to recount the misfortunes of each of his victims one by one. I will, therefore, by your leave, merely relate typical instances.

21] There is a man of Centuripa named Nympho, an active, hardworking man, a careful and experienced farmer. He had a large farm, which he held as leasehold, a common practice in Sicily even for well-to-do persons such as he is; and he had invested a large sum in equipment to keep the place going. But he was treated by Verres with such overwhelming injustice that he not only deserted his farm, but actually fled from Sicily, and came here to Rome, along with

From L. H. G. Greenwood, trans., CICERO: THE VERRINE ORATIONS (Cambridge, Mass., n.d.), vol. ii, pp. 61–67, 79–95, 255–259, 275–277. Reprinted by permission of Harvard University Press and The Loeb Classical Library.

many others whose exile was due to Verres. Verres had caused a collector to state that Nympho had not made any return of the acreage he had under crop, as was required by that precious edict of his, the sole purpose of which was to secure gains of this kind for him. Nympho having declared his readiness to defend his conduct before an impartial court, Verres appointed some excellent fellows to try the case: that same medico of his, Cornelius, *alias* Artemidorus, who in his own town of Perga had formerly been Verres' leader and instructor in the spoliation of Diana's temple there; his diviner Volusius, and his crier Valerius. Nympho was sentenced before he had fairly taken his place in court. To what penalty, you may ask. The edict fixed no penalty and he was sentenced to pay all the corn he had on his threshing-floors. Thus did this tithe-collector Apronius carry off from Nympho's farm not the due tithe, not some portion of corn removed to a hiding-place, but 7000 good bushels of wheat, as a penalty for infringing the edict, and not by any right his contract gave him.

22] The wife of a well-born citizen of Menae named Xeno had an estate which was let to a tenant. The tenant, unable to endure the ill-treatment he received from the collectors, had deserted his farm. Verres authorized the prosecution of Xeno on his favourite fatal charge of not making a proper return of acreage. Xeno denied liability; the estate, he pointed out, had been let to another person. Verres directed the court to find Xeno guilty *if it shall appear that the acreage of the farm in question exceeds the area stated by the tenant.* Xeno argued not only that he had not been farming the land — which was in itself a valid defence — but that he was not the owner or the lessor of the estate in question; that it belonged to his wife; that she managed her own business, and had let the place herself. His defence was conducted by Marcus Cossutius, a man of high distinction and held in great respect. Verres none the less committed him for trial, fixing the penalty at £500.[1] Though Xeno was aware that the court to try his case was being made up from that company of bandits, he none the less agreed to accept its verdict. Thereupon Verres, speaking loudly so that Xeno should hear him, ordered his temple slaves to keep the man under arrest while the case was proceeding, and to bring him before himself as soon as it was settled; adding that Xeno might be rich enough to be indifferent to the penalty if he were found guilty, but would probably not be indifferent to a flogging as well. Intimidated by this violence, Xeno paid the collectors as much as he was ordered by Verres to pay.

23] Polemarchus, a good respectable inhabitant of Murgentia, was ordered to pay a tithe of 700 bushels on a farm of 50 acres. Because he refused, he was marched off to appear before Verres, in Verres' own house; and as our friend was still in bed, the prisoner was brought into the bedroom, a privilege otherwise extended only to collectors and women. There he was knocked about and kicked so brutally that, after refusing to settle for 700 bushels, he promised to pay 1000.

Eubulidas Grospus of Centuripa is a man whose character and birth, and also his wealth, make him the chief man in his own town. Know, then, gentlemen, that this most honoured member of an honoured community was left not merely with no more corn, but with no more life and blood in his body, than the will and pleasure of Apronius saw fit to leave him. Violence, suffering and blows induced him to pay not the amount of corn that he should have paid but the amount he was forced to pay.

In the same city there were three brothers working in partnership, whose names were Sostratus, Numenius and Nymphodorus. They fled from their land because they were ordered to pay over more than the total yield of their harvest; whereupon Apronius invaded the farm with a band of followers, seized all the stuff, carried off the slaves, and drove off the live stock. Nymphodorus went later to see him at Aetna, and pleaded to have his own property restored to him. While he was doing so, Apronius ordered him to be seized and suspended from a wild olive-tree that grows in the market-place of Aetna. Gentlemen, this friend and ally of Rome, this farmer and landowner of yours, hung there from that tree, in the market-place of a town in our empire, for as long as Apronius chose to let him hang. . . .

*　　*　　*

27] So much for his treatment of individuals: let us now ask how he treated communities. Gentlemen, you have heard of the evidence of a great many towns, and you shall hear that of the rest. Let me first tell you briefly of the loyal and reputable people of Agyrium. This town is one of the most important in Sicily, and its inhabitants were, till Verres became governor, prosperous and efficient farmers. Our friend Apronius came to Agyrium as purchaser of the tithe-rights over its corn-lands. On arriving there with his attendants, full of violence and threats of violence, he proceeded to ask for a large sum of money, so that he might make his profit and depart: he did not wish to have any trouble, he said, but would like to take his money and go off as soon as he could to deal with some other town. The Sicilians are, all of them, a far from contemptible race, if only our magistrates would leave them alone; they are really quite fine fellows, thoroughly honest and well-behaved; and this is notably true of the community of which I am speaking. They told the villain that they would pay him the amount of tithe that was due from them; but they would not pay him a bonus as well, especially as he had paid a high price for the tithe-rights. Apronius reported this to the party whose interests were concerned.

28] Immediately, as though some conspiracy against the State had been occurring, or the governor's representative beaten, the magistrates and five chief citizens of Agyrium were summoned by Verres. They reached Syracuse; there Apronius was ready for them, and alleged that the actual persons who had come there had broken the governor's regulations. They asked him how: he would tell that, he replied, to the members of the court. Yonder model of equity proceeded to intimidate these unfortunate persons with his usual threat of selecting the court from his own staff. They replied stoutly that they would stand their trial. Verres thrust on them Cornelius Artemidorus the medico, and Cornelius Tlepolemus the painter, and others like them, as members of the court: not one of them a Roman citizen: they were rascally Greeks who were formerly temple-robbers, and had become Cornelii suddenly.[2] The men from Agyrium saw that, before a court like this, Apronius would have no trouble in establishing any charge he might bring. They chose to be found guilty, and thus to bring odium and disgrace to Verres, rather than accept the terms and conditions their accuser demanded. They asked how he would state the charge on which they were to be tried. He replied "That they had broken the regulation"; and that he would pronounce sentence according to the verdict on this. They chose to face an unfair charge, and an unscrupulous court, rather than to submit to any terms dictated by the man himself. Then he sent Timarchides secretly to them with a warning that if they were wise they would agree to a settlement. They still refused. "Oh? would you rather be sentenced to pay £500 apiece, then?" Yes, they said, they would. Then Verres said, loudly enough for all to hear, "Anyone found guilty will be flogged to death." At that, with tears in their eyes, they began to pray and entreat that they might be allowed to vacate their own farms and hand them over to Apronius with their crops and their harvests, if only they might get off without torture and disgrace.

These, gentlemen, were the conditions under which Verres sold those tithes. Hortensius may say, if he will, that Verres sold the tithes for a high price.

29] When Verres was governor of Sicily, the position of the farmers was such that they thought themselves well treated if they were allowed to vacate their farms and hand them over to Apronius; they were only too eager to escape the numerous sufferings they saw in front of them. The edict required them to hand over as much corn as Apronius might declare due from them. Even if he declared more due than the whole of their crop? Yes: by Verres' edict that was what the magistrates had to extract from them. Well, the farmer had power to claim back from the collector. He had; and his claim was heard by — Artemidorus. What if the farmer paid over less than Apronius demanded? He was prosecuted before a court, with a fourfold penalty if convicted. From whom was this court selected? From the highly respectable members of the governor's admirable staff. Is that all? No; I next charge you with making an under-statement of your acreage; stand your trial for breaking the regulations. Trial before what court? Before a court taken from the staff aforesaid. And finally: if you are found guilty, or rather, *when* you are found guilty — for before such a court what doubt could there be of it? — you must be flogged to death. Under such terms and such conditions, will anyone be so simple as to think that those sales were sales of tithes? as to suppose that the farmer was allowed to keep nine-tenths of his corn? as not to see that the farmers' goods and property and fortunes simply went to enrich that pirate of a governor?

The threat of flogging, then, terrified these men of Agyrium into promising to do what they were ordered to do.

30] And now hear what Verres did order them to do, and then conceal if you can your certainty of what all Sicily saw clearly, that it was the governor himself who was the purchaser of those tithe-rights, or rather, who was the farmers' master and tyrant. He ordered the people of Agyrium to take over, as a community, the collection of the tithe, paying Apronius a bonus as well. — If Apronius bought those tithe-rights dear, may I ask you, Verres — since you are the man who looked into the value of these things so carefully, and tell us you sold those rights so dear — why should you think the purchaser ought to be paid a bonus? Oh well, you did think so: but why did you *order* that payment? What can "extortion of money" be — that clearly criminal act — if this

violent abuse of your authority to force unwilling persons to
pay another person a bonus — in other words, to pay him money —
if this is *not* extortion? — Very well. They were ordered to pay a
small trifle of bonus to the governor's particular friend Apronius. You
shall believe, gentlemen, that it was Apronius to whom this was
paid, if you make up your mind that it *was* a bonus for Apronius and
not plunder for the governor. — You order them to take over the
tithe-collection, and to pay Apronius a bonus of *thirty-three thousand*
bushels of wheat. What? From the land of one town, this one town
is forced, by the governor's orders, to make Apronius a present of
enough corn to supply the populace of Rome for nearly a month!
What, you sold the tithes at a high price — when such a profit as that
was made over to the man who bought them? If you had made careful inquiry into the value of those tithes when you were selling them,
I am very sure the town would have added another ten thousand
bushels then, rather than £6000³ afterwards.

You will think this a profitable robbery, gentlemen. Listen to the
rest of the story, and give me your careful attention: it will not then
seem so strange to you that sheer necessity has made the people of
Sicily turn for help to their patrons, to our consuls and our senate,
to our laws and our courts of law. As a fee for the approval by
Apronius of the wheat thus presented to him, Verres ordered the
people of Agyrium to pay Apronius one sesterce per bushel.

31] What have we here? Besides the extortion by order, as a so-called
bonus, of that great quantity of wheat, is a money fee as well exacted
for the approval of that wheat? Why, could Apronius, could anyone
at all, possibly reject Sicilian wheat, even if it were to be taken over
for army stores? and, moreover, there was nothing to prevent him
from taking it over, if he chose, direct from the floors where it lay. All
that corn is extorted and handed over by your orders. That is not
enough: a money payment is ordered as well. The payment is made
— and *that* will not do. A further sum of money is extorted for the
tithes of barley, for which you order the presentation of a bonus of
£300.⁴ And so we find this tyrannical governor, by the use of threats
and violence, officially robbing a single town of 33,000 bushels of
wheat and £600⁵ into the bargain.

Are these things hidden? Could they be hidden, though all the
world should seek to hide them? You have done them openly. The
people of the district heard your orders given. Your extortions were
effected before the eyes of the public. The officials and the five
chief citizens of Agyrium, whom you hailed into court in order to

enrich yourself, went home and reported your actions and your orders to their own senate. That report, in accordance with the local law, was entered in their public records. The men of high standing who represent them are here in Rome, and have stated in the witness-box what I have stated here. I ask the Court to listen to that official entry in the records, and then to the official evidence of the town. — Read them, please. *The passage from the town records, and the official evidence of the town, are read aloud.* — You will have noticed, gentlemen, when these witnesses were speaking, how Apollodorus Pyragus, the chief citizen of his community, wept as he gave his evidence. Never, he told you, since the name of Rome had been a familiar sound in Sicilian ears, had the people of Agyrium once spoken or acted against the humblest Roman citizen — the people whose great wrongs, and whose sharp sufferings, were now forcing them to hear public testimony against a Roman governor. By God, Verres, this single town is enough to beat down your defence, so impressive is these men's loyalty, so sharp the pain of their wrongs, so scrupulous their testimony. But indeed not one town only, but all the towns of Sicily have been crushed with similar wrongs and injuries, and have sent their representatives and their public testimonies to assist your prosecutors.

32] Let us now, therefore, turn to Herbita, and see how Verres despoiled and ravaged that reputable and hitherto prosperous community. What good folk they are! excellent farmers; men to whom the disputes and litigations of city life are things unknown. — You foul rascal, your duty was to show them consideration, to forward their interests, to do your utmost to preserve such men from harm. — In Verres' first year, the tithes of that district were sold for 18,000 pecks of wheat. They were sold to Atidius, another of this man's assistants in the tithe business. Ostensibly as a district judge, he arrived at Herbita with an escort of temple slaves, and a lodging was provided for him at the expense of the town. Thereupon the town was forced to give him a bonus of 38,800 pecks of wheat — when the tithes had been sold for 18,000 pecks! It was forced as a community to pay him that huge bonus at a time when the individual farmers had already fled from their farms, plundered and driven away by the illegal assaults of the collectors. In the second year, Apronius bought the tithes for 25,800 pecks of wheat; and on his arrival in person at Herbita with the band of highwaymen that formed his bodyguard, the inhabitants as a body were made to bestow on him a bonus of 21,000 pecks of wheat and an additional fee of £20.[6] As for the fee, it may possibly have been given to Apronius himself as the pay for his trouble — and his unblushing knavery: but that great quantity of wheat, at least, we shall all feel sure found its way, like the corn at Agyrium, to the corn-pirate who sits yonder. 33] In the third year he adopted a practice that may fairly be described as "royal." It is the custom of the native kings in Persia and Syria, we are told, to have a number of wives, and to these wives they assign towns in the following fashion: one town is to provide for a lady's girdle, another for her necklace, another for her hair-ornaments; and thus they keep whole populations not merely in the secret but in the service of their pleasures. Even such, as I will now explain, were the lawless pleasures of yonder self-styled King of the Sicilians.

Aeschrio of Syracuse has a wife named Pipa, whose name the vicious practices of Verres have made a by-word throughout Sicily: couplets referring to this woman were constantly being scribbled over the dais and above his Excellency's head. This Aeschrio, Pipa's honorary husband, was put up to be the new tax-gatherer for the tithes of Herbita. The people of Herbita were aware that, if no advance were made on the figure that Aeschrio might offer, they would be robbed of as much as that unprincipled woman might choose to demand; and therefore they bid up to the highest figure they thought they could manage to pay. Aeschrio outbid them, feeling quite sure that, with Verres governor of Sicily, there was no danger of a lady tithe-collector's losing money. The tithes were knocked down for 8100 bushels — for nearly as much again as the year before. This meant complete ruin for the farmers; all the more so because they had been hard hit and all but crushed in the two previous years. Verres perceived that the price was so high that no larger amount could possibly be squeezed out of the people of Herbita; so he reduced the total figure by 600 bushels, and ordered the sale price to be entered as 7500 bushels instead of 8100.

* * *

89] Because of Roman greed and Roman injustice, all our provinces are mourning, all our free communities are complaining, and even foreign kingdoms are protesting. As far as the bounds of Ocean there is no spot now so distant or so obscure that the wanton and oppressive deeds of Romans have not penetrated thither. Not against the onset of the armies of the world in war, but against its groans and tears and lamentation, can Rome hold out no longer. When such

are the facts, and such the prevailing moral standards, if any prosecuted person, upon his crimes being clearly demonstrated, shall plead
that others have done the like, he will not find himself without
precedents: but Rome will find herself without hope of escaping
doom, if the precedents set by one scoundrel are to secure the acquit-
tal and impunity of another. Are you satisfied that our governors
shall govern as they do? satisfied that our allies should for the future
be treated as you see that in recent years they have been treated?
Then why am I wasting my labour here, why do you still sit on, why
do you not rise and go while I am still addressing you? Would you,
on the other hand, do something to reduce the unscrupulous and unprincipled villainy of such men as that? Then waver no longer between the advantage of sparing one rascal for the sake of a number
of rascals, and that of punishing one rascal and thereby checking the
rascality of many others.

90] Yet what, after all, are these numerous precedents? In so important a trial on so serious a charge, when the advocate for the
defence begins to plead that something has "often been done," his
hearers expect to be told of precedents drawn from the annals of the
past, recorded by the sculptor's chisel and the historian's pen, clothed
with all the dignity of bygone days; for these, it is found, most delight our ears and most convince our judgements. I ask my learned
friend — will he tell us of a Scipio, a Cato, a Laelius, and assert that
they have done the same? However little I may approve such actions,
I cannot hold out against the authority of such men. Or failing these,
will he bring forward the men of our own day — the elder Catulus,
Marius, Scaevola, Scaurus, Metellus? all of them men who governed
provinces and requisitioned corn for their maintenance. The authority
of such men is great indeed — great enough to cover even the suspicion of misconduct. But not even from such men as these of our
own day can he produce any authority for commuting corn as Verres
did. Whither, then, to what precedents, will he refer me? Will he
pass over the careers of men who lived when moral standards were
high, when public opinion was respected, when our law-courts were
honestly administered, and refer me to the dissolute and unbridled
profligacy of the present day, and seek to defend his client by quoting
the examples set by men whom the people of this land regard as
deserving exemplary punishment? Not that I refuse to consider even
the standards that now prevail among us, provided that we take as
our guides precedents that the national conscience approves, and not
such as it condemns. For such, I need not look long or far afield. I

have before me, as he has, two members of this Court, Publius Servilius and Quintus Catulus, two of the leading men in Rome, who are so highly respected, and distinguished by service so eminent, that they rank with those famous men of the distant past of whom I have already spoken. We are looking for precedents — for modern precedents: so be it. Not long ago, both these men were commanding armies. Let my learned friend mark — since modern precedents are to his taste — let him mark what these men did. Incredible! Catulus made use of his corn and required no money. Servilius, who held his command for five years, and had he been a Verres could have amassed a vast sum of money, felt himself debarred from doing anything that he had not seen done by his father or by his famous uncle Metellus. And shall it be left to Gaius Verres to argue that what is profitable is proper, and to justify by the example of others his doing what none but scoundrels have ever done?

*   *   *

97] I wish, indeed, that Verres could seek to meet this charge with some plea that however unfounded was at least civilized and customary. You would be sitting to try this case with less danger both to yourselves and to all our provinces. If he had been denying that he exacted that money as he did, and if you had believed him, people would feel that you had believed the man, not approved the action. But he cannot possibly deny it; all Sicily is pressing the charge; there is not one of all its many farmers from whom "maintenance" money has not been wrung. And I wish he could say even this, that the whole business was no concern of his, since his quaestors had managed everything to do with corn. But even this he is debarred from saying, because we have been hearing read aloud his own letter written to the communities demanding the 3 denarii a peck. What then *is* his plea? "I have done what you attack me for doing; I have amased great sums of maintenance money: but it was permissible for me to do so, and — if you will look ahead — it will be permissible for you." Gentlemen, it is a dangerous thing for our provinces that your verdict should establish the principle of this injustice; and it will be fatal for our order if the nation should believe that men who may themselves incur the penalties of the law are incapable of conscientiously upholding the law when they sit as judges in our courts.

And further, gentlemen, when Verres was governor, not only was there no limit to the rate of commutation, but there was none to the amount of corn demanded: it was not the amount due to him that he demanded, but the amount that suited his inclinations. I will put before you, on the authority of the official records and official evidence of the communities, the total amount of the corn demanded for maintenance; and you will find it five times as much as he was legally entitled to demand from the communities for that purpose. The man both fixed an intolerably high rate for commutation, and at the same time demanded an amount of corn immensely in excess of what the law allowed him. Can shameless impudence go further?

NOTES

1. 50,000 sesterces, $2,500.
2. I.e., they had taken Roman names unjustifiably.
3. 600,000 sesterces, $30,000.
4. 30,000 sesterces, $1,500.
5. 60,000 sesterces, $3,000.
6. 2,000 sesterces, $100.

6

Caesar, Statesman and Man

SUETONIUS (ca. A.D. 70–140), possibly a Native of Hippo (Bône, Algeria) in Africa, started life as a teacher and scholar. Patronized by Pliny the Younger, he began an equestrian career under Trajan and became minister of archives in the years 114 to 117. Hadrian made him minister of correspondence, but his official career ended upon his dismissal in 121–122. He devoted the remainder of his life to research and writing. Although his Lives of the Twelve Caesars does not rise to Tacitean heights of subtlety and literary brilliance, it is nonetheless an important work because of its reliance on archival sources and because it created a subsequently popular genre of historical biography. The following selections from the Life of Julius Caesar show the radical nature of the dictator's reforms as well as his manysided assertive personality. They explain in part why a successful reorganization of the government awaited a more devious statesman.

Suetonius, Life of Julius Caesar, 40-44, 54-60, 62-70, 72-79

40] CAESAR next turned his attention to domestic reforms.[1] First he reorganized the Calendar which the Pontiffs had allowed to fall into such disorder, by intercalating days or months as it suited them, that the harvest and vintage festivals no longer corresponded with the appropriate seasons. He linked the year to the course of the sun by lengthening it from 355 days to 365, abolishing the short extra month intercalated after every second February, and adding an entire day every fourth year. But to make the next first of January fall at the right season, he drew out this particular year by two extra months, inserted between November and December, so that it consisted of fifteen, including the intercalary one inserted after February in the old style.

From Suetonius, THE TWELVE CAESARS, translated by Robert Graves (Baltimore, 1957), pp. 27–29, 32–36, 36–39, 39–43. Copyright © 1957 International Authors N.V. Reprinted by permission of Willis Kingsley Wing.

41] He brought the Senate up to strength by creating new patricians, and increased the yearly quota of praetors, aediles, and quaestors, as well as of minor officials; reinstating those degraded by the Censors or condemned for corruption by a jury. Also, he arranged with the commons that, apart from the Consul, half the magistrates should be popularly elected and half nominated by himself. Allowing even the sons of proscribed men to stand, he circulated brief directions to the voters. For instance: "Caesar the Dictator to such-and-such a tribe of voters: I recommend So-and-so to you for office." He limited jury service to knights and senators, disqualifying the Treasury tribunes — these were commoners who collected the tribute and paid the army.

Caesar changed the old method of registering voters: he made the City landlords help him to complete the list, street by street, and reduced from 320,000 to 150,000 the number of householders who might draw free grain. To do away with the nuisance of having to summon everyone for enrolment periodically, he made the praetors keep their register up to date by replacing the names of dead men with those of others not yet listed.

42] Since the population of Rome had been considerably diminished by the transfer of 80,000 men to overseas colonies, he forbade any citizen between the ages of twenty and forty to absent himself from Italy for more than three years in succession. Nor might any senator's son travel abroad unless as a member of some magistrate's household or staff; and at least a third of the cattlemen employed by graziers had to be free-born. Caesar also granted the citizenship to all medical practitioners and professors of liberal arts resident in Rome, thus inducing them to remain and tempting others to follow suit.

He disappointed popular agitators by cancelling no debts, but in the end decreed that every debtor should have his property assessed according to pre-war valuation and, after deducting the interest already paid directly, or by way of a banker's guarantee, should satisfy his creditors with whatever sum that might represent. Since prices had risen steeply, this left debtors with perhaps a fourth part of their property. Caesar dissolved all workers' guilds except the ancient ones, and increased the penalties for crime; and since wealthy men had less compunction about committing major offences, because the worst that could happen to them was a sentence of exile, he punished murderers of fellow-citizens (as Cicero records) by the seizure of either their entire property, or half of it.

43] In his administration of justice he was both conscientious and severe, and went so far as to degrade senators found guilty of extortion. Once, when an ex-praetor married a woman on the day after her divorce from another man, he annulled the union, although adultery between them was not suspected.

He imposed a tariff on foreign manufactures; forbade the use, except on stated occasions, of litters, and the wearing of either scarlet robes or pearls by those below a certain rank and age. To implement his laws against luxury he placed inspectors in different parts of the market to seize delicacies offered for sale in violation of his orders; sometimes he even sent lictors and guards into dining-rooms to remove illegal dishes, already served, which his watchmen had failed to intercept.

44] Caesar continually undertook great new works for the embellishment of the City, or for the Empire's protection and enlargement. His first projects were a temple of Mars, the biggest in the world, to build which he would have had to fill up and pave the lake where the naval sham-fight had been staged; and an enormous theatre sloping down from the Tarpeian Rock on the Capitoline Hill.

Another task he set himself was the reduction of the Civil Code to manageable proportions, by selecting from the unwieldy mass of statutes only the most essential, and publishing them in a few volumes. Still another was to provide public libraries, by commissioning Marcus Varro to collect and classify Greek and Latin books on a comprehensive scale. His engineering schemes included the draining of the Pomptine Marshes and of Lake Fucinus; also a highway running from the Adriatic across the Apennines to the Tiber; and a canal to be cut through the Isthmus of Corinth. In the military field he planned an expulsion of the Dacians from Pontus and Thrace, which they had recently occupied, and then an attack on Parthia by way of Lesser Armenia; but decided not to risk a pitched battle until he had familiarized himself with Parthian tactics. . . .

*   *   *

54] He was not particularly honest in money matters, either while a provincial governor or while holding office at Rome. Several memoirs record that as Governor-General of Western Spain he not only begged his allies for money to settle his debts, but wantonly sacked several Lusitanian towns, though they had accepted his terms and opened their gates to welcome him.

In Gaul he plundered large and small temples of their votive offerings, and more often gave towns over to pillage because their inhabitants were rich than because they had offended him. As a result he collected larger quantities of gold than he could handle, and began selling it for silver, in Italy and the provinces, at 750 denarii to the pound — which was about two-thirds of the official exchange rate.

In the course of his first consulship he stole 3,000 lb of gold from the Capitol, and replaced it with the same weight of gilded bronze. He sold alliances and thrones for cash, making King Ptolemy XII of Egypt give him and Pompey nearly 1,500,000 gold pieces; and later paid his Civil War army, and the expenses of his triumphs and entertainments, by open extortion and sacrilege.

55] Caesar equalled, if he did not surpass, the greatest orators and generals the world had ever known. His prosecution of Dolabella unquestionably placed him in the first rank of advocates; and Cicero, discussing the matter in his *Brutus,* confessed that he knew no more eloquent speaker than Caesar 'whose style is chaste, pellucid, and grand, not to say noble.' Cicero also wrote to Cornelius Nepos:

'Very well, then! Do you know any man who, even if he has concentrated on the art of oratory to the exclusion of all else, can speak better than Caesar? Or anyone who makes so many witty remarks? Or whose vocabulary is so varied and yet so exact?' . . .

56] He left memoirs of his war in Gaul, and of his civil war against Pompey; but no one knows who wrote those of the Alexandrian, African, and Spanish campaigns. Some say that it was his friend Oppius; others that it was Hirtius, who also finished 'The Gallic War,' left incomplete by Caesar, adding a final book. Cicero, also in the *Brutus,* observes: 'Caesar wrote admirably; his memoirs are cleanly, directly and gracefully composed, and divested of all rhetorical trappings. And while his sole intention was to supply historians with factual material, the result has been that several fools have been pleased to primp up his narrative for their own glorification; but every writer of sense has given the subject a wide berth.'

Hirtius says downrightly: 'These memoirs are so highly rated by all judicious critics that the opportunity of enlarging and improving on them, which he purports to offer historians, seems in fact withheld from them. And, as his friends, we admire this feat even more than strangers can: they appreciate the faultless grace of his style, we know how rapidly and easily he wrote.'

Asinius Pollio, however, believes that the memoirs show signs of carelessness and inaccuracy: Caesar, he holds, did not always check the truth of the reports that came in, and was either disingenuous or

forgetful in describing his own actions. Pollio adds that Caesar must
have planned a revision.

Among his literary remains are two books of *An Essay on Analogy,* two more of *Answers to Cato,* and a poem, *The Journey.* He
wrote *An Essay on Analogy* while coming back over the Alps after
holding assizes in Cisalpine Gaul; *Answers to Cato* in the year that he
won the battle of Munda; and *The Journey* during the twenty-four
days he spent on the road between Rome and Western Spain.

Many of the letters and despatches sent by him to the Senate also
survive, and he seems to have been the first statesman who reduced
such documents to book form; previously, Consuls and governor-
generals had written right across the page, not in neat columns. Then
there are his letters to Cicero; and his private letters to friends, the
more confidential passages of which he wrote in cypher: to understand their apparently incomprehensible meaning one must number
the letters of the alphabet from 1 to 22, and then replace each of
the letters that Caesar has used with the one which occurs four numbers lower — for instance, D stands for A.

It is said that in his boyhood and early youth he also wore pieces
called *In Praise of Hercules* and *The Tragedy of Oedipus* and *Collected Sayings;* but nearly a century later the Emperor Augustus sent
Pompeius Macer, his Surveyor of Libraries, a brief, frank letter forbidding him to circulate these minor works.

57] Caesar was a most skilful swordsman and horseman, and
showed surprising powers of endurance. He always led his army,
more often on foot than in the saddle, went bareheaded in sun and
rain alike, and could travel for long distances at incredible speed in a
gig, taking very little luggage. If he reached an unfordable river he
would either swim or propel himself across it on an inflated skin;
and often arrived at his destination before the messengers whom he
had sent ahead to announce his approach.

58] It is a disputable point which was the more remarkable when
he went to war: his caution or his daring. He never exposed his army
to ambushes, but made careful reconnaissances; and refrained from
crossing over into Britain until he had collected reliable information
(for Gaius Volusenus) about the harbours there, the best course to
steer, and the navigational risks. On the other hand, when news
reached him that his camp in Germany was being besieged, he dis-
guised himself as a Gaul and picked his way through the enemy
outposts to take command on the spot.

He ferried his troops across the Adriatic from Brindisi to Dyrrhachium in the winter season, running the blockade of Pompey's fleet. And one night, when Mark Antony had delayed the supply of reinforcements, despite repeated pleas, Caesar muffled his head with a cloak and secretly put to sea in a small boat, alone and incognito; forced the helmsman to steer into the teeth of a gale, and narrowly escaped shipwreck.

59] Religious scruples never deterred him for a moment. At the formal sacrifice before he launched his attack on Scipio and King Juba, the victim escaped; but he paid no heed to this most unlucky sign and marched off at once. He had also slipped and fallen as he disembarked on the coast of Africa, but turned an unfavourable omen into a favourable one by clasping the ground and shouting: 'Africa, I have tight hold of you!' Then, to ridicule the prophecy according to which it was the Scipios' fate to be perpetually victorious in Africa, he took about with him a contemptible member of the Cornelian branch of the Scipio family nicknamed 'Salvito' — or 'Greetings! but off with him!' — the 'Greetings!' being an acknowledgement of his distinguished birth, the 'Off with him!' a condemnation of his disgusting habits.

60] Sometimes he fought after careful tactical planning, sometimes on the spur of the moment — at the end of a march, often; or in miserable weather, when he would be least expected to make a move. Towards the end of his life, however, he took fewer chances; having come to the conclusion that his unbroken run of victories ought to sober him, now that he could not possibly gain more by winning yet another battle than he would lose by a defeat. It was his rule never to let enemy troops rally when he had routed them, and always therefore to assault their camp at once. If the fight were a hard-fought one he used to send the chargers away — his own among the first — as a warning that those who feared to stand their ground need not hope to escape on horseback.

* * *

62] If Caesar's troops gave ground he would rally them in person, catching individual fugitives by the throat and forcing them round to face the enemy again; even if they were panic-striken — as when one standard-bearer threatened him with the sharp butt of his Eagle and another, whom he tried to detain, ran off leaving the Eagle in his hand.

63] Caesar's reputation for presence of mind is fully borne out by the instances quoted. After Pharsalus, he had sent his legions ahead of him into Asia and was crossing the Hellespont in a small ferry-boat, when Lucius Cassius with ten naval vessels approached. Caesar made no attempt to escape but rowed towards the flagship and demanded Cassius's surrender; Cassius gave it and stepped aboard Caesar's craft.

64] Again, while attacking a bridge at Alexandria, Caesar was forced by a sudden enemy sortie to jump into a row-boat. So many of his men followed him that he dived into the sea and swam 200 yards until he reached the nearest Caesarean ship — holding his left hand above water the whole way to keep certain documents dry; and towing his purple cloak behind him with his teeth, to save this trophy from the Egyptians.

65] He judged his men by their fighting record, not by their morals or social position, treating them all with equal severity — and equal indulgence; since it was only in the presence of the enemy that he insisted on strict discipline. He never gave forewarning of a march or a battle, but kept his troops always on the alert for sudden orders to go wherever he directed. Often he made them turn out when there was no need at all, especially in wet weather or on public holidays. Sometimes he would say: 'Keep a close eye on me!' and then steal away from camp at any hour of the day or night, expecting them to follow. It was certain to be a particularly long march, and hard on stragglers.

66] If rumours about the enemy's strength were causing alarm, his practice was to heighten morale, not by denying or belittling the danger, but on the contrary by further exaggerating it. For instance, when his troops were in a panic before the battle of Thapsus at the news of King Juba's approach, he called them together and announced: 'You may take it from me that the King will be here within a few days, at the head of ten infantry legions, thirty thousand cavalry, a hundred thousand lightly armed troops, and three hundred elephants. This being the case, you may as well stop asking questions and making guesses. I have given you the facts, with which I am familiar. Any of you who remain unsatisfied will find themselves aboard a leaky hulk and being carried across the sea wherever the winds may decide to blow them.'

67] Though turning a blind eye to much of this misbehaviour, and never laying down any fixed scale of penalties, he allowed no deserter or mutineer to escape severe punishment. Sometimes, if a victory had been complete enough, he relieved the troops of all military duties and let them carry on as wildly as they pleased. One of his boasts was: 'My men fight just as well when they are stinking of perfume.' He always addressed them not with 'My men,' but with 'Comrades. . . ,' which put them into a better humour; and he equipped them splendidly. The silver and gold inlay of their weapons both improved their appearance on parade and made them more careful not to get disarmed in battle, these being objects of great value. Caesar loved his men dearly; when news came that Titurius's command had been massacred, he swore neither to cut his hair nor to trim his beard until they had been avenged.

68] By these means he won the devotion of his army as well as making it extraordinarily gallant. At the outbreak of the Civil War every centurion in every legion volunteered to equip a cavalryman from his savings; and the private soldiers unanimously offered to serve under him without pay or rations, pooling their money so that nobody should go short. Throughout the entire struggle not a single Caesarean deserted, and many of them, when taken prisoners, preferred death to the alternative of serving with the Pompeians. Such was their fortitude in facing starvation and other hardships, both as besiegers and as besieged, that when Pompey was shown at Dyrrhachium the substitute for bread, made of grass, on which they were feeding, he exclaimed: 'I am fighting wild beasts!' Then he ordered the loaf to be hidden at once, not wanting his men to find out how tough and resolute the enemy were, and so lose heart.

Here the Caesareans suffered their sole reverse, but proved their stout-heartedness by begging to be punished for the lapse; whereupon he felt called upon to console rather than upbraid them. In other battles, they beat enormously superior forces. Shortly before the defeat at Dyrrhachium, a single company of the Sixth Legion held a redoubt against four Pompeian legions, though almost every man had been wounded by arrow-shot — 130,000 arrows were afterwards collected on the scene of the engagement. This high level of courage is less surprising when individual examples are considered: for the centurion Cassius Scaeva, blinded in one eye, wounded in thigh and shoulder, and with no less than 120 holes in his shield, continued to defend the approaches to the redoubt. Nor was his by any means an exceptional case. At the naval battle of Marseilles, a private soldier named Gaius Acilius grasped the stern of an enemy ship and, when someone lopped off his right hand, nevertheless boarded her and drove the enemy back with the boss of his shield only — a feat rivalling that of the Athenian Cynaegeirus (brother of the poet Aeschylus), who showed similar courage when maimed in trying to detain a Persian ship after the victory at Marathon.

69] Caesar's men did not mutiny once during the Gallic War, which lasted thirteen years. In the Civil Wars they were less dependable, but whenever they made insubordinate demands he faced them boldly, and always brought them to heel again — not by appeasement but by sheer exercise of personal authority. At Piacenza, although Pompey's armies were as yet undefeated, he disbanded the entire Ninth Legion with ignominy, later recalling them to the Colours in response to their abject pleas; this with great reluctance and only after executing the ringleaders.

70] At Rome, too, when the Tenth Legion agitated for their discharge and bounty and were terrorizing the City, Caesar defied the advice of his friends and at once confronted the mutineers in person. Again he would have disbanded them ignominiously, though the African war was still being hotly fought; but by addressing them as 'Citizens' he readily regained their affections. A shout went up: 'We are your soldiers, Caesar, not civilians!' and they clamoured to serve under him in Africa: a demand which he nevertheless disdained to grant. He showed his contempt for the more disaffected soldiers by withholding a third part of the prize-money and land which had been set aside for them.

*   *   *

72] He showed consistent affection to his friends. Gaius Oppius, travelling by his side once through a wild forest, suddenly fell sick; but Caesar insisted on his using the only shelter that offered — a woodcutter's hut, hardly large enough for a single occupant — while he and the rest of his staff slept outside on the bare ground. Having attained supreme power he raised some of his friends, including men of humble birth, to high office and brushed aside criticism by saying: 'If bandits and cut-throats had helped to defend my honour, I should have shown them gratitude in the same way.'

73] Yet, when given the chance, he would always cheerfully come to terms with his bitterest enemies. He supported Gaius Memmius's candidature for the consulship, though they had both spoken most damagingly against each other. When Gaius Calvus, after his cruel lampoons of Caesar, made a move towards reconciliation through mutual friends, Caesar met him more than half way by writing him a friendly letter. Valerius Catullus had also libelled him in his verse about Mamurra, yet Caesar, while admitting that these were a permanent blot of his name, accepted Catullus's apology and invited him to dinner that same afternoon, and never interrupted his friendship with Catullus's father.

74] Caesar was not naturally vindictive; and if he crucified the pirates who had held him to ransom, this was only because he had sworn in their presence to do so; and he first mercifully cut their throats. He could never bring himself to take vengeance on Cornelius Phagites, even though in his early days, while he was sick and a fugitive from Sulla, Cornelius had tracked him down night after night and demanded large sums of hush-money. On discovering that Philemon, his slave-secretary, had been induced to poison him, Caesar ordered a simple execution, without torture. When Publius Clodius was accused of adultery with Caesar's wife Pompeia, in sacrilegious circumstances, and both her mother-in-law Aurelia and her sister-in-law Julia had given the court a detailed and truthful account of the affair, Caesar himself refused to offer any evidence. The Court then asked him why, in that case, he had divorced Pompeia. He replied: 'Because I cannot have members of my household suspected, even if they are innocent.'

75] Nobody can deny that during the Civil War, and after, he behaved with wonderful restraint and clemency. Whereas Pompey declared that all who were not actively with him were against him and would be treated as public enemies, Caesar announced that all who were not actively against him were with him. He allowed every centurion whom he had appointed on Pompey's recommendation to join the Pompeian forces if he pleased. At Lerida, in Spain, the articles of capitulation were being discussed between Caesar and the Pompeian generals Afranius and Petreius, and the rival armies were fraternizing, when Afranius suddenly decided not to surrender and massacred every Caesarean soldier found in his camp. Yet after capturing both generals a few days later, Caesar could not bring himself to pay Afranius back in the same coin; but let him go free. During the battle of Pharsalus he shouted to his men: 'Spare your fellow-Romans!' and then allowed them to save one enemy soldier apiece, whoever he might be. My researches show that not a single Pompeian was killed at Pharsalus, once the fighting had ended, except Afranius and Faustus and young Lucius Caesar. It is thought that not even these three fell victims to his vengeance, though Afranius and Faustus had taken up arms again after he had spared their lives, and Lucius Caesar had cruelly cut the throats of his famous relative's slaves and freedmen, even butchering the wild beasts brought by him to Rome for a public show! Eventually, towards the end of his career, Caesar invited back to Italy all exiles whom he had not yet pardoned, permitting them to hold magistracies and command armies; and went so far as to restore the statues of Sulla and Pompey, which the City crowds had thrown down and smashed. He also preferred to discourage rather than punish any plots against his life, or any slanders on his name. All that he would do when he detected such plots, or became aware of secret nocturnal meetings, was to announce openly that he knew about them. As for slanderers, he contented himself with warning them in public to keep their mouths shut; and goodnaturedly took no action either against Aulus Caecina for his most libellous pamphlet or against Pitholaus for his scurrilous verses.

76] Yet other deeds and sayings of Caesar's may be set to the debit account, and justify the conclusion that he deserved assassination. Not only did he accept unconstitutional honours, such as a life-consulship, a life-dictatorship, a perpetual Censorship, the title 'Emperor' put before his name, and the title 'Father of his Country' appended to it, also a statue standing among those of the ancient kings, and a raised couch placed in the orchestra at the Theatre; but took other honours which, as a mere mortal, he should certainly have refused. These included a golden throne in the Senate House, and another on the tribunal; a ceremonial chariot and litter for carrying his statue in the religious procession around the Circus; temples, altars and divine images; a priest of his own cult; a new college of Lupercals to celebrate his divinity; and the renaming of the seventh month as 'July.' Few, in fact, were the honours which he was not pleased to accept or assume.

His third and fourth consulships were merely titular; the dictatorship conferred on him at the same time supplied all the authority he needed. And in both years he substituted two new Consuls for himself during the last quarter, meanwhile letting only tribunes and aediles of the people be elected, and appointing prefects instead of praetors to govern the City during his absence.

One of the Consuls died suddenly on New Year's Eve and, when someone asked to hold office for the remaining few hours, Caesar granted his request. He showed equal scorn of constitutional precedent by choosing magistrates several years ahead, decorating ten former praetors with the emblems of consular rank, and admitting to the Senate men of foreign birth, including semi-civilized Gauls who had been granted Roman citizenship. He placed his own slaves in charge of the Mint and the public revenues, and sent one of his favourites, a freedman's son, to command the three legions stationed at Alexandria.

77] Titus Ampius has recorded some of Caesar's public statements which reveal a similar presumption: that the Republic was nothing —

a mere name without form or substance; that Sulla had proved himself a dunce by resigning his dictatorship; and that, now his own word was law, people ought to be more careful how they approached him. Once, when a soothsayer reported that a sacrificial beast had been found to have no heart — an unlucky omen indeed — Caesar told him arrogantly: 'The omens will be as favourable as I wish them to be; meanwhile I am not at all surprised that a beast should lack the organ which inspires our finer feelings.'

78] What made the Romans hate him so bitterly was that when, one day, the entire Senate, armed with an imposing list of honours that they had just voted him, came to where he sat in front of the Temple of Mother Venus, he did not rise to greet them. According to some accounts he would have risen had not Cornelius Balbus prevented him; according to others, he made no such move and grimaced angrily at Gaius Trebatius who suggested this courtesy. The case was aggravated by a memory of Caesar's behaviour during one of his triumphs: he had ridden past the benches reserved for the tribunes of the people, and shouted in fury at a certain Pontius Aquila, who had kept his seat: 'Hey, there, Aquila the tribune! Do you want me to restore the Republic?' For several days after this incident he added to every undertaking he gave: 'With the kind consent of Pontius Aquila.'

79] This open insult to the Senate was emphasized by an even worse example of his scorn for the Constitution. As he returned to Rome from the Alban Hill, where the Latin Festival had been celebrated, a member of the crowd set a laurel wreath bound with a royal white fillet on the head of his statue. Two tribunes of the people, Epidius Marullus and Caesetius Flavus, ordered the fillet to be removed at once and the offender imprisoned. But Caesar reprimanded and summarily degraded them both: either because the suggestion that he should be crowned King had been so rudely rejected, or else because — this was his own version — they had given him no chance to reject it himself and so earn deserved credit. From that day forward, however, he lay under the odious suspicion of having tried to revive the title of King; though, indeed, when the commons greeted him with 'Long live the King!' he now protested: 'No, I am Caesar, not King'; and though, again, when he was addressing the crowd from the Rostra at the Lupercalian Festival, and Mark Antony, the Consul, made several attempts to crown him, he refused the offer each time and at last sent the crown away for dedication to Capitoline Juppiter. What made matters worse was a persistent rumour that

Caesar intended to move the seat of government to Troy or Alexandria, carrying off all the national resources, drafting every available man in Italy for military service, and letting his friends govern what was left of the City. At the next meeting of the House (it was further whispered), Lucius Cotta would announce a decision of the Fifteen who had charge of the Sibylline Books, that since these prophetic writings stated clearly: 'Only a king can conquer the Parthians,' the title of King must be conferred on Caesar.

NOTE

1. 46 B.C.

7

The Deeds of Augustus

AUGUSTUS composed the following document in the period 8 B.C.–A.D. 6,
kept revising it until the end of his reign, and ordered it inscribed on
bronze pillars outside his tomb in the Campus Martius upon his death.
Copies were made, and the inscription appeared in various public places
throughout the Empire to advertise the accomplishments of the first
emperor and to stimulate the loyalty of Rome's subjects to the imperial
regime. An almost complete text of the document was found in the
Temple of Rome and Augustus at Ankara, whence its common appella-
tion, Monumentum Ancyranum. The Res Gestae is probably the most
important political apologia to have survived from antiquity. The emperor
describes with sober accuracy his many acts for the good of the state. At
the same time, since he was too consummate a politician to be completely
truthful, his references to his own early career as a revolutionary and to
the true monarchic basis of his power are oblique and ambiguous.

Augustus, Res Gestae

BELOW is a copy of the accomplishments of the deified Augustus
by which he brought the whole world under the empire of
the Roman people, and of the moneys expended by him on the state
and the Roman people, as inscribed on two bronze pillars set up in
Rome.

1] At the age of nineteen, on my own initiative and my own expense, I raised an army by means of which I liberated the Republic,
which was oppressed by the tyranny of a faction. For which reason
the senate, with honorific decrees, made me a member of its order in
the consulship of Gaius Pansa and Aulus Hirtius,[1] giving me at the
same time consular rank in voting, and granted me the *imperium*. It
ordered me as propraetor, together with the consuls, to see to it that
the state suffered no harm. Moreover, in the same year, when both
consuls had fallen in war, the people elected me consul and a
triumvir for the settlement of the commonwealth.

From N. Lewis and M. Reinhold, ROMAN CIVILIZATION (New York,
1955), vol. ii, pp. 9–19. Reprinted by permission of the Columbia University Press.

2] Those who assassinated my father[2] I drove into exile, avenging their crime by due process of law; and afterwards when they waged war against the state, I conquered them twice on the battlefield.[3]

3] I waged many wars throughout the whole world by land and by sea, both civil and foreign, and when victorious I spared all citizens who sought pardon. Foreign peoples who could safely be pardoned I preferred to spare rather than to extirpate. About 500,000 Roman citizens were under military oath to me. Of these, when their terms of service were ended, I settled in colonies or sent back to their own municipalities a little more than 300,000, and to all of these I allotted lands or granted money as rewards for military service. I captured 600 ships, exclusive of those which were of smaller class than triremes.

4] Twice I celebrated ovations, three times curule triumphs, and I was acclaimed *imperator* twenty-one times. When the senate decreed additional triumphs to me, I declined them on four occasions. I deposited in the Capitol laurel wreaths adorning my *fasces*, after fulfilling the vows which I had made in each war. For successes achieved on land and on sea by me or through my legates under my auspices the senate decreed fifty-five times that thanksgiving be offered to the immortal gods. Moreover, the number of days on which, by decree of the senate, such thanksgiving was offered, was 890. In my triumphs there were led before my chariot nine kings or children of kings. At the time I wrote this document, I had been consul thirteen times, and I was in the thirty-seventh year of my tribunician power.[4]

5] The dictatorship offered to me in the consulship of Marcus Marcellus and Lucius Arruntius[5] by the people and by the senate, both in my absence and in my presence, I refused to accept. In the midst of a critical scarcity of grain I did not decline the supervision of the grain supply, which I so administered that within a few days I freed the whole people from imminent panic and danger by my expenditures and efforts. The consulship, too, which was offered to me at that time as an annual office for life, I refused to accept.

6] In the consulship of Marcus Vinicius and Quintus Lucretius, and again in that of Publius Lentulus and Gnaeus Lentulus, and a third time in that of Paullus Fabius Maximus and Quintus Tubero,[6] though the Roman senate and people unitedly agreed that I should be elected sole guardian of the laws and morals with supreme authority, I refused to accept any office offered me which was contrary to the traditions of our ancestors. The measures which the senate desired at that time to be taken by me I carried out by virtue of the tribunician power.[7] In this power I five times voluntarily requested and was given a colleague by the senate.

7] I was a member of the triumvirate for the settlement of the commonwealth for ten consecutive years.[8] I have been ranking senator for forty years, up to the day on which I wrote this document. I have been *pontifex maximus,* augur, member of the college of fifteen for performing sacrifices, member of the college of seven for conducting religious banquets, member of the Arval Brotherhood, one of the Titii sodales, and a fetial.

8] In my fifth consulship I increased the number of patricians, by order of the people and the senate. Three times I revised the roll of senators. And in my sixth consulship, with Marcus Agrippa as my colleague, I conducted a census of the people. I performed the *lustrum* after an interval of forty-two years. At this *lustrum* 4,063,000 Roman citizens were recorded. Then a second time, acting alone, by virtue of the consular power, I completed the taking of the census in the consulship of Gaius Censorinus and Gaius Asinius. At this *lustrum* 4,233,000 Roman citizens were recorded. And a third time I completed the taking of the census in the consulship of Sextus Pompeius and Sextus Appuleius, by virtue of the consular power and with my son Tiberius Caesar as my colleague. At this *lustrum* 4,937,000 Roman citizens were recorded. By new legislation which I sponsored I restored many traditions of our ancestors which were falling into desuetude in our generation; and I myself handed down precedents in many spheres for posterity to imitate.

9] The senate decreed that vows for my health should be offered up every fifth year by the consuls and priests. In fulfillment of these vows, games were often celebrated during my lifetime, sometimes by the four most distinguished colleges of priests, sometimes by the consuls. Moreover, the whole citizen body, with one accord, both individually and as members of municipalities, prayed continuously for my health at all the shrines.

10] My name was inserted, by decree of the senate, in the hymn of the Salian priests. And it was enacted by law that I should be sacrosanct in perpetuity and that I should possess the tribunician power as long as I live. I declined to become *pontifex maximus* in place of a colleague[9] while he was still alive, when the people offered me that priesthood, which my father had held. A few years later, in the consulship of Publius Sulpicius and Gaius Valgius, I accepted this priesthood, when death removed the man who had taken possession of it at a time of civil disturbance; and from all Italy a multitude flocked to my election such as had never previously been recorded at Rome.

11] To commemorate my return from Syria, the senate consecrated an altar to Fortune the Home-bringer before the temple of Honor and Virtue at the Porta Capena, on which altar it decreed that the pontiffs and Vestal Virgins should make a yearly sacrifice on the anniversary of the day in the consulship of Quintus Lucretius and Marcus Vinicius[10] on which I returned to the city from Syria, and it designated that day *Augustalia* from my name.

12] On this occasion, by decree of the senate, a portion of the praetors and tribunes of the plebs, together with the consul Quintus Lucretius and the leading men, was sent to Campania to meet me, an honor which up to this time has been decreed to no one but myself. When I returned to Rome from Spain and Gaul in the consulship of Tiberius Nero and Publius Quintilius,[11] after successfully settling the affairs of those provinces, the senate, to commemorate my return, ordered an altar of the Augustan Peace[12] to be consecrated in the Campus Martius, on which it decreed that the magistrates, priests, and Vestal Virgins should make an annual sacrifice.

13] The temple of Janus Quirinus, which our ancestors desired to be closed whenever peace with victory was secured by sea and by land throughout the entire empire of the Roman people, and which before I was born is recorded to have been closed only twice since the founding of the city, was during my principate three times ordered by the senate to be closed.

14] My sons Gaius and Lucius Caesar,[13] whom fortune took from me in their youth, were, in my honor, made consuls designate by the Roman senate and people when they were fifteen years old, with permission to enter that magistracy after a period of five years. The senate further decreed that from the day on which they were introduced into the Forum they should attend its debates. Moreover, the whole body of Roman *equites* presented each of them with silver shields and spears and saluted each as *princeps iuventutis*.[14]

15] To the Roman plebs I paid 300 sesterces apiece in accordance with the will of my father;[15] and in my fifth consulship I gave each 400 sesterces in my own name out of the spoils of war; and a second time in my tenth consulship I paid out of my own patrimony a largess of 400 sesterces to every individual; in my eleventh consulship I made twelve distributions of food out of grain purchased at my own expense; and in the twelfth year of my tribunician power for the third time I gave 400 sesterces to every individual. These largesses of mine reached never less than 250,000 persons. In the eighteenth year of my tribunician power and my twelfth consulship I gave sixty *denarii* to each of 320,000 persons of the urban plebs. And in my fifth consulship I gave out of the spoils of war 1,000 sesterces apiece to my soldiers settled in colonies. This largess on the occasion of my triumph was received by about 120,000 persons in the colonies. In my thirteenth consulship I gave sixty *denarii* apiece to those of the plebs who at that time were receiving public grain; the number involved was a little more than 200,000 persons.

16] I reimbursed municipalities for the lands which I assigned to my soldiers in my fourth consulship, and afterwards in the consulship of Marcus and Gnaeus Lentulus the augur. The sums involved were about 600,000,000 sesterces which I paid for Italian estates, and about 260,000,000 sesterces which I paid for provincial lands. I was the first and only one to take such action of all those who up to my time established colonies of soldiers in Italy or in the provinces. And afterwards, in the consulship of Tiberius Nero and Gnaeus Piso, and likewise of Gaius Antistius and Decimus Laelius, and of Gaius Calvisius and Lucius Passienus, and of Lucius Lentulus and Marcus Messalla, and of Lucius Caninius and Quintus Fabricius, I granted bonuses in cash to the soldiers whom after the completion of their terms of service I sent back to their municipalities; and for this purpose I expended about 400,000,000 sesterces.

17] Four times I came to the assistance of the treasury with my own money, transferring to those in charge of the treasury 150,000,000 sesterces. And in the consulship of Marcus Lepidus and Lucius Arruntius I transferred out of my own patrimony 170,000,000 sesterces to the soldiers' bonus fund, which was established on my advice for the purpose of providing bonuses for soldiers who had completed twenty or more years of service.

18] From the year in which Gnaeus Lentulus and Publius Lentulus were consuls, whenever the provincial taxes fell short, in the case sometimes of 100,000 persons and sometimes of many more, I made up their tribute in grain and in money from my own grain stores and my own patrimony.

19] I built the following structures: the senate house and the Chalcidicum adjoining it; the temple of Apollo on the Palatine with its porticoes; the temple of the deified Julius; the Lupercal; the portico at the Circus Flaminius, which I allowed to be called Octavia after the name of the man who had built an earlier portico on the same site; the state box at the Circus Maximus; the temples of Jupiter the

Smiter and Jupiter the Thunderer on the Capitoline; the temple of Quirinus; the temples of Minerva and Queen Juno and of Jupiter Freedom on the Aventine; the temple of the Lares at the head of the Sacred Way; the temple of the Penates on the Velia; the temple of Youth and the temple of the Great Mother on the Palatine.

20] I repaired the Capitol and the theater of Pompey with enormous expenditures on both works, without having my name inscribed on them. I repaired the conduits of the aqueducts which were falling into ruin in many places because of age, and I doubled the capacity of the aqueduct called Marcia by admitting a new spring into its conduit. I completed the Julian Forum and the basilica which was between the temple of Castor and the temple of Saturn, works begun and far advanced by my father, and when the same basilica was destroyed by fire, I enlarged its site and began rebuilding the structure, which is to be inscribed with the names of my sons; and in case it should not be completed while I am still alive, I left instructions that the work be completed by my heirs. In my sixth consulship I repaired eighty-two temples of the gods in the city, in accordance with a resolution of the senate, neglecting none which at that time required repair. In my seventh consulship I reconstructed the Flaminian Way from the city as far as Ariminum, and also all the bridges except the Mulvian and the Minucian.

21] On my own private land I built the temple of Mars Ultor and the Augustan Forum from spoils of war. On ground bought for the most part from private owners I built the theater adjoining the temple of Apollo which was to be inscribed with the name of my son-in-law Marcus Marcellus. In the Capitol, in the temple of the deified Julius, in the temple of Apollo, in the temple of Vesta, and in the temple of Mars Ultor I consecrated gifts from spoils of war which cost me about 100,000,000 sesterces. In my fifth consulship I remitted to the municipalities and colonies of Italy 35,000 pounds of crown gold which they were collecting in honor of my triumphs; and afterwards, whenever I was acclaimed *imperator,* I did not accept the crown gold, though the municipalities and colonies decreed it with the same enthusiasm as before.

22] I gave a gladiatorial show three times in my own name, and five times in the names of my sons or grandsons; at these shows about 10,000 fought. Twice I presented to the people in my own name an exhibition of athletes invited from all parts of the world, and a third time in the name of my grandson. I presented games in my own name four times, and in addition twenty-three times in the place of other magistrates. On behalf of the college of fifteen, as master of that college, with Marcus Agrippa as my colleague, I celebrated the Secular Games in the consulship of Gaius Furnius and Gaius Silanus. In my thirteenth consulship I was the first to celebrate the Games of Mars, which subsequently the consuls, in accordance with a decree of the senate and a law, have regularly celebrated in the succeeding years. Twenty-six times I provided for the people, in my own name or in the names of my sons or grandsons, hunting spectacles of African wild beasts in the circus or in the Forum or in the amphitheaters; in these exhibitions about 3,500 animals were killed.

23] I presented to the people an exhibition of a naval battle across the Tiber where the grove of the Caesars now is, having had the site excavated 1,800 feet in length and 1,200 feet in width. In this exhibition thirty beaked ships, triremes or biremes, and in addition a great number of smaller vessels engaged in combat. On board these fleets, exclusive of rowers, there were about 3,000 combatants.

24] When I was victorious I replaced in the temples of all the communities of the province of Asia the ornaments which my opponent in the war had seized for his private use after despoiling the temples. About eighty silver statues of myself, represented on foot, on horseback, or in chariot, stood in the city; these I myself removed, and out of the money therefrom I set up golden offerings in the temple of Apollo in my own name and in the names of those who had honored me with the statues.

25] I brought peace to the sea by suppressing the pirates.[16] In that war I turned over to their masters for punishment nearly 30,000 slaves who had run away from their owners and taken up arms against the state. The whole of Italy voluntarily took an oath of allegiance to me and demanded me as its leader in the war in which I was victorious at Actium. The same oath was taken by the provinces of the Gauls, the Spains, Africa, Sicily, and Sardinia. More than 700 senators served at that time under my standards; of that number eighty-three attained the consulship and about 170 obtained priesthoods, either before that date or subsequently, up to the day on which this document was written.

26] I extended the frontiers of all the provinces of the Roman people on whose boundaries were peoples subject to our empire. I restored peace to the Gallic and Spanish provinces and likewise to Germany, that is to the entire region bounded by the Ocean from Gades to the mouth of the Elbe river. I caused peace to be restored in the Alps, from the region nearest to the Adriatic Sea as far as the Tuscan Sea, without undeservedly making war against any people. My fleet sailed the Ocean from the mouth of the Rhine eastward as far as the territory of the Cimbrians, to which no Roman previously had penetrated either by land or by sea. The Cimbrians, the Charydes, the Semnones, and other German peoples of the same region through their envoys sought my friendship and that of the Roman people. At my command and under my auspices two armies were led almost at the same time into Ethiopia and into Arabia which is called Felix;[17] and very large forces of the enemy belonging to both peoples were killed in battle, and many towns were captured. In Ethiopia a penetration was made as far as the town of Napata, which is next to Meroe; in Arabia the army advanced into the territory of the Sabaeans to the town of Mariba.

27] I added Egypt to the empire of the Roman people. Although I might have made Greater Armenia into a province when its king Artaxes was assassinated, I preferred, following the precedent of our ancestors, to hand over this kingdom, acting through Tiberius Nero, who was then my stepson, to Tigranes, son of King Artavasdes and grandson of King Tigranes. And afterwards, when this same people revolted and rebelled, after I subdued it through my son Gaius, I handed it over to the rule of King Ariobarzanes, son of Artabazus, king of the Medes, and after his death to his son Artavasdes. When the latter was killed, I dispatched to that kingdom Tigranes, a scion of the royal family of Armenia. I recovered all the provinces extending beyond the Adriatic Sea eastward, and also Cyrenae, which were for the most part already in the possession of kings, as I had previously recovered Sicily and Sardinia, which had been seized in the slave war.

28] I established colonies of soldiers in Africa, Sicily, Macedonia, in both Spanish provinces, in Achaea, Asia, Syria, Narbonese Gaul, and Pisidia. Italy, moreover, has twenty-eight colonies established by me, which in my lifetime have grown to be famous and populous.

29] A number of military standards lost by other generals I recovered, after conquering the enemy, from Spain, Gaul, and the Dalmatians. The Parthians I compelled to restore to me the spoils and standards of three Roman armies and to seek the friendship of the Roman people as suppliants. The standards, moreover, I deposited in the inner shrine of the temple of Mars Ultor.

30] Through Tiberius Nero, who was then my stepson and legate, I conquered and subjected to the empire of the Roman people the Pannonian tribes, to which before my principate no army of the

Roman people had ever penetrated; and I extended the frontier of Illyricum to the bank of the Danube River. An army of the Dacians which had crossed to our side of the river was conquered and destroyed under my auspices, and later on, my army crossed the Danube and compelled the Dacian tribes to submit to the orders of the Roman people.

31] Royal embassies from India, never previously seen before any Roman general, were often sent to me. Our friendship was sought through ambassadors by the Bastarnians and Scythians and by the kings of the Sarmatians, who live on both sides of the Don River, and by the kings of the Albanians and of the Iberians and of the Medes.

32] The following kings fled to me as suppliants: Tiridates and afterwards Phraates son of King Phraates, kings of the Parthians; Artavasdes, king of the Medes; Artaxares, king of the Adiabenians; Dumnobellaunus and Tincommius, kings of the Britons; Maelo, king of the Sugumbrians, and Segimerus[?], king of the Marcomannian Suebians. Phraates son of Orodes, king of the Parthians, sent to me in Italy all his sons and grandsons, not because he was conquered in war, but seeking our friendship through pledge of his children. Under my principate numerous other peoples, with whom previously there had existed no exchange of embassies and friendship, experienced the good faith of the Roman people.

33] The peoples of the Parthians and of the Medes, through ambassadors who were the leading men of these peoples, received from me the kings for whom they asked: the Parthians, Vonones son of King Phraates, grandson of King Orodes; the Medes, Ariobarzanes son of King Artavasdes, grandson of King Ariobarzanes.

34] In my sixth and seventh consulships,[18] after I had put an end to the civil wars, having attained supreme power by universal consent, I transferred the state from my own power to the control of the Roman senate and people. For this service of mine I received the title of Augustus by decree of the senate, and the doorposts of my house were publicly decked with laurels, the civic crown was affixed over my doorway, and a golden shield was set up in the Julian senate house, which, as the inscription on the shield testifies, the Roman senate and people gave me in recognition of my valor, clemency, justice, and devotion. After that time I excelled all in authority, but I possessed no more power than the others who were my colleagues in each magistracy.

35] When I held my thirteenth consulship, the senate, the equestrian order, and the entire Roman people gave me the title of "father of the country" and decreed that this title should be inscribed in the vestibule of my house, in the Julian senate house, and in the Augustan Forum on the pedestal of the chariot which was set up in my honor by decree of the senate. At the time I wrote this document I was in my seventy-sixth year.

NOTES

1. 44/43 B.C., when he ranged himself with the senate against Antony.
2. Julius Caesar, his adoptive father.
3. Two battles of Philippi, 42 B.C.
4. A.D. 14.
5. 22 B.C.
6. 19, 18, and 11 B.C.
7. Moral and social legislation beginning in 18 B.C.
8. 43–33 B.C.
9. The reference is to the third triumvir, Lepidus, who lived in retirement until his death in 12 B.C.
10. 19 B.C.
11. 13 B.C.
12. Altar of Peace dedicated in 9 B.C.
13. Augustus adopted his two grandsons, sons of his daughter, Julia, and his prime minister, Agrippa.
14. Leaders of an organization of equestrian youths.
15. One sesterce, about five cents.
16. The war with Sextus Pompey, Gnaeus Pompey's son, concluded in 36 B.C.
17. The Yemen.
18. 28 and 27 B.C.

8

Roman Poetry

THE SELECTIONS from the following poets of the first centuries before and after Christ suggest the variety of the Roman artistic genius. Lucretius' (98–53 B.C.) On the Nature of the Universe illustrates an essentially Epicurean quest for peace of mind, which led him to an un-Roman quietistic life of withdrawal from society. The selections from the three Augustan poets demonstrate the creativity of the Golden Age. Patriotic inspiration is implicit in the excerpts from Vergil's (70–19 B.C.) Aeneid, in which the shade of Anchises causes Aeneas to behold a vision of Rome's future heroes. The Ode from Horace (65–8 B.C.) expresses gratitude for the establishment of peace, while his Hymn for the Centennial, performed at the inauguration of the "New Era" in 17 B.C., evokes a typically Augustan religious solemnity. Ovid's (43 B.C.–A.D. 17) charming Art of Love reveals the Romans as flesh-and-blood people and permits a glimpse of one aspect of their social life, while Juvenal's (ca. A.D. 55–125) bitter satire describes the sycophantic nature of "high society" about A.D. 100.

a Lucretius, On the Nature of the Universe, II, 1-61; III, 787-867

II, 1–61]

'TIS SWEET, when, down the mighty main, the winds
Roll up its waste of waters, from the land
To watch another's labouring anguish far,
Not that we joyously delight that man
Should thus be smitten, but because 'tis sweet
To mark what evils we ourselves be spared;
'Tis sweet, again, to view the mighty strife
Of armies embattled yonder o'er the plains,
Ourselves no sharers in the peril; but naught

From Lucretius, OF THE NATURE OF THINGS, metrical translation by William Ellery Leonard (New York and London, 1921, Everyman's Library edition), pp. 45–47, 129–131. Reprinted by permission of E. P. Dutton & Co., Inc. and J. M. Dent and Sons Ltd.

There is more goodly than to hold the high
Serene plateaus, well fortressed by the wise,
Whence thou may'st look below on other men
And see them ev'rywhere wand'ring, all dispersed
In their lone seeking for the road of life;
Rivals in genius, or emulous in rank,
Pressing through days and nights with hugest toil
For summits of power and mastery of the world.
O wretched minds of men! O blinded hearts!
In how great perils, in what darks of life
Are spent the human years, however brief! —
O not to see that nature for herself
Barks after nothing, save that pain keep off,
Disjoined from the body, and that mind enjoy
Delightsome feeling, far from care and fear!
Therefore we see that our corporeal life
Needs little, altogether, and only such
As takes the pain away, and can besides
Strew underneath some number of delights.
More grateful 'tis at times (for nature craves
No artifice nor luxury), if forsooth
There be no golden images of boys
Along the halls, with right hands holding out
The lamps ablaze, the lights for evening feasts,
And if the house doth glitter not with gold
Nor gleam with silver, and to the lyre resound
No fretted and gilded ceilings overhead,
Yet still to lounge with friends in the soft grass
Beside a river of water, underneath
A big tree's boughs, and merrily to refresh
Our frames, with no vast outlay — most of all
If the weather is laughing and the times of the year
Besprinkle the green of the grass around with flowers.
Nor yet the quicker will hot fevers go,
If on a pictured tapestry thou toss,
Or purple robe, than if 'tis thine to lie
Upon the poor man's bedding. Wherefore, since
Treasure, nor rank, nor glory of a reign
Avail us naught for this our body, thus
Reckon them likewise nothing for the mind:
Save then perchance, when thou beholdest forth

Thy legions swarming round the Field of Mars,
Rousing a mimic warfare — either side
Strengthened with large auxiliaries and horse,
Alike equipped with arms, alike inspired;
Or save when also thou beholdest forth
Thy fleets to swarm, deploying down the sea:
For then, by such bright circumstance abashed,
Religion pales and flees thy mind; O then
The fears of death leave heart so free of care.
But if we note how all this pomp at last
Is but a drollery and a mocking sport,
And of a truth man's dread, with cares at heels,
Dreads not these sounds of arms, these savage swords,
But among kings and lords of all the world
Mingles undaunted, nor is overawed
By gleam of gold nor by the splendour bright
Of purple robe, canst thou then doubt that this
Is aught, but power of thinking? — when, besides
The whole of life but labours in the dark.
For just as children tremble and fear all
In the viewless dark, so even we at times
Dread in the light so many things that be
No whit more fearsome than what children feign,
Shuddering, will be upon them in the dark.
This terror then, this darkness of the mind,
Not sunrise with its flaring spokes of light,
Nor glittering arrows of morning can disperse,
But only nature's aspect and her law.

III, 787–867]

TARTARUS, out-belching from his mouth the surge
Of horrible heat — the which are nowhere, nor
Indeed can be: but in this life is fear
Of retributions just and expiations
For evil acts: the dungeon and the leap
From that dread rock of infamy, the stripes,
The executioners, the oaken rack,
The iron plates, bitumen, and the torch.
And even though these are absent, yet the mind,
With a fore-fearing conscience, plies its goads
And burns beneath the lash, nor sees meanwhile

What terminus of ills, what end of pine
Can ever be, and feareth lest the same
But grow more heavy after death. Of truth,
The life of fools is Acheron on earth.
   This also to thy very self sometimes
Repeat thou mayst: "Lo, even good Ancus left
The sunshine with his eyes, in divers things
A better man than thou, O worthless hind;
And many other kings and lords of rule
Thereafter have gone under, once who swayed
O'er mighty peoples. And he also, he —
Who whilom paved a highway down the sea,
And gave his legionaries thoroughfare
Along the deep, and taught them how to cross
The pools of brine afoot, and did contemn,
Trampling upon it with his cavalry,
The bellowings of ocean — poured his soul
From dying body, as his light was ta'en
And Scipio's son, the thunderbolt of war,
Horror of Carthage, gave his bones to earth,
Like to the lowliest villein in the house.
Add finders-out of sciences and arts;
Add comrades of the Heliconian dames,
Among whom Homer, sceptered o'er them all,
Now lies in slumber sunken with the rest.
Then, too, Democritus, when ripened eld
Admonished him his memory waned away,
Of own accord offered his head to death.
Even Epicurus went, his light of life
Run out, the man in genius who o'er-topped
The human race, extinguishing all others,
As sun, in ether arisen, all the stars.
Wilt thou, then, dally, thou complain to go? —
For whom already life's as good as dead,
Whilst yet thou livest and lookest? — who in sleep
Wastest thy life — time's major part, and snorest
Even when awake, and ceasest not to see
The stuff of dreams, and bearest a mind beset
By baseless terror, nor discoverest oft
What's wrong with thee, when, like a sotted wretch,
Thou'rt jostled along by many crowding cares,
And wanderest reeling round, with mind aswim."

If men, in that same way as on the mind
They *feel* the load that wearies with its weight,
Could also *know* the causes whence it comes,
And why so great the heap of ill on heart,
O not in this sort would they live their life,
As now so much we see them, knowing not
What 'tis they want, and seeking ever and ever
A change of place, as if to drop the burden.
The man who sickens of his home goes out,
Forth from his splendid halls, and straight — returns,
Feeling i'faith no better off abroad.
He races, driving his Gallic ponies along,
Down to his villa, madly, — as in haste
To hurry help to a house afire. — At once
He yawns, as soon as foot has touched the threshold,
Or drowsily goes off in sleep and seeks
Forgetfulness, or maybe bustles about
And makes for town again. In such a way
Each human flees himself — a self in sooth,
As happens, he by no means can escape;
And willy-nilly he cleaves to it and loathes,
Sick, sick, and guessing not the cause of ail.
Yet should he see but *that,* O chiefly then,
Leaving all else, he'd study to divine
The nature of things, since here is in debate
Eternal time and not the single hour,
Mortal's estate in whatsoever remains
After great death.

b Vergil, Aeneid, VI, 752–901

 ANCHISES ceased; and 'midst their gatherings
And murmuring crowd, draws son and Sybil both
With him, and mounts a hillock, whence he might
View all in long array confronting him,

From Vergil, THE AENEID, translated by T. H. Delabère-Muy and edited by Moses Hadas (New York, 1961), pp. 158–163. Copyright © 1961 by Bantam Books, Inc. All rights reserved. Reprinted by permission of Bantam Books, Inc.

And notes the features of them as they come.
  "Now hear: What fame henceforward shall attend
The Dardan offspring, what Italian-born
Descendants wait us, souls illustrious,
And to our name hereafter to succeed,
I will rehearse, and show you your fates.
  That youth, you will note, who leans on pointless spear,
Next place by lot he holds to reach the light;
Italian blood commingling in his veins,
He first shall rise to air of upper world
Silvius, an Alban name, your youngest born;
Whom late your wife Lavinia shall rear,
Within the woods, for you advanced in years,
To be a king and parent of our kings,
From whom our line within the Long White Town
Shall bear dominion. He that comes the next
Procas, the glory of the Trojan race,
Capys and Numitor, and who by name
Shall recall you, Aeneas Silvius,
Matchless alike in goodness and in arms,
If ever over Alba he shall take the rule.
What warriors! what vigor they display,
Behold! and how enshadowed are their brows
With civic oakleaf! These shall build for you
Nomentum, Gabii, and Fidenae's town,
These on the mountains set Collatia's towers,
Pometii, and the camp of Inuus,
Bola and Cora. These shall be their names
Then, — for they now are lands without a name.
  Nay more, Mars' offspring, Romulus, will join
His grandsire's company, whom Ilia
His mother, daughter of Assaracus,
Shall rear. Do you see how on his head there stand
The double plumes? and how his sire himself
Stamps him already of the gods above
With his own mark of honor? Lo, my son,
'Neath this one's rule shall that renownèd Rome
Wide as the lands extend her sway, and raise
To heaven her pride, and, one alone, wall round
Seven citadels, blessed in her warrior sons;
Just as car-borne the Berecynthian Queen
Crownèd with towers through Phrygian cities rides,

Rejoicing in her progeny of gods,
And clasps a hundred grandsons to her side,
All denizens of heaven and all of them
Holding the lofty places of the sky.
Now, hither now, turn both your eyes to view
This race to come, and Romans who are your own.
Caesar is here and all Iulus' sons
Beneath heaven's lofty pole to pass in time.
This is the hero — this is he of whom
Full many times in promise you were told,
Augustus Caesar, offspring of a god,
Who once again shall found the golden age
In Latium over the fields that Saturn ruled
In days gone by; and will advance his sway
Over Garamantes' and over Indian tribes.
Beyond the constellations lies a land,
Beyond the ways of sun and year, and there
Sky-bearing Atlas on his shoulder whirls
The heavens with fiery constellations set.
Even now before his coming Caspian realms
Shudder to hear the message of the gods,
Maeotia too, and tremblingly the mouths
Of Nile's seven rivers pour their troubled streams.
Not even Alcides roamed over earth so far,
Even though he slew the brazen-footed stag,
Or brought repose to Erymanthus' glades,
And with his bow made Lerna's monster quake;
Nor Liber who victorious guides his team,
Vine tendrils for his reins, what time he drives
His tigers down from Nysa's lofty peak.
And shrink we still from widening valor's roll
By deeds, or does our fear restrain us still
From planting foot upon Ausonian land?

　　But who is he afar, conspicuous
With boughs of olive, bearing holy things?
I recognize the locks and hoary chin
Of Roman king, who shall with laws set firm
Our rising town; sent forth to lordly rule
From scanty Cures, and its barren soil.

And after him shall Tullus come, and break
His country's spell of ease, and rouse to arms
Our sluggish warriors and battalions grown
Already all unused to victories.
And close behind him, of more boastful mien,
Comes Ancus, and even now too he delights
More than is well in popular applause.
And would you also see the Tarquin kings?
And the avenger Brutus' lofty soul?
See too the people's sovereignty restored?
He shall be first to wield a consul's power
And the unrelenting axes; and, their sire,
Shall call his sons to meet their punishment
For lighting war anew — unhappy he —
All for the sake of glorious liberty.
However those deeds our after-folk shall tell,
Love of his land and boundless thirst for praise
With him will overcome. Nay more, behold
Far off the Decii, and the Drusi there,
Torquatus also with unpitying axe,
Camillus too, who bears the standards back.
But those you see glistening-armed alike,
Souls now at one, and while in thrall of night,
Alas! what cruel war between the pair,
What battles, and what carnage will they stir,
Should they the light of earthly life attain!
The Sire-in-law from ranges of the Alps,
And from Monoecus' stronghold coming down;
The son against him ranged with Eastern host!
Never, never, my children, let your hearts grow used
To wars so fierce, nor turn your stalwart strength
To rend the bowels of your fatherland;
You who draw your descent from Olympus,
Be you the first to spare. Your weapons
Fling from your hands, offspring mine!
　　He there — his triumph over Corinth won,
A victor to the lofty Capitol,
Renowned for slaughtered Greeks shall drive his car;
He, Argos, ay and Agamemnon's town
Mycenae, even Aeacides himself,

Valiant Achilles' offspring, shall overthrow,
Take vengeance for his ancestors of Troy,
And for Minerva's desecrated shrines.
Who, mighty Cato, could leave you unsung.
Or you, O Cossus? Who the Gracchan clan?
Or war's two thunderbolts the Scipios twain
The bane of Carthage? or Fabricius, rich
Upon his scanty sustenance; or you,
Serranus, in your furrow sowing seed?
Whither, Fabii, do you whirl me along,
Spent in my song? You are that Maximus
Who, singly, by delaying does restore
Our fortunes for us. Others, well I know,
Will forge the living bronze more gracefully,
Will from the marble lifelike features chase,
Plead causes better, and with pointer trace
The journeyings of the heavens, and indicate
The rising constellations: be thy thought,
Roman, to hold the nations in your sway.
These shall your arts be; terms of peace to name,
To spare the vanquished and war down the proud."
   So speaks the Sire, and, while they wonder, adds
These words: "See how Marcellus proudly strides,
Conspicuous for princeliest trophies won,
And towers victorious over all the chiefs!
This knight shall prove of Roman state the stay
'Midst the fierce broil of rising, shall lay low
Carthage, and rebel Gaul, and dedicate
To sire Quirinus spoils the third time won."
And here Aeneas (for he now did mark
Walking with him a youth of noble mien
And arms resplendent yet whose brow was sad,
And downcast was the look within his eye)
"Who sire is this, who thus accompanies
The hero as he goes? A son is he,
Or one of his descendants' noble line?
What hum of his companions all around!
What mirror of perfection in himself!
But round his head black night is hovering
With gloomy shade." Tears welling forth the while,

Then Sire Anchises thus reply began:
"O son, enquire not of the bitter grief
Of your descendants. This one shall the fates
But show to earth, and let him be no more.
Ye gods, to you Rome's scions would have seemed
Too mighty, had these gifts been theirs to keep.
What bitter wail of heroes shall that plain
Waft onward to the mighty town of Mars!
What funeral obsequies will you behold
Tiber, when you shall glide by that fresh tomb!
Nor ever shall youth of Ilian race uplift
So high the hopes of Latin ancestors;
Nor ever shall the land of Romulus
So vaunt herself of any son she bears.
Woe for this goodness, for his early faith,
And his right arm in war invincible!
None ever should have scathless crossed his path
When armed, were he afoot to meet his foe,
Or spurring in the flank his foaming steed.
Ah, hapless youth, you too, if any way
You can but burst your cruel fate apart,
Shall a Marcellus be. Full-handed bring
Lilies; that I their purple flowers may strew,
Pile them at least by my descendant's shade,
And with these gifts mine idle tribute pay."
Thus everywhere in all the place they roam
Throughout the misty plains, and scan them all.
And when Anchises through each separate scene
Had led his son, and set his soul aflame
With longing for the fame of coming days,
Then to the hero he relates the wars
That he must wage forthwith, portrays to him
Laurentine races, and Latinus' town,
And how to escape each peril or endure.
  Sleep has twin portals; one, as story tells,
A gate of horn, for easy issuing
Of truthful visions given; the other one
Shining and all of dazzling ivory wrought,
But false the dreams the Manes send through this
To world above. Anchises with these words

There then takes leave of son and Sibyl both,
And by the gate of ivory sends them forth.
He to the vessels speeds the shortest way,
And back to his companions fares again,
Then to Caieta's harbor sails along
Straight by the shore. The anchor from the prow
Is cast; the sterns are grounding on the beach.

c   *Horace*

Ode iv, 15]

 PHOEBUS, as I was about to celebrate
battles and cities conquered, twanged on the lyre,
        warning me not to hoist a small sail
                on the Tuscan sea. Your era, Caesar,

has brought plentiful harvests back to the fields,
and restored to our shrine of Jove the banners
        torn from the high and mighty poles
                of the Parthians, and closed Janus' temple,

for no war was on, and imposed restrictions
on the freedom that wandered beyond proper
        boundaries, and expelled wrongdoing,
                and recalled the ancestral way of life

by which the Latin name and the power of
Italy grew, and the fame of the empire
        and its majesty stretched from the sun's
                western bed to the place of his rising.

While the state is in Caesar's charge, no civil
madness, no disturbance shall drive away peace,
        nor shall hatred, that forges its swords
                and transforms poor towns into enemies.

From Joseph P. Clancy, trans., THE ODES AND EPODES OF HORACE (Chicago, 1960), pp. 186–187, 188–190. Copyright © 1960 by The University of Chicago. Reprinted by permission of The University of Chicago Press.

Nor shall those who drink the Danube's deep waters
break the Julian laws, nor shall the Getae,
   the Seres, the faithless Parthians,
      nor those born near the river Tanais.

All of us, on working days and holy days,
among the gifts of laughter-loving Bacchus,
   accompanied by wives and children,
      will first, as is proper, pray to the gods,

then, in the way of our fathers, to the sound
of Lydian flutes we will hymn our heroes
   and their noble achievements and Troy,
      Anchises, and kind Venus' descendants.

Hymn for the Centennial}

Phoebus, and Diana, ruler of forests,
the sky's bright beauty, O honored gods, to be
honored forever, grant our prayers in this
   time of devotion,

when the words of the Sybil have commanded
a choir of chosen virgins and chaste young boys
to chant a hymn to the gods who are gladdened
   by our seven hills.

Lifegiving Sun, whose bright chariot brings forth
the day and hides it again, who are reborn
new and the same, may you see nothing greater
   than Rome, the City.

Be gracious, Ilithyia, whose concern
is the time of childbirth, protect the mothers,
or, if you wish, we shall call you Lucina
   or Genitalis.

Goddess, guide our growing young ones, and bless the
decrees of the city fathers concerning
weddings, and may the laws of marriage bring forth
   many new children,

so that ten times eleven years, the proper
cycle, may bring back singing and public games

crowded into three bright days and as many
    nights of rejoicing.

And you, the Fates, whose predictions were truthful,
may the constant order of things obey your
commands, and may you add good destinies to
    those now accomplished.

May the earth be fertile for harvests and herds
and give to Ceres her garland of wheat ears;
may the crops be nourished by Jupiter's good
    breezes and showers.

Put your weapons away, be mild and gentle,
listen to the prayers of boys, Apollo;
moon goddess, crescent queen of constellations,
    listen to virgins.

If Rome is your doing, and the Tuscan coast
was won by a company from Ilium,
survivors, told to change homes and city by
    prosperous voyage,

for whom virtuous Aeneas, unharmed in
the burning of Troy, outlived his homeland,
paved the way to freedom, and would give them more
    than they left behind:

gods, help the young to learn to do what is right,
gods, help the old to be serene and quiet,
grant to Romulus' people wealth, children, and
    every honor

And the petitions, with the blood of white bulls,
of Anchises' and Venus' bright descendant,
may they be answered: may he triumph in war,
    sparing the conquered.

Now the Mede is afraid of our men, mighty
on land and sea, and their Roman axes;
now Scythians and Indians, once so proud,
    plead for our answer.

Now Faith and Peace and Honor and ancestral
Decency and slighted Virtue venture to

return, and blessed Plenty appears once more
with her brimming horn.

Phoebus, the prophet, graced with his gleaming bow,
and held in reverence by the nine Muses,
who eases with his power of healing the
exhausted body.

when he sees and blesses Palatine altars,
the Roman state and Latin prosperity
he preserves forever, through future cycles
and better ages;

and she who rules Algidus and Aventine,
Diana, hears the prayers of the Fifteen
Guardians, and listens and is kind to the
children's petitions.

This is the wish of Jove and of all the gods:
that is the good and certain hope we carry
home, we the chorus, trained to chant Phoebus' and
Diana's praises.

d Ovid, Art of Love, I, 30-170

VENUS, give aid to my song!
Keep far away, stern looks and all of modesty's emblems,
Headdresses worn by the pure, skirts hiding feet in their folds.
What is the theme of my song? A little pleasant indulgence.
What is the theme of my song? Nothing that's very far wrong.

First, my raw recruit, my inexperienced soldier,
Take some trouble to find the girl whom you really can love.
Next, when you see what you like your problem will be how to win
her.
Finally, strive to make sure mutual love will endure.
That's as far as I go, the territory I cover,
Those are the limits I set: take them or leave them alone.

From Ovid, THE ART OF LOVE, translated by Rolfe Humphries (Bloom-ington, Ind., 1958), pp 106–110. Reprinted by permission of Indiana University Press.

While you are footloose and free to play the field at your pleasure,
    Watch for the one you can tell, "I want no other but you!"
She is not going to come to you floating down from the heavens:
    For the right kind of a girl you must keep using your eyes.
Hunters know where to spread their nets for the stag in his covert,
    Hunters know where the boar gnashes his teeth in the glade.
Fowlers know brier and bush, and fishermen study the waters
    Baiting the hook for the cast just where the fish may be found.
So you too, in your hunt for material worthy of loving,
    First will have to find out where the game usually goes.
I will not tell you to sail searching far over the oceans,
    I will not tell you to plod any long wearisome road.
Perseus went far to find his dusky Indian maiden.
    That was a Grecian girl Paris took over the sea.
Rome has all you will need, so many beautiful lovelies
    You will be bound to say, "Here is the grace of the world!"
Gargara's richness of field, Methymna's abundance of vineyard,
    All the fish of the sea, all the birds in the leaves,
All the stars in the sky, are less than the girls Rome can offer;
    Venus is mother and queen here in the town of her son.
If you are fond of them young, you will find them here by the thou-
      sands,
    Maids in their teens, from whom you will have trouble to choose.
Maybe a bit more mature, a little bit wiser? Believe me,
    These will outnumber the first as they come trooping along.

Take your time, walk slow, when the sun approaches the lion.
    There are porticoes, marbled under the shade,
Pompey's, Octavia's, or the one in Livia's honor,
    Or the Danaid's own, tall on the Palatine hill.
Don't pass by the shrine of Adonis, sorrow to Venus,
    Where, on the Sabbath day, Syrians worship, and Jews.
Try the Memphian fane of the Heifer, shrouded in linen;
    Isis makes many a girl willing as Io for Jove.
Even the courts of the law, the bustle and noise of the forum,
    (This may be hard to believe) listen to whispers of love.
Hard by the marble shrine of Venus, the Appian fountain,
    Where the water springs high in its rush to the air,
There, and more than once, your counsellor meets with his betters,
    All his forensic arts proving of little avail;

Others he might defend; himself he cannot; words fail him,
  Making objections in vain; Cupid says, *Overruled!*
Venus, whose temple is near, laughs at the mortified creature,
  Lawyer a moment ago, in need of a counselor now.
Also, the theater's curve is a very good place for your hunting,
  More opportunity here, maybe, than anywhere else.
Here you may find one to love, or possibly only have fun with,
  Someone to take for a night, someone to have and to hold.
Just as a column of ants keeps going and coming forever,
  Bearing their burdens of grain, just as the flight of the bees
Over the meadows and over the fields of the thyme and the clover,
  So do the women come, thronging the festival games,
Elegant, smart, and so many my sense of judgment is troubled.
  Hither they come, to see; hither they come, to be seen.
This is a place for the chase, not the chaste, and Romulus knew it,
  Started it all, in fact; think of the Sabine girls.
There were no awnings, then, over the benches of marble,
  There were no crimson flowers staining the platform's floor,
Only the natural shade from the Palatine trees, and the stage-set
  Quite unadorned, and the folk sitting on steps of sod,
Shading their foreheads with leaves, studying, watching intently,
  Each for the girl he would have, none of them saying a word.
Then, while the Tuscan flute was sounding its primitive measure,
  While the dancer's foot thrice beat the primitive ground,
While the people roared in uninhibited cheering,
  Romulus gave the sign. They had been waiting. They knew.
Up they leaped, and their noise was proof of their vigorous spirit.
  Never a virgin there was free from the lust of a hand.
Just as the timid doves fly from the swooping of eagles,
  Just as the newest lamb tries to escape from the wolf,
So those girls, fearing men, went rushing in every direction;
  Every complexion, through fright, turning a different hue.
Though their fear was the same, it took on different guises:
  Some of them tore their hair; some of them sat stricken dumb.
One is silent in grief, another calls for her mother,
  One shrieks out, one is still; one runs away, and one stays.
So, they are all carried off, these girls, the booty of husbands,
  While, in many, their fear added endowments of charm.
If one struggled too much, or refused to go with her captor,
  He'd pick her up from the ground, lift her aloft in his arms,

Saying, "Why do you spoil your beautiful eyes with that crying?
    Wasn't your mother a wife? That's all I want you to be."
Romulus, you knew the way to give rewards to your soldiers!
    Give me rewards such as these, I would enlist for the wars.
So, to this very day, the theater keeps its tradition:
    Danger is lurking there still, waiting for beautiful girls.

Furthermore, don't overlook the meetings when horses are running;
    In the crowds at the track opportunity waits.
There is no need for a code of finger-signals or nodding.
    Sit as close as you like; no one will stop you at all.
In fact, you will have to sit close — that's one of the rules, at a race
    track.
    Whether she likes it or not, contact is part of the game.
Try to find something in common, to open the conversation;
    Don't care too much what you say, just so that every one hears.
Ask her, "Whose colors are those?" — that's good for an opening
    gambit.
    Put your own bet down, fast, on whatever she plays.
Then, when the gods come along in procession, ivory, golden,
    Outcheer every young man, shouting for Venus, the queen.
Often it happens that dust may fall on the blouse of the lady.
    If such dust should fall, carefully brush it away.
Even if there's no dust, brush off whatever there isn't.
    Any excuse will do: why do you think you have hands?
If her cloak hangs low, and the ground is getting it dirty,
    Gather it up with care, lift it a little, so!
Maybe, by way of reward, and not without her indulgence,
    You'll be able to see ankle or possibly knee.
Then look around and glare at the fellow who's sitting behind you,
    Don't let him crowd his knees into her delicate spine.
Girls, as everyone knows, adore these little attentions:
    Getting the cushion just right, that's in itself quite an art;
Yes, and it takes a technique in making a fan of your program
    Or in fixing a stool under the feet of a girl.
Such is the chance of approach the race track can offer a lover.
    There is another good ground, the gladiatorial shows.
On that sorrowful sand Cupid has often contested,
    And the watcher of wounds often has had it himself.
While he is talking, or touching a hand, or studying entries,

Asking which one is ahead after his bet has been laid,
Wounded himself, he groans to feel the shaft of the arrow;
    He is a victim himself, no more spectator, but show.

e Juvenal, Satire 5

TREBIUS, if you persist in these ways, so utterly shameless
    That you think it is the highest good to live on another man's
table,
If you can stand for treatment the cheapest satellites never
Would have endured at the unjust board of an earlier Caesar,
Then I'd not trust your word under oath. I know, it takes little,
Little enough, to keep a belly content; if that's lacking,
Is there no place on the sidewalk, no room on one of the bridges,
No smaller half of a beggar's mat where you could be standing?
Is a free meal worth its cost in insult, your hunger
So demanding? By God, it would be more honest to shiver
No matter where you are, and gnaw on mouldy dog-biscuit.
First, get this into your head: an invitation to dinner
Means a payment in full for all of your previous service.
One meal is your share of the profit of this great friendship. Your
    master
Puts it on your account, a rare enough entry, sufficient,
Just the same, to balance his books. Perhaps two months later
It may please him again to invite his neglected client
Lest the lowest place at the lowest table be empty.
"Join us," he says. The height of good luck! What more could you
    ask for?
Trebius has good cause to break off his sleep, to come running,
Shoelaces not yet tied, worried that some one else,
Or every one else, may arrive before he does with his greetings,
While the stars fade out in the early hours of the morning,
While the planets wheel, sluggish and cold in the heavens.

What a dinner it is! Blotting paper would shudder
To sop up wine like this, which turns the guests into madmen.

From Juvenal, THE SATIRES, translated by Rolfe Humphries (Blooming-
ton, Ind., 1958), pp. 55–62. Reprinted by permission of Indiana University Press.

"You bastard!" "You son of a bitch!" These are preliminaries
To the main event, a battle royal, the freedmen
Versus the rest of you, with goblets and crockery flying.
You stop a jug with your face, pick up a napkin to wipe it,
Find your bloody nose has turned the damask to crimson,
While your host drinks wine drawn off when the consuls were
    bearded,
    Juice of grapes that were trod during wars a hundred years past.
Will he send one thimbleful to his cardiac friend? No. Never.
Tomorrow he'll drink again, a vintage from Setian or Alban
Mountains, the jar so black with soot and dust that he cannot
Tell where it came from, what year, such wine as Paetus and Priscus,
Chaplet-crowned haters of Tyrants, would drink on republican birth-
    days
Honoring Brutus and Cassius.
                                        Your noble patron, this Virro,
Holds cups encrusted with amber, saucers jagged with beryl,
Never letting them go; to you no gold is entrusted,
Or, if it ever is, a watcher leans over your shoulder
Keeping count of each jewel, watching your sharpened nails.
Pardon precautions like these, but his jasper is wonderful, truly.
Virro, and many like him, transfer from their rings to their goblets
Stones like these, the kind Aeneas wore on his scabbard.
You will drink from a cup that is cracked and fit for the junk pile,
Tradable, maybe, for sulphur, one of those four-nozzled vessels
Named after Nero's fool, the cobbler Beneventum.

If his stomach's inflamed from the food and wine, he is given
Water, sterilized first by boiling, then cooled in the snow.
You did not get the same wine, I complained; that's half the story,
The water is different, too. You are handed the cup by the fellow
Who runs in front of his car, a Gaetulian out of the stables,
Or by the bony hand of some black Moor, not a person
You'd enjoy meeting at night where the tombs line the roads of the
    city.
Standing in front of your host is the very flower of Asia,
Bought for a higher price than the whole estates of old kings,
Tullus, the fighter, and Ancus, were worth. In fact, you could throw
    in
All of the goods of all of the kings of the Rome of the legends.
This being so, if you thirst, look for your African server.
His expensive boy cannot mix a drink for a poor man,

But he's so lovely, so young! When do you think he will listen,
Whether it's hot or cold you request? Oh no, it's beneath him
To serve an old client; he's irked that you ask, or sit while he's
    standing.
Every great house is full of these supercilious slave boys.
Look at this one, who grumbles, handing you the hard bread
Made of the coarsest bran, or the mouldy jawbreaking crackers.
But our lord receives the tenderest, snowiest, finest
Proof of the kneader's art. Respect the breadbasket, please!
Keep hands off! If you reach — such nerve is hard to imagine —
Some one will cry, "Put it down! You shameless guest, can't you ever
Learn which kind is yours, and tell your bread by its color?"
Was it for this, you'll think, that you left your wife in the morning,
Ran up hill through the cold, with the hail rattling down in the
    springtime,
With your porous cloak distilling water in buckets?
In comes a lobster, immense, in fact, too large for the platter,
Waving its tail in contempt at the crowd, as it rides along, highborne,
To the table's head, with asparagus for a garnish.
What do you get? One prawn, half an egg — the kind of a supper
People leave at the tombs of the dead by way of a token.
He soaks his fish in the best olive oil; you get some pale coleslaw
Reeking of stuff that would smell very fine if used in a lantern,
Grease that has ridden the Nile in the meanest African lighters.
Used as a lotion, it gives you absolute privacy, bathing,
Guaranteed, furthermore, as a preventive of snake bite.
Virro will have a mullet, from Corsica or Taormina,
Since our seas are fished out, so desperate are our gluttons.
Too many nets are spread near home, and our Tuscan fishes
Never attain full size, so the provinces have to supply them.
That's where the market is found by the legacy-hunters, Laenas
Makes his purchases there, and Aurelia sells, at a profit.
Virro is given a lamprey, the greatest that Sicily ever
Sent to our coast; when the wind from the south is still in his prison,
Drying his wings, all craft despise the wrath of Charybdis.
You get an eel, so-called, but it looks much more like a blacksnake,
Or you may get a pike from the Tiber, mottled with ice-spots,
A riverbank denizen, fat from the rush of the sewers,
Tough enough to swim uptown as far as Subura.

A word in the ear of our host, if he'd be so kind as to listen:
"No one asks for such gifts as Seneca, Piso, or Cotta

Sent to their humble friends, when giving was reckoned an honor
Greater than titles or symbols of power. All we can ask for
Is that you dine with us on decent terms, just another
Citizen like ourselves. Do this — all right, all right, we can't stop you
Being rich for yourself and poor to your friends. They all do it."

What comes in now? Goose liver, tremendous, and also a capon
Big as a goose, and a boar, worthy of blond Meleager's
Steel, served piping hot, and truffles, assuming the season
Right for their growth, with enough spring thunder to swell their
        production.
What did that gourmet say? Alledius, I think his name was —
"Keep your wheat for yourself, O Libya; unyoke your oxen,
Just so you send us your truffles!"
                                Meanwhile, to make you more angry,
You will behold the carver, the sleight-of-hand master, performing,
Prancing around, and waving his knife like a wand. How important,
So his master says, to make the right gestures when carving
Rabbit or fowl! Shut your mouth, don't act like a freeborn Roman,
Don't think those three words of your name have any real meaning.
Do you want to be dragged from the house by the heels, like Cacus
        the monster
After the beating he took from Hercules? When will Virro
Pass the cup? He won't. And he won't risk any pollution
Touching his lips to the rim which a wretch like you has infected.
Which of you has the nerve, is so abandoned or silly
As to say to that prince "Drink up!" When your jacket is shabby
There are many remarks it is better to leave unspoken,
But should a god, or some chap who looked like a god, be more
        kindly
Than your fates ever were, and give you the cool twenty thousand
Suiting the rank of knight, how quickly you'd find yourself Some
        One,
Not a nobody now, but Virro's most intimate crony.
"Something for Trebius there! Give Trebius one more helping!
Brother, wouldn't you like a cut from the loin?" Money, money,
You are the one he calls brother, the one he gives homage and
        honor.
One word of caution, though: if you want to be patron and prince,
Let no little Aeneas go playing about in your hallways,
Let no small princess appear as father's small sweetheart.

Nothing will bring you more friends than a wife who is certified
  barren,
But, the way things are now, should your wife present you with
  triplets,
Virro'd be utterly charmed with your chattering brood, and to show
  it,
Order for each a little green shirt, and peanuts, and pennies,
When the small parasites come and hang around at his table.
Toadstools the poor will get, but Virro is feasted on mushrooms
Such as Claudius ate, before the one his wife gave him.
(Since then, he ate no more.) To himself and the rest of the Virros
Fruit will be served. Such fruit you'd be happy with even a smell of,
Fruit such as grew in the days when Autumn was never-ending,
Fruit you would think had been robbed from the girls of the Golden
  Orchards.
You get a rotten old apple, the kind that is given a monkey
All rigged out with a helmet and shield, and afraid of a whipping
While he is being trained to toss the spear from a goat's back.

Maybe you think that Virro is cheap. That's hardly the reason.
He does this to hurt, on purpose. What comedy ever,
What buffoon, is more fun than a gut that rumbles in protest?
So, in case you don't know, all this is done to compel you,
Force you, to tears of rage, and the grinding of squeaky molars.
You're a free man (you think) and the guest of a royal good fellow.
He knows, too damn well, you're the slave of the smell of his kitchen.
Oh, he's perfectly right. Only a slave would endure him
More than once. I don't care how poor you were in your childhood,
Whether you wore on your neck amulets golden or leather.
You are sucked in, now, by the hope of a dinner. "He'll give us,
Surely," you say, "at least the remains of a rabbit, the scraps
Off a wild-boar's haunch, or a picked-over carcass of capon."
So you sit there dumb, all of you, silent, expectant,
Bread in your hand untouched, ready to spring into action.
He's a wise man to treat you like this, for if you can stand it,
You can stand anything else, and, by God, I think that you ought to!
Some day you'll offer your shaved-off heads to be slapped, and a
  flogging
Won't seem fearful at all. You have done what you could to deserve
  them,
Trebius. Such a feast! And such a wonderful friendship!

9

The Neronian Terror

CORNELIUS TACITUS, Rome's greatest historian (ca. A.D. 50–120), was probably a native of Narbonese Gaul and, pursuing a typical senatorial career, attained a consulship in A.D. 97. He profited by the liberal regimes of the first good emperors to write outspoken history. His standards of factual accuracy were high but his primary interest was in recounting gloomy events at Rome and he did not do justice to the material benefits accruing to the provinces even under bad emperors. His pessimism and anti-imperial bias are understandable, since his own class suffered persecution under the first-century emperors. The following selection from the Annals, describing the celebrated Pisonian conspiracy of A.D. 65 against Nero, illustrates his interests. The event itself reveals a basic weakness of imperial rule: the necessity of a recourse to violence by responsible elements (in this case a motley group of praetorian guardsmen, equestrians, senators, and philosophers) to depose an unworthy emperor.

Tacitus, Annals, XV, 48-70

48] SILIUS NERVA and Atticus Vestinus then entered on the consulship, and now a conspiracy was planned, and at once became formidable, for which senators, knights, soldiers, even women, had given their names with eager rivalry, out of hatred of Nero as well as a liking for Caius Piso. A descendant of the Calpurnian house, and embracing in his connections through his father's noble rank many illustrious families, Piso had a splendid reputation with the people from his virtue or semblance of virtue. His eloquence he exercised in the defence of fellow-citizens, his generosity towards friends, while even for strangers he had a courteous address and demeanour. He had, too, the fortuitous advantages of tall stature and a handsome face. But solidity of character and moderation in pleasure were wholly alien to him. He indulged in laxity, in display,

From A. J. Church and W. J. Brodribb, trans., and Moses Hadas, ed., THE COMPLETE WORKS OF TACITUS (New York, 1942), pp. 382–396. Copyright © 1942 by Random House, Inc. Reprinted by permission of Random House, Inc.

and occasionally in excess. This suited the taste of that numerous class who, when the attractions of vice are so powerful, do not wish for strictness or special severity on the throne.

49] The origin of the conspiracy was not in Piso's personal ambition. But I could not easily narrate who first planned it, or whose prompting inspired a scheme into which so many entered. That the leading spirits were Subrius Flavus, tribune of a prætorian cohort, and Sulpicius Asper, a centurion, was proved by the fearlessness of their death. Lucanus Annæus,[1] too, and Plautius Lateranus, imported into it an intensely keen resentment. Lucanus had the stimulus of personal motives, for Nero tried to disparage the fame of his poems and, with the foolish vanity of a rival, had forbidden him to publish them. As for Lateranus, a consul-elect, it was no wrong, but love of the State which linked him with the others. Flavius Scævinus and Afranius Quintianus, on the other hand, both of senatorial rank, contrary to what was expected of them, undertook the beginning of this daring crime. Scævinus, indeed, had enfeebled his mind by excess, and his life, accordingly, was one of sleepy languor. Quintianus, infamous for his effeminate vice, had been satirised by Nero in a lampoon, and was bent on avenging the insult.

50] So, while they dropped hints among themselves or among their friends about the emperor's crimes, the approaching end of empire, and the importance of choosing some one to rescue the State in its distress, they associated with them Tullius Senecio, Cervarius Proculus, Vulcatius Araricus, Julius Augurinus, Munatius Gratus, Antonius Natalis, and Marcius Festus, all Roman knights. Of these Senecio, one of those who was specially intimate with Nero, still kept up a show of friendship, and had consequently to struggle with all the more dangers. Natalis shared with Piso all his secret plans. The rest built their hopes on revolution. Besides Subrius and Sulpicius, whom I have already mentioned, they invited the aid of military strength, of Gavius Silvanus and Statius Proximus, tribunes of prætorian cohorts, and of two centurions, Maximus Scaurus and Venetus Paulus. But their mainstay, it was thought, was Fænius Rufus, the commander of the guard, a man of esteemed life and character, to whom Tigellinus[2] with his brutality and shamelessness was superior in the emperor's regard. He harassed him with calumnies, and had often put him in terror by hinting that he had been Agrippina's paramour, and from sorrow at her loss was intent on vengeance. And so, when the conspirators were assured by his own repeated language that the commander of the prætorian guard had come over to their side, they once more eagerly discussed the time and place of the fatal deed. It was said that Subrius Flavus had formed a sudden resolution to attack Nero when singing on the stage, or when his house was in flames and he was running hither and thither, unattended, in the darkness. In the one case was the opportunity of solitude; in the other, the very crowd which would witness so glorious a deed, had roused a singularly noble soul; it was only the desire of escape, that foe to all great enterprises, which held him back.

51] Meanwhile, as they hesitated in prolonged suspense between hope and fear, a certain Epicharis (how she informed herself is uncertain, as she had never before had a thought of anything noble) began to stir and upbraid the conspirators. Wearied at last of their long delay, she endeavoured, when staying in Campania, to shake the loyalty of the officers of the fleet at Misenum, and to entangle them in a guilty complicity. She began thus. There was a captain in the fleet, Volusius Proculus, who had been one of Nero's instruments in his mother's murder, and had not, as he thought, been promoted in proportion to the greatness of his crime. Either, as an old acquaintance of the woman, or on the strength of a recent intimacy, he divulged to her his services to Nero and their barren result to himself, adding complaints, and his determination to have vengeance, should the chance arise. He thus inspired the hope that he could be persuaded, and could secure many others. No small help was to be found in the fleet, and there would be numerous opportunities, as Nero delighted in frequent enjoyment of the sea off Puteoli and Misenum.

Epicharis accordingly said more, and began the history of all the emperor's crimes. "The Senate," she affirmed, "had no power left it; yet means had been provided whereby he might pay the penalty of having destroyed the State. Only let Proculus gird himself to do his part and bring over to their side his bravest soldiers, and then look for an adequate recompense." The conspirators' names, however, she withheld. Consequently the information of Proculus was useless, even though he reported what he had heard to Nero. For Epicharis being summoned and confronted with the informer easily silenced him, unsupported as he was by a single witness. But she was herself detained in custody, for Nero suspected that even what was not proved to be true, was not wholly false.

52] The conspirators, however, alarmed by the fear of disclosure, resolved to hurry on the assassination at Baiæ, in Piso's villa, whither

the emperor, charmed by its loveliness, often went, and where, un-
guarded and without the cumbrous grandeur of his rank, he would
enjoy the bath and the banquet. But Piso refused, alleging the odium
of an act which would stain with an emperor's blood, however bad
he might be, the sanctity of the hospitable board and the deities who
preside over it. "Better," he said, "in the capital, in that hateful man-
sion which was piled up with the plunder of the citizens, or in public,
to accomplish what on the State's behalf they had undertaken."

So he said openly, with however a secret apprehension that Lucius
Silanus might, on the strength of his distinguished rank and the
teachings of Caius Cassius, under whom he had been trained, aspire
to any greatness and seize on empire, which would be promptly
offered him by all who had no part in the conspiracy, and who
would pity Nero as the victim of a crime. Many thought that Piso
shunned also the enterprising spirit of Vestinus, the consul, who
might, he feared, rise up in the cause of freedom, or, by choosing
another emperor, make the State his own gift. Vestinus, indeed, had
no share in the conspiracy, though Nero on that charge gratified an
old resentment against an innocent man.

53] At last they decided to carry out their design on that day of the
circus games, which is celebrated in honour of Ceres,[3] as the emperor,
who seldom went out, and shut himself up in his house or gardens,
used to go to the entertainments of the circus, and access to him was
the easier from his keen enjoyment of the spectacle. They had so
arranged the order of the plot, that Lateranus was to throw himself
at the prince's knees in earnest entreaty, apparently craving relief
for his private necessities, and, being a man of strong nerve and huge
frame, hurl him to the ground and hold him down. When he was
prostrate and powerless, the tribunes and centurions and all the
others who had sufficient daring were to rush up and do the murder,
the first blow being claimed by Scævinus, who had taken a dagger
from the Temple of Safety, or, according to another account, from
that of Fortune, in the town of Ferentum, and used to wear the
weapon as though dedicated to some noble deed. Piso, meanwhile,
was to wait in the sanctuary of Ceres, whence he was to be summoned by Fænius, the commander of the guard, and by the others,
and then conveyed into the camp, accompanied by Antonia, the
daughter of Claudius Cæsar, with a view to evoke the people's
enthusiasm. So it is related by Caius Pliny. Handed down from whatever source, I had no intention of suppressing it, however absurd it
may seem, either that Antonia should have lent her name at her life's

peril to a hopeless project, or that Piso, with his well-known affection for his wife, should have pledged himself to another marriage, but for the fact that the lust of dominion inflames the heart more than any other passion.

54] It was however wonderful how among people of different class, rank, age, sex, among rich and poor, everything was kept in secrecy till betrayal began from the house of Scævinus. The day before the treacherous attempt, after a long conversation with Antonius Natalis, Scævinus returned home, sealed his will, and, drawing from its sheath the dagger of which I have already spoken, and complaining that it was blunted from long disuse, he ordered it to be sharpened on a stone to a keen and bright point. This task he assigned to his freedman Milichus. At the same time he sat down to a more than usually sumptuous banquet, and gave his favourite slaves their freedom, and money to others. He was himself depressed, and evidently in profound thought, though he affected gaiety in desultory conversation. Last of all, he directed ligatures for wounds and the means of stanching blood to be prepared by the same Milichus, who either knew of the conspiracy and was faithful up to this point, or was in complete ignorance and then first caught suspicions, as most authors have inferred from what followed. For when his servile imagination dwelt on the rewards of perfidy, and he saw before him at the same moment boundless wealth and power, conscience and care for his patron's life, together with the remembrance of the freedom he had received, fled from him. From his wife, too, he had adopted a womanly and yet baser suggestion; for she even held over him a dreadful thought, that many had been present, both freedmen and slaves, who had seen what he had; that one man's silence would be useless, whereas the rewards would be for him alone who was first with the information.

55] Accordingly at daybreak Milichus went to the Servilian gardens, and, finding the doors shut against him, said again and again that he was the bearer of important and alarming news. Upon this he was conducted by the gate-keepers to one of Nero's freedmen, Epaphroditus, and by him to Nero, whom he informed of the urgent danger, of the formidable conspiracy, and of all else which he had heard or inferred. He showed him too the weapon prepared for his destruction, and bade him summon the accused.

Scævinus on being arrested by the soldiers began his defence with the reply that the dagger about which he was accused, had of old been regarded with a religious sentiment by his ancestors, that it

had been kept in his chamber, and been stolen by a trick of his
freedman. He had often, he said, signed his will without heeding
the observance of particular days, and had previously given presents
of money as well as freedom to some of his slaves, only on this
occasion he gave more freely, because, as his means were now
impoverished and his creditors were pressing him, he distrusted the
validity of his will. Certainly his table had always been profusely
furnished, and his life luxurious, such as rigid censors would hardly
approve. As to the bandages for wounds, none had been prepared at
his order, but as all the man's other charges were absurd, he added
an accusation in which he might make himself alike informer and
witness.

He backed up his words by an air of resolution. Turning on his
accuser, he denounced him as an infamous and depraved wretch,
with so fearless a voice and look that the information was beginning
to collapse, when Milichus was reminded by his wife that Antonious
Natalis had had a long secret conversation with Scævinus, and that
both were Piso's intimate friends.

56] Natalis was therefore summoned, and they were separately
asked what the conversation was, and what was its subject. Then a
suspicion arose because their answers did not agree, and they were
both put in irons. They could not endure the sight and the threat of
torture. Natalis however, taking the initiative, knowing as he did
more of the whole conspiracy, and being also more practised in
accusing, first confessed about Piso, next added the name of Annæus
Seneca,[4] either as having been a messenger between him and Piso, or
to win the favour of Nero, who hated Seneca and sought by every
means for his ruin. Then Scævinus too, when he knew the disclosure
of Natalis, with like pusillanimity, or under the impression that
everything was now divulged, and that there could be no advantage
in silence, revealed the other conspirators. Of these, Lucanus, Quintianus, and Senecio long persisted in denial; after a time, when
bribed by the promise of impunity, anxious to excuse their reluctance,
Lucanus named his mother Atilla, Quintianus and Senecio, their chief
friends, respectively, Glitius Gallus and Annius Pollio.

57] Nero, meanwhile, remembering that Epicharis was in custody
on the information of Volusius Proculus, and assuming that a
woman's frame must be unequal to the agony, ordered her to be torn
on the rack. But neither the scourge nor fire, nor the fury of the
men as they increased the torture that they might not be a woman's
scorn, overcame her positive denial of the charge. Thus the first day's

inquiry was futile. On the morrow, as she was being dragged back on a chair to the same torments (for with her limbs all dislocated she could not stand), she tied a band, which she had stript off her bosom, in a sort of noose to the arched back of the chair, put her neck in it, and then straining with the whole weight of her body, wrung out of her frame its little remaining breath. All the nobler was the example set by a freedwoman at such a crisis in screening strangers and those whom she hardly knew, when freeborn men, Roman knights, and senators, yet unscathed by torture, betrayed, every one, his dearest kinsfolk. For even Lucanus and Senecio and Quintianus failed not to reveal their accomplices indiscriminately, and Nero was more and more alarmed, though he had fenced his person with a largely augmented guard.

58] Even Rome itself he put, so to say, under custody, garrisoning its walls with companies of soldiers and occupying with troops the coast and the river-banks. Incessantly were there flying through the public places, through private houses, country fields, and the neighbouring villages, horse and foot soldiers, mixed with Germans, whom the emperor trusted as being foreigners. In long succession, troops of prisoners in chains were dragged along and stood at the gates of his gardens. When they entered to plead their cause, a smile of joy on any of the conspirators, a casual conversation, a sudden meeting, or the fact of having entered a banquet or a public show in company, was construed into a crime, while to the savage questionings of Nero and Tigellinus were added the violent menaces of Fænius Rufus, who had not yet been named by the informers, but who, to get the credit of complete ignorance, frowned fiercely on his accomplices. When Subius Flavus at his side asked him by a sign whether he should draw his sword in the middle of the trial and perpetrate the fatal deed, Rufus refused, and checked the man's impulse as he was putting his hand to his sword-hilt.

59] Some there were who, as soon as the conspiracy was betrayed, urged Piso, while Milichus' story was being heard, and Scævinus was hesitating, to go to the camp or mount the Rostra and test the feelings of the soldiers and of the people. "If," said they, "your accomplices join your enterprise, those also who are yet undecided, will follow, and great will be the fame of the movement once started, and this in any new scheme is all-powerful. Against it Nero has taken no precaution. Even brave men are dismayed by sudden perils; far less will that stage-player, with Tigellinus forsooth and his concubines in his train, raise arms against you. Many things are accomplished on trial which cowards think arduous. It is vain to expect secrecy and fidelity from the varying tempers and bodily constitutions of such a host of accomplices. Torture or reward can overcome everything. Men will soon come to put you also in chains and inflict on you an ignominious death. How much more gloriously will you die while you cling to the State and invoke aid for liberty. Rather let the soldiers fail, the people be traitors, provided that you, if prematurely robbed of life, justify your death to your ancestors and descendants."

Unmoved by these considerations, Piso showed himself a few moments in public, then sought the retirement of his house, and there fortified his spirit against the worst, till a troop of soldiers arrived, raw recruits, or men recently enlisted, whom Nero had selected, because he was afraid of the veterans, imbued, though they were, with a liking for him. Piso expired by having the veins in his arms severed. His will, full of loathsome flatteries of Nero, was a concession to his love of his wife, a base woman, with only a beautiful person to recommend her, whom he had taken away from her husband, one of his friends. Her name was Atria Galla; that of her former husband, Domitius Silus. The tame spirit of the man, the profligacy of the woman, blazoned Piso's infamy.

60] In quick succession Nero added the murder of Plautius Lateranus, consul-elect, so promptly that he did not allow him to embrace his children or to have the brief choice of his own death. He was dragged off to a place set apart for the execution of slaves, and butchered by the hand of the tribune Statius, maintaining a resolute silence, and not reproaching the tribune with complicity in the plot.

Then followed the destruction of Annæus Seneca, a special joy to the emperor, not because he had convicted him of the conspiracy, but anxious to accomplish with the sword what poison had failed to do. It was, in fact, Natalis alone who divulged Seneca's name, to this extent, that he had been sent to Seneca when ailing, to see him and remonstrate with him for excluding Piso from his presence, when it would have been better to have kept up their friendship by familiar intercourse; that Seneca's reply was that mutual conversations and frequent interviews were to the advantage of neither, but still that his own life depended on Piso's safety. Gavius Silvanus, tribune of a prætorian cohort, was ordered to report this to Seneca and to ask him whether he acknowledged what Natalis said and his own answer. Either by chance or purposely Seneca had returned on that day from

Campania, and had stopped at a country-house four miles from Rome. Thither the tribune came next evening, surrounded the house with troops of soldiers, and then made known the emperor's message to Seneca as he was at dinner with his wife, Pompeia Paulina, and two friends.

61] Seneca replied that Natalis had been sent to him and had complained to him in Piso's name because of his refusal to see Piso, upon which he excused himself on the ground of failing health and the desire of rest. "He had no reason," he said, for "preferring the interest of any private citizen to his own safety, and he had no natural aptitude for flattery. No one knew this better than Nero, who had oftener experienced Seneca's freespokenness than his servility." When the tribune reported this answer in the presence of Poppæa[5] and Tigellinus, the emperor's most confidential advisers in his moments of rage, he asked whether Seneca was meditating suicide. Upon this the tribune asserted that he saw no signs of fear, and perceived no sadness in his words or in his looks. He was accordingly ordered to go back and to announce sentence of death. Fabius Rusticus tells us that he did not return the way he came, but went out of his course to Fænius, the commander of the guard, and having explained to him the emperor's orders, and asked whether he was to obey them, was by him admonished to carry them out, for a fatal spell of cowardice was on them all. For this very Silvanus was one of the conspirators, and he was now abetting the crimes which he had united with them to avenge. But he spared himself the anguish of a word or of a look, and merely sent in to Seneca one of his centurions, who was to announce to him his last doom.

62] Seneca, quite unmoved, asked for tablets on which to inscribe his will, and, on the centurion's refusal, turned to his friends, protesting that as he was forbidden to requite them, he bequeathed to them the only, but still the noblest possession yet remaining to him, the pattern of his life, which, if they remembered, they would win a name for moral worth and steadfast friendship. At the same time he called them back from their tears to manly resolution, now with friendly talk, and now with the sterner language of rebuke. "Where," he asked again and again, "are your maxims of philosophy, or the preparation of so many years' study against evils to come? Who knew not Nero's cruelty? After a mother's and a brother's murder, nothing remains but to add the destruction of a guardian and a tutor."

63] Having spoken these and like words, meant, so to say, for all, he embraced his wife; then softening awhile from the stern resolution of the hour, he begged and implored her to spare herself the burden of perpetual sorrow, and, in the contemplation of a life virtuously spent, to endure a husband's loss with honourable consolations. She declared, in answer, that she too had decided to die, and claimed for herself the blow of the executioner. Thereupon Seneca, not to thwart her noble ambition, from an affection too which would not leave behind him for insult one whom he dearly loved, replied: "I have shown you ways of smoothing life; you prefer the glory of dying. I will not grudge you such a noble example. Let the fortitude of so courageous an end be alike in both of us, but let there be more in your decease to win fame."

Then by one and the same stroke they sundered with a dagger the arteries of their arms. Seneca, as his aged frame, attenuated by frugal diet, allowed the blood to escape but slowly, severed also the veins of his legs and knees. Worn out by cruel anguish, afraid too that his sufferings might break his wife's spirit, and that, as he looked on her tortures, he might himself sink into irresolution, he persuaded her to retire into another chamber. Even at the last moment his eloquence failed him not; he summoned his secretaries, and dictated much to them which, as it has been published for all readers in his own words, I forbear to paraphrase.

64] Nero meanwhile, having no personal hatred against Paulina and not wishing to heighten the odium of his cruelty, forbade her death. At the soldiers' prompting, her slaves and freedmen bound up her arms, and stanched the bleeding, whether with her knowledge is doubtful. For as the vulgar are ever ready to think the worst, there were persons who believed that, as long as she dreaded Nero's relentlessness, she sought the glory of sharing her husband's death, but that after a time, when a more soothing prospect presented itself, she yielded to the charms of life. To this she added a few subsequent years, with a most praiseworthy remembrance of her husband, and with a countenance and frame white to a degree of pallor which denoted a loss of much vital energy.

Seneca meantime, as the tedious process of death still lingered on, begged Statius Annæus, whom he had long esteemed for his faithful friendship and medical skill, to produce a poison with which he had some time before provided himself, the same drug which extinguished the life of those who were condemned by a public sentence of the people of Athens. It was brought to him and he drank it in vain, chilled as he was throughout his limbs, and his frame closed against the efficacy of the poison. At last he entered a pool of heated water, from which he sprinkled the nearest of his slaves, adding the exclamation, "I offer this liquid as a libation to Jupiter the Deliverer." He was then carried into a bath, with the steam of which he was suffocated, and he was burnt without any of the usual funeral rites. So he had directed in a codicil of his will, when even in the height of his wealth and power he was thinking of his life's close.

65] There was a rumour that Sabrius Flavus had held a secret consultation with the centurions, and had planned, not without Seneca's knowledge, that when Nero had been slain by Piso's instrumentality, Piso also was to be murdered, and the empire handed over to Seneca, as a man singled out for his splendid virtues by all persons of integrity. Even a saying of Flavus was popularly current, "that it mattered not as to the disgrace if a harp-player were removed and a tragic actor succeeded him." For as Nero used to sing to the harp, so did Piso in the dress of a tragedian.

66] The soldiers' part too in the conspiracy no longer escaped discovery, some in their rage becoming informers to betray Fænius Rufus, whom they could not endure to be both an accomplice and a judge. Accordingly Scævinus, in answer to his browbeating and menaces, said with a smile that no one knew more than he did, and actually urged him to show gratitude to so good a prince. Fænius could not meet this with either speech or silence. Halting in his words and visibly terror-stricken, while the rest, especially Cervarius Proculus, a Roman knight, did their utmost to convict him, he was, at the emperor's bidding, seized and bound by Cassius, a soldier, who because of his well-known strength of limb was in attendance.

67] Shortly afterwards, the information of the same men proved fatal to Subrius Flavus. At first he grounded his defence on his moral contrast to the others, implying that an armed soldier, like himself, would never have shared such an attempt with unarmed and effeminate associates. Then, when he was pressed, he embraced the glory of a full confession. Questioned by Nero as to the motives which had led him on to forget his oath of allegiance, "I hated you," he replied; "yet not a soldier was more loyal to you while you deserved to be loved. I began to hate you when you became the murderer of your mother and your wife, a charioteer, an actor, and an incendiary." I have given the man's very words, because they were not, like those of Seneca, generally published, though the rough and vigorous sentiments of a soldier ought to be no less known.

Throughout the conspiracy nothing, it was certain, fell with more terror on the ears of Nero, who was as unused to be told of the crimes he perpetrated as he was eager in their perpetration. The punishment of Flavus was intrusted to Veianius Niger, a tribune. At his direction, a pit was dug in a neighbouring field. Flavus, on seeing it, censured it as too shallow and confined, saying to the soldiers around him, "Even this is not according to military rule." When bidden to offer his neck resolutely, "I wish," said he, "that your stroke may be as resolute." The tribune trembled greatly, and having only just severed his head at two blows, vaunted his brutality to Nero, saying that he had slain him with a blow and a half.

68] Sulpicius Asper, a centurion, exhibited the next example of fortitude. To Nero's question why he had conspired to murder him, he briefly replied that he could not have rendered a better service to his infamous career. He then underwent the prescribed penalty. Nor did the remaining centurions forget their courage in suffering their punishment. But Fænius Rufus had not equal spirit; he even put his laments into his will.

Nero waited in the hope that Vestinus also, the consul, whom he thought an impetuous and deeply disaffected man, would be involved in the charge. None however of the conspirators had shared their counsels with him, some from old feuds against him, most because they considered him a reckless and dangerous associate. Nero's hatred of him had had its origin in intimate companionship, Vestinus seeing through and despising the emperor's cowardice, while Nero feared the high spirit of his friend, who often bantered him with that rough humour which, when it draws largely on facts, leaves a bitter memory behind it. There was too a recent aggravation in the circumstance of Vestinus having married Statilia Messalina, without being ignorant that the emperor was one of her paramours.

69] As neither crime nor accuser appeared, Nero, being thus unable to assume the semblance of a judge, had recourse to the sheer might of despotism, and despatched Gerellanus, a tribune, with a cohort of soldiers, and with orders to forestall the designs of the consul, to seize what he might call his fortress, and crush his train of chosen youths. For Vestinus had a house towering over the Forum, and a host of handsome slaves of the same age. On that day he had performed all his duties as consul, and was entertaining some guests, fearless of danger, or perhaps by way of hiding his fears, when the soldiers entered and announced to him the tribune's summons. He rose without a moment's delay, and every preparation was at once made. He shut himself into his chamber; a physician was at his side; his veins were opened; with life still strong in him, he was carried into a bath, and plunged into warm water, without uttering a word of pity for himself. Meanwhile the guards surrounded those who had sat at his table, and it was only at a late hour of the night that they were dismissed, when Nero, having pictured to himself and laughed over their terror at the expectation of a fatal end to their banquet, said that they had suffered enough punishment for the consul's entertainment.

70] Next he ordered the destruction of Marcus Annæus Lucanus. As the blood flowed freely from him, and he felt a chill creeping through his feet and hands, and the life gradually ebbing from his extremities, though the heart was still warm and he retained his mental power, Lucanus recalled some poetry he had composed in which he had told the story of a wounded soldier dying a similar kind of death, and he recited the very lines. These were his last words. After him, Senecio, Quintianus, and Scævinus perished, not in the manner expected from the past effeminacy of their life, and then the remaining conspirators, without deed or word deserving record.

NOTES

1. The poet Lucan, Seneca's nephew, a Stoic of republican inclinations.
2. The other praetorian prefect.
3. April, 65.
4. The famous Stoic philosopher, formerly regent in Nero's youth.
5. Poppaea Sabina, the emperor's wife.

10

Roman Education

THE SPANIARD Quintilian (ca. A.D. 35–95) was the leading rhetorician of the first century A.D. and numbered among his students the sons of Rome's elite. His Institutes of Oratory is the most complete treatise on the education to which many children of the upper classes were exposed. The first school of rhetoric opened in 94 B.C., but such formal training did not become popular until the imperial period, when it rivaled the traditional curriculum based on philosophy. Quintilian alludes to this competition when he states that the true orator is by definition a philosopher. Although he was not unaware of the importance of liberal arts other than literature, he insisted that all training had forensic eloquence as its aim. Quintilian himself would have been appalled at the baleful effects that rhetoric later had on Roman letters, since he demanded that the orator have something worthwhile to say.

Quintilian, Institutes of Oratory, Book I, "Preface," 1-4, 8, 10

PREFACE] MY AIM, then is the education of the perfect orator. The first essential for such an one is that he should be a good man, and consequently we demand of him not merely the possession of exceptional gifts of speech, but of all the excellencies of character as well. For I will not admit that the principles of upright and honourable living should, as some have held, be regarded as the peculiar concern of philosophy. The man who can really play his part as a citizen and is capable of meeting the demands both of public and private business, the man who can guide a state by his counsels, give it a firm basis by his legislation and purge its vices by his decisions as a judge, is assuredly no other than the orator of our quest. Wherefore, although I admit I shall make use of certain of the principles laid down in philosophical textbooks, I would insist that such

From H. E. Butler, trans., THE INSTITUTIO ORATORIA OF QUINTILIAN (Cambridge, Mass., 1920), vol. i, pp. 9–15, 25–27, 39–43, 47–53, 57–65, 147–153, 161–163. Reprinted by permission of Harvard University Press and The Loeb Classical Library.

principles have a just claim to form part of the subject-matter of this work and do actually belong to the art of oratory. I shall frequently be compelled to speak of such virtues as courage, justice, self-control; in fact scarcely a case comes up in which some one of these virtues is not involved; every one of them requires illustration and consequently makes a demand on the imagination and eloquence of the pleader. I ask you then, can there be any doubt that, wherever imaginative power and amplitude of diction are required, the orator has a specially important part to play? These two branches of knowledge were, as Cicero has clearly shown, so closely united, not merely in theory but in practice, that the same men were regarded as uniting the qualifications of orator and philosopher. Subsequently this single branch of study split up into its component parts, and thanks to the indolence of its professors was regarded as consisting of several distinct subjects. As soon as speaking became a means of livelihood and the practice of making an evil use of the blessings of eloquence came into vogue, those who had a reputation for eloquence ceased to study moral philosophy, and ethics, thus abandoned by the orators, became the prey of weaker intellects. As a consequence certain persons, disdaining the toil of learning to speak well, returned to the task of forming character and establishing rules of life and kept to themselves what is, if we *must* make a division, the better part of philosophy, but presumptuously laid claim to the sole possession of the title of philosopher, a distinction which neither the greatest generals nor the most famous statesmen and administrators have ever dared to claim for themselves. For they preferred the performance to the promise of great deeds. I am ready to admit that many of the old philosophers inculcated the most excellent principles and practised what they preached. But in our own day the name of philosopher has too often been the mask for the worst vices. For their attempt has not been to win the name of philosopher by virtue and the earnest search for wisdom; instead they have sought to disguise the depravity of their characters by the assumption of a stern and austere mien accompanied by the wearing of a garb differing from that of their fellow men. Now as a matter of fact we all of us frequently handle those themes which philosophy claims for its own. Who, short of being an utter villain, does not speak of justice, equity and virtue? Who (and even common country-folk are no exception) does not make some inquiry into the causes of natural phenomena? As for the special uses and distinctions of words, they should be a subject of study common to all

who give any thought to the meaning of language. But it is surely
the orator who will have the greatest mastery of all such depart-
ments of knowledge and the greatest power to express it in words.
And if ever he had reached perfection, there would be no need to
go to the schools of philosophy for the precepts of virtue. As things
stand, it is occasionally necessary to have recourse to those authors
who have, as I said above, usurped the better part of the art of
oratory after its desertion by the orators and to demand back what
is ours by right, not with a view to appropriating their discoveries,
but to show them that they have appropriated what in truth belonged
to others. Let our ideal orator then be such as to have a genuine title
to the name of philosopher: it is not sufficient that he should be
blameless in point of character (for I cannot agree with those who
hold this opinion): he must also be a thorough master of the science
and the art of speaking, to an extent that perhaps no orator has yet
attained. Still we must none the less follow the ideal, as was done
by not a few of the ancients, who, though they refused to admit that
the perfect sage had yet been found, none the less handed down
precepts of wisdom for the use of posterity. Perfect eloquence is
assuredly a reality, which is not beyond the reach of human intellect.
Even if we fail to reach it, those whose aspirations are highest, will
attain to greater heights than those who abandon themselves to
premature despair of ever reaching the goal and halt at the very
foot of the ascent. . . .

1] . . . I prefer that a boy should begin with Greek, because Latin,
being in general use, will be picked up by him whether we will or
no; while the fact that Latin learning is derived from Greek is a
further reason for his being first instructed in the latter. I do not
however desire that this principle should be so superstitiously observed that he should for long speak and learn only Greek, as is
done in the majority of cases. Such a course gives rise to many faults
of language and accent; the latter tends to acquire a foreign intona-
tion, while the former through force of habit becomes impregnated
with Greek idioms, which persist with extreme obstinacy even when
we are speaking another tongue. The study of Latin ought therefore
to follow at no great distance and in a short time proceed side by
side with Greek. The result will be that, as soon as we begin to give
equal attention to both languages, neither will prove a hindrance to
the other. . . .

2] But the time has come for the boy to grow up little by little, to
leave the nursery and tackle his studies in good earnest. This there-

fore is the place to discuss the question as to whether it is better to have him educated privately at home or hand him over to some large school and those whom I may call public instructors. The latter course has, I know, won the approval of most eminent authorities and of those who have formed the national character of the most famous states. It would, however, be folly to shut our eyes to the fact that there are some who disagree with this preference for public education owing to a certain prejudice in favour of private tuition. These persons seem to be guided in the main by two principles. In the interests of morality they would avoid the society of a number of human beings at an age that is specially liable to acquire serious faults: I only wish I could deny the truth of the view that such education has often been the cause of the most discreditable actions. Secondly they hold that whoever is to be the boy's teacher, he will devote his time more generously to one pupil than if he has to divide it among several. The first reason certainly deserves serious consideration. If it were proved that schools, while advantageous to study, are prejudicial to morality, I should give my vote for virtuous living in preference to even supreme excellence of speaking. But in my opinion the two are inseparable. I hold that no one can be a true orator unless he is also a good man and, even if he could be, I would not have it so. I will therefore deal with this point first.

It is held that schools corrupt the morals. It is true that this is sometimes the case. But morals may be corrupted at home as well. There are numerous instances of both, as there are also of the preservation of a good reputation under either circumstance. The nature of the individual boy and the care devoted to his education make all the difference. Given a natural bent toward evil or negligence in developing and watching over modest behaviour in early years, privacy will provide equal opportunity for sin. The teacher employed at home may be of bad character, and there is just as much danger in associating with bad slaves as there is with immodest companions of good birth. On the other hand if the natural bent be towards virtue, and parents are not afflicted with a blind and torpid indifference, it is possible to choose a teacher of the highest character (and those who are wise will make this their first object), to adopt a method of education of the strictest kind and at the same time to attach some respectable man or faithful freedman to their son as his friend and guardian, that his unfailing companionship may improve the character even of those who gave rise to apprehension.

Yet how easy were the remedy for such fears. Would that we did not too often ruin our children's character ourselves! We spoil them from the cradle. That soft upbringing, which we call kindness, saps all the sinews both of mind and body. If the child crawls on purple, what will he not desire when he comes to manhood? Before he can talk he can distinguish scarlet and cries for the very best brand of purple. We train their palates before we teach their lips to speak. They grow up in litters: if they set foot to earth, they are supported by the hands of attendants on either side. We rejoice if they say something over-free, and words which we should not tolerate from the lips even of an Alexandrian page are greeted with laughter and a kiss. We have no right to be surprised. It was we that taught them: they hear us use such words, they see our mistresses and minions; every dinner party is loud with foul songs, and things are presented to their eyes of which we should blush to speak. Hence springs habit, and habit in time becomes second nature. The poor children learn these things before they know them to be wrong. They become luxurious and effeminate, and far from acquiring such vices at schools, introduce them themselves. . . .

. . . Still I do not wish a boy to be sent where he will be neglected. But a good teacher will not burden himself with a larger number of pupils than he can manage, and it is further of the very first importance that he should be on friendly and intimate terms with us and make his teaching not a duty but a labour of love. Then there will never be any question of being swamped by the number of our fellow-learners. Moreover any teacher who has the least tincture of literary culture will devote special attention to any boy who shows signs of industry and talent; for such a pupil will redound to his own credit. But even if large schools are to be avoided, a proposition from which I must dissent if the size be due to the excellence of the teacher, it does not follow that all schools are to be avoided. It is one thing to avoid them, another to select the best.

Having refuted these objections, let me now explain my own views. It is above all things necessary that our future orator, who will have to live in the utmost publicity and in the broad daylight of public life, should become accustomed from his childhood to move in society without fear and habituated to a life far removed from that of the pale student, the solitary and recluse. His mind requires constant stimulus and excitement, whereas retirement such as has just been mentioned induces languor and the mind becomes mildewed like things that are left in the dark, or else flies to the opposite extreme and becomes puffed up with empty conceit; for he who has no standard of comparison by which to judge his own powers will necessarily rate them too high. Again when the fruits of his study have to be displayed to the public gaze, our recluse is blinded by the sun's glare, and finds everything new and unfamiliar, for though he has learnt what is required to be done in public, his learning is but the theory of a hermit. I say nothing of friendships which endure unbroken to old age having acquired the binding force of a sacred duty: for initiation in the same studies has all the sanctity of initiation in the same mysteries of religion. And where shall he acquire that instinct which we call common feeling, if he secludes himself from that intercourse which is natural not merely to mankind but even to dumb animals? Further, at home he can only learn what is taught to himself, while at school he will learn what is taught others as well. He will hear many merits praised and many faults corrected every day: he will derive equal profit from hearing the indolence of a comrade rebuked or his industry commended. Such praise will incite him to emulation, he will think it a disgrace to be outdone by his contemporaries and a distinction to surpass his seniors. All such incentives provide a valuable stimulus, and though ambition may be a fault in itself, it is often the mother of virtues. I remember that my own masters had a practice which was not without advantages. Having distributed the boys in classes, they made the order in which they were to speak depend on their ability, so that boy who had made most progress in his studies had the privilege of declaiming first. The performances on these occasions were criticised. To win commendation was a tremendous honour, but the prize most eagerly coveted was to be the leader of the class. Such a position was not permanent. Once a month the defeated competitors were given a fresh opportunity of competing for the prize. Consequently success did not lead the victor to relax his efforts, while the vexation caused by defeat served as an incentive to wipe out the disgrace. I will venture to assert that to the best of my memory this practice did more to kindle our oratorical ambitions than all the exhortations of our instructors, the watchfulness of our *paedagogi* and the prayers of our parents. Further while emulation promotes progress in the more advanced pupils, beginners who are still of tender years derive greater pleasure from imitating their comrades than their masters, just because it is easier. For children still in the elementary stages of education can scarce dare hope to reach that complete eloquence which they understand to be their goal: their ambition will not soar so high, but they will imitate the vine which has to grasp the lower branches of the tree on which

it is trained before it can reach the topmost boughs. So true is this
that it is the master's duty as well, if he is engaged on the task of
training unformed minds and prefers practical utility to a more
ambitious programme, not to burden his pupils at once with tasks
to which their strength is unequal, but to curb his energies and
refrain from talking over the heads of his audience. Vessels with
narrow mouths will not receive liquids if too much be poured into
them at a time, but are easily filled if the liquid is admitted in a
gentle stream or, it may be, drop by drop; similarly you must consider how much a child's mind is capable of receiving: the things
which are beyond their grasp will not enter their minds, which have
not opened out sufficiently to take them in. It is a good thing therefore that a boy should have companions whom he will desire first
to imitate and then to surpass: thus he will be led to aspire to higher
achievement. I would add that the instructors themselves cannot
develop the same intelligence and energy before a single listener as
they can when inspired by the presence of a numerous audience. . . .
3] . . . Still, all our pupils will require some relaxation, not merely
because there is nothing in this world that can stand continued
strain and even unthinking and inanimate objects are unable to
maintain their strength, unless given intervals of rest, but because
study depends on the good will of the student, a quality that cannot be secured by compulsion. Consequently if restored and refreshed
by a holiday they will bring greater energy to their learning and
approach their work with greater spirit of a kind that will not submit
to be driven. I approve of play in the young; it is a sign of a lively
disposition; nor will you ever lead me to believe that a boy who is
gloomy and in a continual state of depression is ever likely to show
alertness of mind in his work, lacking as he does the impulse most
natural to boys of his age. Such relaxation must not however be
unlimited: otherwise the refusal to give a holiday will make boys
hate their work, while excessive indulgence will accustom them to
idleness. There are moreover certain games which have an educational value for boys, as for instance when they compete in posing
each other with all kinds of questions which they ask turn and turn
about. Games too reveal character in the most natural way, at least
that is so if the teacher will bear in mind that there is no child so
young as to be unable to learn to distinguish between right and
wrong, and that the character is best moulded, when it is still guilt-
less of deceit and most susceptible to instruction: for once a bad
habit has become engrained, it is easier to break than bend. There
must be no delay, then, in warning a boy that his actions must be

unselfish, honest, self-controlled, and we must never forget the words of Virgil,

"So strong is custom formed in early years."

I disapprove of flogging, although it is the regular custom and meets with the acquiescence of Chrysippus, because in the first place it is a disgraceful form of punishment and fit only for slaves, and is in any case an insult, as you will realise if you imagine its infliction at a later age. Secondly if a boy is so insensible to instruction that reproof is useless, he will, like the worst type of slave, merely become hardened to blows. Finally there will be absolutely no need of such punishment if the master is a thorough disciplinarian. As it is, we try to make amends for the negligence of the boy's *paedagogus*, not by forcing him to do what is right, but by punishing him for not doing what is right. And though you may compel a child with blows, what are you to do with him when he is a young man no longer amenable to such threats and confronted with tasks of far greater difficulty? Moreover when children are beaten, pain or fear frequently have results of which it is not pleasant to speak and which are likely subsequently to be a source of shame, a shame which unnerves and depresses the mind and leads the child to shun and loathe the light. Further if inadequate care is taken in the choices of respectable governors and instructors, I blush to mention the shameful abuse which scoundrels sometimes make of their right to administer corporal punishment or the opportunity not infrequently offered to others by the fear thus caused in the victims. I will not linger on this subject; it is more than enough if I have made my meaning clear. I will content myself with saying that children are helpless and easily victimised, and that therefore no one should be given unlimited power over them. I will now proceed to describe the subjects in which the boy must be trained, if he is to become an orator, and to indicate the age at which each should be commenced. 4] As soon as the boy has learned to read and write without difficulty, it is the turn for the teacher of literature. My words apply equally to Greek and Latin masters, though I prefer that a start should be made with a Greek: in either case the method is the same. This profession may be most briefly considered under two heads, the art of speaking correctly and the interpretation of the poets; but there is more beneath the surface than meets the eye. For the art of writing is combined with that of speaking, and correct reading precedes interpretation, while in each of these cases criticism has its work to perform. The old school of teachers indeed carried their criticism so far that they were not content with obelising lines or rejecting books whose titles they regarded as spurious, as though they were expelling a supposititious child from the family circle, but also drew up a canon of authors, from which some were omitted altogether. Nor is it sufficient to have read the poets only; every kind of writer must be carefully studied, not merely for the subject matter, but for the vocabulary; for words often acquire authority from their use by a particular author. Nor can such training be regarded as complete if it stop short of music, for the teacher of literature has to speak of metre and rhythm: nor again if he be ignorant of astronomy, can he understand the poets; for they, to mention no further points, frequently give their indications of time by reference to the rising and setting of the stars. Ignorance of philosophy is an equal drawback, since there are numerous passages in almost every poem based on the most intricate questions of natural philosophy, while among the Greeks we have Empedocles and among our own poets Varro and Lucretius, all of whom have expounded their philosophies in verse. No small powers of eloquence also are required to enable the teacher to speak appropriately and fluently on the various points which have just been mentioned. For this reason those who criticise the art of teaching literature as trivial and lacking in substance put themselves out of court. Unless the foundations of oratory are well and truly laid by the teaching of literature, the superstructure will collapse. The study of literature is a necessity for boys and the delight of old age, the sweet companion of our privacy and the sole branch of study which has more solid substance than display. . . .

*   *   *

8] Reading remains for consideration. In this connexion there is much that can only be taught in actual practice, as for instance when the boy should take breath, at what point he should introduce a pause into a line, where the sense ends or begins, when the voice should be raised or lowered, what modulation should be given to each phrase, and when he should increase or slacken speed, or speak with greater or less energy. In this portion of my work I will give but one golden rule: to do all these things, he must understand what he reads. But above all his reading must be manly, combining dignity and charm; it must be different from the reading of prose, for poetry is song and poets claim to be singers. But this fact does not justify degeneration into sing-song or the effeminate modulations now in vogue: there is an excellent saying on this point attributed to Gaius Caesar while he was still a boy: "If you are singing, you sing badly: if you are reading, you sing." Again I do not, like some teachers, wish character as revealed by speeches to be indicated as it is by the comic actor, though I think that there should be some modulation of the voice to distinguish such passages from those where the poet is speaking in person. There are other points where there is much need of instruction: above all, unformed minds which are liable to be all the more deeply impressed by what they learn in their days of childish ignorance, must learn not merely what is eloquent; it is even more important that they should study what is morally excellent.

It is therefore an admirable practice which now prevails, to begin by reading Homer and Vergil, although the intelligence needs to be further developed for the full appreciation of their merits: but there is plenty of time for that since the boy will read them more than once. In the meantime let his mind be lifted by the sublimity of heroic verse, inspired by the greatness of its theme and imbued with the loftiest sentiments. The reading of tragedy also is useful, and lyric poets will provide nourishment for the mind, provided not merely the authors be carefully selected, but also the passages from their works which are to be read. For the Greek lyric poets are often licentious and even in Horace there are passages which I should be unwilling to explain to a class. Elegiacs, however, more especially erotic elegy, and hendecasyllables, which are merely sections of Sotadean verse (concerning which latter I need give no admonitions), should be entirely banished, if possible; if not absolutely banished, they should be reserved for pupils of a less impressionable age. As to comedy, whose contribution to eloquence may be of no small importance, since it is concerned with every kind of character and emotion, I will shortly point out in its due place what use can in my opinion be made of it in the education of boys. As soon as we have no fear of contaminating their morals, it should take its place among the subjects which it is specially desirable to read. I speak of Menander, though I would not exclude others. For Latin authors will also be of some service. But the subjects selected for lectures to boys should be those which will enlarge the mind and provide the greatest nourishment to the intellect. Life is quite long enough for the subsequent study of those other subjects which are concerned with matters of interest solely to learned men. But even the old Latin poets may be of great value, in spite of the fact that their strength lies in their natural talent rather than in their art: above all they will contribute richness of vocabulary: for the

vocabulary of the tragedians is full of dignity, while in that of the
comedians there is a certain elegance and Attic grace. They are, too,
more careful about dramatic structure than the majority of moderns,
who regard epigram as the sole merit of every kind of literary work.
For purity at any rate and manliness, if I may say so, we must certainly go to these writers, since to-day even our style of speaking is
infected with all the faults of modern decadence. Finally we may
derive confidence from the practice of the greatest orators of drawing
upon the early poets to support their arguments or adorn their
eloquence. For we find, more especially in the pages of Cicero, but
frequently in Asinius and other orators of that period, quotations
from Ennius, Accius, Pacuvius, Lucilius, Terence, Caecilius and
others, inserted not merely to show the speaker's learning, but to
please his hearers as well, since the charms of poetry provide a
pleasant relief from the severity of forensic eloquence. Such quotations have the additional advantage of helping the speaker's case,
for the orator makes use of the sentiments expressed by the poet as
evidence in support of his own statements. But while my earlier
remarks have special application to the education of boys, those
which I have just made apply rather to persons of riper years; for
the love of letters and the value of reading are not confined to one's
schooldays, but end only with life.

In lecturing the teacher of literature must give attention to minor
points as well: he will ask his class after analysing a verse to give
him the parts of speech and the peculiar features of the feet which
it contains: these latter should be so familiar in poetry as to make
their presence desired even in the prose of oratory. He will point
out what words are barbarous, what improperly used, and what are
contrary to the laws of language. . . .

*   *   *

10] . . . For there are other subjects of education which must be
studied simultaneously with literature. These being independent
studies are capable of completion without a knowledge of oratory,
while on the other hand they cannot by themselves produce an
orator. The question has consequently been raised as to whether they
are necessary for this purpose. What, say some, has the knowledge
of the way to describe an equilateral triangle on a given straight
line got to do with pleading in the law-courts or speaking in the
senate? Will an acquaintance with the names and intervals of the
notes of the lyre help an orator to defend a criminal or direct the

policy of his country? They will perhaps produce a long list of orators who are most effective in the courts but have never sat under a geometrician and whose understanding of music is confined to the pleasure which their ears, like those of other men, derive from it. To such critics I reply, and Cicero frequently makes the same remark in his Orator, that I am not describing any orator who actually exists or has existed, but have in my mind's eye an ideal orator, perfect down to the smallest detail. For when the philosophers describe the ideal sage who is to be consummate in all knowledge and a very god incarnate, as they say, they would have him receive instruction not merely in the knowledge of things human and divine, but would also lead him through a course of subjects, which in themselves are comparatively trivial, as for instance the elaborate subtleties of formal logic: not that acquaintance with the so called "horn" or "crocodile" problems can make a man wise, but because it is important that he should never trip even in the smallest trifles. So too the teacher of geometry, music or other subjects which I would class with these, will not be able to create the perfect orator (who like the philosopher ought to be a wise man), but none the less these arts will assist in his perfection. I may draw a parallel from the use of antidotes and other remedies applied to the eyes or to wounds. We know that these are composed of ingredients which produce many and sometimes contrary effects, but mixed together they make a single compound resembling no one of its component parts, but deriving its peculiar properties from all: so too dumb insects produce honey, whose taste is beyond the skill of man to imitate, from different kinds of flowers and juices. Shall we marvel then, if oratory, the highest gift of providence to man, needs the assistance of many arts, which, although they do not reveal or intrude themselves in actual speaking, supply hidden forces and make their silent presence felt? "But" it will be urged "men have proved fluent without their aid." Granted, but I am in quest of an orator. "Their contribution is but small." Yes, but we shall never attain completeness, if minor details be lacking. And it will be agreed that though our ideal of perfection may dwell on a height that is hard to gain, it is our duty to teach all we know, that achievement may at least come somewhat nearer the goal. But why should our courage fail? The perfect orator is not contrary to the laws of nature, and it is cowardly to despair of anything that is within the bounds of possibility. . . .

11

International Trade

THE Red Sea Guide Book, a unique account of Roman commerce with Arabia and India, appears to be the work of a Greek mariner and trader who lived and wrote in Egypt about A.D. 110. His narrative was based not only on his personal experiences but was also compiled from the logs of traders active at an earlier date. The guide book describes routes coasting the shores of the Red Sea and thence to India, and contains practical information for traders, including typical imports and exports. The Near Eastern trade was extremely important, since it provided the Empire with luxuries, whose import produced a large unfavorable balance of trade. The export of specie mentioned in the guide book has been confirmed archaeologically by the discovery of numerous hoards of Roman coins in India.

The Red Sea Guide Book, 1-29, 38-39, 41, 45-49, 56-57

1][1] OF THE designated ports on the Erythræan[2] Sea, and the market-towns around it, the first is the Egyptian port of Mussel Harbor. To those sailing down from that place, on the right hand, after eighteen hundred stadia,[3] there is Berenice. The harbors of both are at the boundary of Egypt, and are bays opening from the Erythræan Sea.

2] On the right-hand coast next below Berenice is the country of the Berbers. Along the shore are the Fish-Eaters, living in scattered caves in the narrow valleys. Further inland are the Berbers, and beyond them the Wild-flesh-Eaters and Calf-Eaters, each tribe governed by its chief; and behind them, further inland, in the country toward the west, there lies a city called Meroe.

3] Below the Calf-Eaters there is a little market-town on the shore after sailing about four thousand stadia from Berenice, called Ptolemais of the Hunts, from which the hunters started for the interior under the dynasty of the Ptolemies. This market-town has

From Wilfred H. Schoff, trans., THE PERIPLUS OF THE ERYTHRÆAN SEA (New York, 1912), pp. 22–23, 37–42, 44–46. Reprinted by permission of David McKay Company, Inc.

the true land-tortoise in small quantity; it is white and smaller in the shells. And here also is found a little ivory, like that of Adulis. But the place has no harbor and is reached only by small boats.

4] Below Ptolemais of the Hunts, at a distance of about three thousand stadia, there is Adulis, a port established by law, lying at the inner end of a bay that runs in toward the south. Before the harbor lies the so-called Mountain Island, about two hundred stadia seaward from the very head of the bay, with the shores of the mainland close to it on both sides. Ships bound for this port now anchor here because of attacks from the land. They used formerly to anchor at the very head of the bay, by an island called Diodorus, close to the shore, which could be reached on foot from the land; by which means the barbarous natives attacked the island. Opposite Mountain Island, on the mainland twenty stadia from shore, lies Adulis, a fair-sized village, from which there is a three-days' journey to Coloe, an inland town and the first market for ivory. From that place to the city of the people called Auxumites[4] there is a five days' journey more; to that place all the ivory is brought from the country beyond the Nile through the district called Cyeneum, and thence to Adulis. Practically the whole number of elephants and rhinoceros that are killed live in the places inland, although at rare intervals they are hunted on the seacoast or even near Adulis. Before the harbor of that market-town, out at sea on the right hand, there lie a great many little sandy islands called Alalæi, yielding tortoise-shell, which is brought to market there by the Fish-Eaters.

5] And about eight hundred stadia beyond there is another very deep bay, with a great mound of sand piled up at the right of the entrance; at the bottom of which the opsian stone[5] is found, and this is the only place where it is produced. These places, from the Calf-Eaters to the other Berber country, are governed by Zoscales; who is miserly in his ways and always striving for more, but otherwise upright, and acquainted with Greek literature.

6] There are imported into these places, undressed cloth made in Egypt for the Berbers; robes from Arsinoe; cloaks of poor quality dyed in colors; double-fringed linen mantles; many articles of flint glass, and others of murrhine,[6] made in Diospolis; and brass, which is used for ornament and in cut pieces instead of coin; sheets of soft copper, used for cooking-utensils and cut up for bracelets and anklets for the women; iron, which is made into spears used against the elephants and other wild beasts, and in their wars. Besides these, small axes are imported, and adzes and swords; copper drinking-cups, round and large; a little coin for those coming to the market;

wine of Laodicea and Italy, not much; olive oil, not much; for the king, gold and silver plate made after the fashion of the country, and for clothing, military cloaks, and thin coats of skin, of no great value. Likewise from the district of Ariaca across the sea, there are imported Indian iron, and steel, and Indian cotton cloth; the broad cloth called *monachê* and that called *sagmatogênê,* and girdles, and coats of skin and mallow-colored cloth, and a few muslins, and colored lac.[7] There are exported from these places ivory, and tortoise-shell and rhinoceros-horn. The most from Egypt is brought to this market from the month of January to September, that is, from Tybi to Thoth; but seasonably they put to sea about the month of September.

7] From this place the Arabian Gulf trends toward the east and becomes narrowest just before the Gulf of Avalites. After about four thousand stadia, for those sailing eastward along the same coast, there are other Berber market-towns, known as the "far-side" ports; lying at intervals one after the other, without harbors but having roadsteads where ships can anchor and lie in good weather. The first is called Avalites; to this place the voyage from Arabia to the far-side coast is the shortest. Here there is a small market-town called Avalites, which must be reached by boats and rafts. There are imported into this place, flint glass, assorted; juice of sour grapes from Diospolis; dressed cloth, assorted, made for the Berbers; wheat, wine, and a little tin. There are exported from the same place, and sometimes by the Berbers themselves crossing on rafts to Ocelis and Muza on the opposite shore, spices, a little ivory, tortoise-shell, and a very little myrrh, but better than the rest. And the Berbers who live in the place are very unruly.

8] After Avalites there is another market-town, better than this, called Malao, distant a sail of about eight hundred stadia. The anchorage is an open roadstead, sheltered by a spit running out from the east. Here the natives are more peaceable. There are imported into this place the things already mentioned, and many tunics, cloaks from Arsinoe, dressed and dyed; drinking-cups, sheets of soft copper in small quantity, iron, and gold and silver coin, not much. There are exported from these places myrrh, a little frankincense (that known as far-side), the harder cinnamon, *duaca,*[8] Indian copal[9] and *macir,*[10] which are imported into Arabia; and slaves, but rarely.

9] Two days' sail, or three, beyond Malao is the market-town of Mundus, where the ships lie at anchor more safely behind a projecting island close to the shore. There are imported into this place the things previously set forth, and from it likewise are exported the merchandise already stated, and the incense called *mocrotu*.[11] And the traders living here are more quarrelsome.

10] Beyond Mundus, sailing toward the east, after another two days' sail, or three, you reach Mosyllum, on a beach, with a bad anchorage. There are imported here the same things already mentioned, also silver plate, a very little iron, and glass. There are shipped from the place a great quantity of cinnamon (so that this market-town requires ships of larger size), and fragrant gums, spices, a little tortoise shell, and *mocrotu* (poorer than that of Mundus), frankincense (the far-side), ivory and myrrh in small quantities.

11] Sailing along the coast beyond Mosyllum, after a two days' course you come to the so-called Little Nile River, and a fine spring, and a small laurel grove, and Cape Elephant. Then the shore recedes into a bay, and has a river, called Elephant, and a large laurel-grove called Acannæ; where alone is produced the far-side frankincense, in great quantity and of the best grade.

12] Beyond this place, the coast trending toward the south, there is the Market and Cape of Spices, an abrupt promontory, at the very end of the Berber coast toward the east. The anchorage is dangerous at times from the ground-swell, because the place is exposed to the north. A sign of an approaching storm which is peculiar to the place, is that the deep water becomes more turbid and changes its color. When this happens they all run to a large promontory called Tabæ, which offers safe shelter. There are imported into this market-town the things already mentioned; and there are produced in it cinnamon (and its different varieties, *gizir, asypha, arebo, magla,* and *moto*) and frankincense.

13] Beyond Tabæ, after four hundred stadia, there is the village of Pano. And then, after sailing four hundred stadia along a promontory, toward which place the current also draws you, there is another market-town called Opone, into which the same things are imported as those already mentioned, and in it the greatest quantity of cinnamon is produced (the *arebo* and *moto*), and slaves of the better sort, which are brought to Egypt in increasing numbers; and a great quantity of tortoise-shell, better than that found elsewhere.

14] The voyage to all these far-side market-towns is made from Egypt about the month of July, that is Epiphi. And ships are also customarily fitted out from the places across this sea, from Ariaca and Barygaza, bringing to these far-side market-towns the products of their own places; wheat, rice, clarified butter, sesame oil, cotton cloth (the *monaché* and the *sagmatogéné*), and girdles, and honey from the reed called *sacchari*.[12] Some make the voyage especially to these market-towns, and others exchange their cargoes while sailing along the coast. This country is not subject to a King, but each market-town is ruled by its separate chief.

15] Beyond Opone, the shore trending more toward the south, first there are the small and great bluffs of Azania; this coast is destitute of harbors, but there are places where ships can lie at anchor, the shore being abrupt; and this course is of six days, the direction being south-west. Then come the small and great beach for another six days' course and after that in order, the Courses of Azania, the first being called Sarapion and the next Nicon; and after that several rivers and other anchorages, one after the other, separately a rest and a run for each day, seven in all, until the Pyralaæ islands and what is called the channel; beyond which, a little to the south of south-west, after two courses of a day and night along the Ausanitic coast, is the island Menuthias, about three hundred stadia from the mainland, low and wooded, in which there are rivers and many kinds of birds and the mountain-tortoise. There are no wild beasts except the crocodiles; but there they do not attack men. In this place there are sewed boats, and canoes hollowed from single logs, which they use for fishing and catching tortoise. In this island they also catch them in a peculiar way, in wicker baskets, which they fasten across the channel-opening between the breakers.

16] Two days' sail beyond, there lies the very last market-town of the continent of Azania, which is called Rhapta; which has its name from the sewed boats (*rhaptôn ploiariôn*) already mentioned; in which there is ivory in great quantity, and tortoise-shell. Along this coast live men of piratical habits, very great in stature, and under separate chiefs for each place. The Mapharitic chief governs it under some ancient right that subjects it to the sovereignty of the state that is become first in Arabia. And the people of Muza now hold it under his authority, and send thither many large ships; using Arab captains and agents, who are familiar with the natives and intermarry with them, and who know the whole coast and understand the language.

17] There are imported into these markets the lances made at Muza especially for this trade, and hatchets and daggers and awls, and various kinds of glass; and at some places a little wine, and wheat, not for trade, but to serve for getting the good-will of the savages. There are exported from these places a great quantity of ivory, but inferior to that of Adulis, and rhinoceros-horn and tortoise-shell (which is in best demand after that from India), and a little palm-oil.

18] And these markets of Azania are the very last of the continent that stretches down on the right hand from Berenice; for beyond these places the unexplored ocean curves around toward the west, and running along by the regions to the south of Aethiopia and Libya and Africa, it mingles with the western sea.

19] Now to the left of Berenice, sailing for two or three days from Mussel Harbor eastward across the adjacent gulf, there is another harbor and fortified place, which is called White Village, from which there is a road to Petra, which is subject to Malichas, King of the Nabatæans. It holds the position of a market-town for the small vessels sent there from Arabia; and so a centurion is stationed there as a collector of one-fourth of the merchandise imported, with an armed force, as a garrison.

20] Directly below this place is the adjoining country of Arabia, in its length bordering a great distance on the Erythræan Sea. Different tribes inhabit the country, differing in their speech, some partially, and some altogether. The land next the sea is similarly dotted here and there with caves of the Fish-Eaters, but the country inland is peopled by rascally men speaking two languages, who live in villages and nomadic camps, by whom those sailing off the middle course are plundered, and those surviving shipwrecks are taken for slaves. And so they too are continually taken prisoners by the chiefs and kings of Arabia; and they are called Carnaites. Navigation is dangerous along this whole coast of Arabia, which is without harbors, with bad anchorages, foul, inaccessible because of breakers and rocks, and terrible in every way. Therefore we hold our course down the middle of the gulf and pass on as fast as possible by the country of Arabia until we come to the Burnt Island; directly below which there are regions of peaceful people, nomadic, pasturers of cattle, sheep and camels.

21] Beyond these places, in a bay at the foot of the left side of this gulf, there is a place by the shore called Muza, a market-town established by law, distant altogether from Berenice for those sailing southward, about twelve thousand stadia. And the whole place is crowded with Arab shipowners and seafaring men, and is busy with the affairs of commerce; for they carry on a trade with the far-side coast and with Barygaza, sending their own ships there.

22] Three days inland from this port there is a city called Saua, in the midst of the region called Mapharitis; and there is a vassal-chief named Cholæbus who lives in that city.

23] And after nine days more there is Saphar, the metropolis, in which lives Charibael, lawful king of two tribes, the Homerites and those living next to them, called the Sabaites; through continual embassies and gifts, he is a friend of the Emperors.

24] The market-town of Muza is without a harbor, but has a good roadstead and anchorage because of the sandy bottom thereabouts, where the anchors hold safely. The merchandise imported there consists of purple cloths, both fine and coarse; clothing in the Arabian style, with sleeves; plain, ordinary, embroidered, or interwoven with gold; saffron, sweet rush, muslins, cloaks, blankets (not many), some plain and others made in the local fashion; sashes of different colors, fragrant ointments in moderate quantity, wine and wheat, not much. For the country produces grain in moderate amount, and a great deal of wine. And to the King and the Chief are given horses and sumpter-mules, vessels of gold and polished silver, finely woven clothing and copper vessels. There are exported from the same place the things produced in the country: selected myrrh, and the Gebanite-Minæan *stacte*,[13] alabaster and all the things already mentioned from Avalites and the far-side coast. The voyage to this place is made best about the month of September, that is Thoth; but there is nothing to prevent it even earlier.

25] After sailing beyond this place about three hundred stadia, the coast of Arabia and the Berber country about the Avalitic gulf now coming close together, there is a channel, not long in extent, which forces the sea together and shuts it into a narrow strait, the passage through which, sixty stadia in length, the island Diodorus divides. Therefore the course through it is beset with rushing currents and with strong winds blowing down from the adjacent ridge of mountains. Directly on this strait by the shore there is a village of Arabs, subject to the same chief, called Ocelis; which is not so much a market-town as it is an anchorage and watering-place and the first landing for those sailing into the gulf.

26] Beyond Ocelis, the sea widening again toward the east and soon giving a view of the open ocean, after about twelve hundred stadia there is Eudæmon Arabia, a village by the shore, also of the Kingdom of Charibael, and having convenient anchorages, and watering-places, sweeter and better than those at Ocelis; it lies at the entrance of a bay, and the land recedes from it. It was called Eudæmon, because in the early days of the city when the voyage was not yet made from India to Egypt, and when they did not dare to sail from Egypt to the ports across this ocean, but all came together at this place, it received the cargoes from both countries, just as Alexandria now receives the things brought both from abroad and from Egypt. But not long before our own time Charibael destroyed the place.

27] After Eudæmon Arabia there is a continuous length of coast, and a bay extending two thousand stadia or more, along which there are Nomads and Fish-Eaters living in villages; just beyond the cape projecting from this bay there is another market-town by the shore, Cana, of the Kingdom of Eleazus, the Frankincense Country; and facing it there are two desert islands, one called Island of Birds, the other Dome Island, one hundred and twenty stadia from Cana. Inland from this place lies the metropolis Sabbatha, in which the King lives. All the frankincense produced in the country is brought by camels to that place to be stored, and to Cana on rafts held up by inflated skins after the manner of the country, and in boats. And this place has a trade also with the far-side ports, with Barygaza and Scythia and Ommana and the neighboring coast of Persia.

28] There are imported into this place from Egypt a little wheat and wine, as at Muza; clothing in the Arabian style, plain and common and most of it spurious; and copper and tin and coral and storax[14] and other things such as go to Muza; and for the King usually wrought gold and silver plate, also horses, images, and thin clothing of fine quality. And there are exported from this place, native produce, frankincense and aloes,[15] and the rest of the things that enter into the trade of the other ports. The voyage to this place is best made at the same time as that to Muza, or rather earlier.

29] Beyond Cana, the land receding greatly, there follows a very deep bay stretching a great way across, which is called Sachalites; and the Frankincense Country, mountainous and forbidding, wrapped in thick clouds and fog, and yielding frankincense from the trees. These incense-bearing trees are not of great height or thickness; they bear the frankincense sticking in drops on the bark, just as the trees among us in Egypt weep their gum. The frankincense is gathered by the King's slaves and those who are sent to this service for punishment. For these places are very unhealthy, and pestilential even to those sailing along the coast; but almost always fatal to those working there, who also perish often from want of food.

* * *

38] Beyond this region, the continent making a wide curve from the east across the depths of the bays, there follows the coast district of Scythia, which lies above toward the north; the whole marshy; from which flows down the river Sinthus,[16] the greatest of all the rivers that flow into the Erythræan Sea, bringing down an enormous volume of water; so that a long way out at sea, before reaching this country, the water of the ocean is fresh from it. Now as a sign of approach to this country to those coming from the sea, there are serpents coming forth from the depths to meet you; and a sign of the places just mentioned and in Persia, are those called *gracæ*. This river has seven mouths, very shallow and marshy, so that they are not navigable, except the one in the middle; at which by the shore, is the market-town, Barbaricum. Before it there lies a small island, and inland behind it is the metropolis of Scythia, Minnagara; it is subject to Parthian princes who are constantly driving each other out.

39] The ships lie at anchor at Barbaricum, but all their cargoes are carried up to the metropolis by the river, to the King. There are imported into this market a great deal of thin clothing, and a little spurious; figured linens, topaz, coral, storax, frankincense, vessels of glass, silver and gold plate, and a little wine. On the other hand there are exported costus,[17] bdellium,[18] lycium,[19] nard,[20] turquoise, lapis lazuli, Seric skins, cotton cloth, silk yarn, and indigo. And sailors set out thither with the Indian Etesian winds, about the month of July, that is Epiphi: it is more dangerous then, but through these winds the voyage is more direct, and sooner completed.

* * *

41] Beyond the gulf of Baraca is that of Barygaza and the coast of the country of Ariaca, which is the beginning of the Kingdom of Nambanus and of all India. That part of it lying inland and adjoining Scythia is called Abiria, but the coast is called Syrastrene. It is a fertile country, yielding wheat and rice and sesame oil and clarified butter, cotton and the Indian cloths made therefrom, of the coarser sorts. Very many cattle are pastured there, and the men are of great stature and black in color. The metropolis of this country is Minnagara, from which much cotton cloth is brought down to Barygaza. In these places there remain even to the present time signs of the expedition of Alexander, such as ancient shrines, walls of forts and great wells. The sailing course along this coast, from Barbaricum to the promontory called Papica, opposite Barygaza, and before Astacampra, is of three thousand stadia.

* * *

45] Now the whole country of India has very many rivers, and very great ebb and flow of the tides; increasing at the new moon, and at the full moon for three days, and falling off during the intervening days of the moon. But about Barygaza it is much greater, so that the bottom is suddenly seen, and now parts of the dry land are sea, and now it is dry where ships were sailing just before; and the rivers, under the inrush of the flood tide, when the whole force of the sea is directed against them, are driven upwards more strongly against their natural current, for many stadia.

46] For this reason entrance and departure of vessels is very dangerous to those who are inexperienced or who come to this market-town for the first time. For the rush of waters at the incoming tide is irresistible, and the anchors cannot hold against it; so that large ships are caught up by the force of it, turned broadside on through the speed of the current, and so driven on the shoals and wrecked; and smaller boats are overturned; and those that have been turned aside among the channels by the receding waters at the ebb, are left on their sides, and if not held on an even keel by props, the flood tide comes upon them suddenly and under the first head of the current they are filled with water. For there is so great force in the rush of the sea at the new moon, especially during the flood tide at night, that if you begin the entrance at the moment when the waters are still, on the instant there is borne to you at the mouth of the river, a noise like the cries of an army heard from afar; and very soon the sea itself comes rushing in over the shoals with a hoarse roar.

47] The country inland from Barygaza is inhabited by numerous tribes, such as the Arattii, the Arachossi, the Gandaræi and the people of Poclais, in which is Bucephalus Alexandria. Above these is the very warlike nation of the Bactrians, who are under their own king. And Alexander, setting out from these parts, penetrated to the Ganges, leaving aside Damirica and the southern part of India; and to the present day ancient drachmæ are current in Barygaza, coming from this country, bearing inscriptions in Greek letters, and the devices of those who reigned after Alexander, Apollodotus and Menander.

48] Inland from this place and to the east, is the city called Ozene, formerly a royal capital; from this place are brought down all things needed for the welfare of the country about Barygaza, and many things for our trade: agate and carnelian, Indian muslins and mallow cloth, and much ordinary cloth. Through this same region and from the upper country is brought the spikenard that comes through Poclais; that is, the Caspapyrene and Paropanisene and Cabolitic and that brought through the adjoining country of Scythia; also costus and bdellium.

49] There are imported into this market-town, wine, Italian preferred, also Laodicean and Arabian; copper, tin, and lead; coral and topaz; thin clothing and inferior sorts of all kinds; bright-colored girdles a cubit wide; storax, sweet clover, flint glass, realgar,[21] antimony, gold and silver coin, on which there is a profit when exchanged for the money of the country; and ointment, but not very costly and not much. And for the King there are brought into those places very costly vessels of silver, singing boys, beautiful maidens for the harem, fine wines, thin clothing of the finest weaves, and the choicest ointments. There are exported from these places spikenard, costus, bdellium, ivory, agate and carnelian, lycium, cotton cloth of all kinds, silk cloth, mallow cloth, yarn, long pepper and such other things as are brought here from the various market-towns. Those bound for this market-town from Egypt make the voyage favorably about the month of July, that is Epiphi.

* * *

56] They send large ships to these market-towns on account of the great quantity and bulk of pepper and malabathrum. There are imported here, in the first place, a great quantity of coin; topaz, thin clothing, not much; figured linens, antimony, coral, crude glass, copper, tin, lead; wine, not much, but as much as at Barygaza; realgar and orpiment;[21] and wheat enough for the sailors, for this is not dealt in by the merchants there. There is exported pepper, which is produced in quantity in only one region near these markets, a district called Cottonara. Besides this there are exported great quantities of fine pearls, ivory, silk cloth, spikenard from the Ganges, malabathrum from the places in the interior, transparent stones of all kinds, diamonds and sapphires, and tortoise-shell; that from Chryse Island, and that taken among the islands along the coast of Damirica. They make the voyage to this place in a favorable season who set out from Egypt about the month of July, that is Epiphi.

57] This whole voyage as above described, from Cana and Eudæmon Arabia, they used to make in small vessels, sailing close around the shores of the gulfs; and Hippalus was the pilot who by observing the location of the ports and the conditions of the sea, first discovered how to lay his course straight across the ocean. For at the same time when with us the Etesian winds are blowing, on the shores of India the wind sets in from the ocean, and this southwest wind is called Hippalus, from the name of him who first discovered the passage across.[22] From that time to the present day ships start, some direct from Cana, and some from the Cape of Spices; and those bound for Damirica throw the ship's head considerably off the wind; while those bound for Barygaza and Scythia keep along shore not more than three days and for the rest of the time hold the same course straight out to sea from that region, with a favorable wind, quite away from the land, and so sail outside past the aforesaid gulfs.

NOTES

1. The itinerary is as follows: Sections 1–18 describe the voyage along the African shores of the Red Sea as far as the Straits of Bab-el-Mandeb and the Indian Ocean; sections 19–25, the Arabian shores to the same point; sections 26–57, the route along the Indian coast south from the Persian Gulf and Indus River. This document is best studied with a classical atlas of the Near East.

2. I.e., Red.

3. One stadium, about 520 feet.

4. The ancient capital of Abyssinia.

5. Obsidian.

6. A cheap colored glass.

7. A dye.

8. A kind of frankincense.

9. A gum or resin used in making varnishes.

10. An aromatic bark.

11. Probably a high grade of frankincense.

12. First mention in Western civilization of sugar as an article of commerce.

13. An aromatic gum.

14. Probably a resin used as incense.

15. A cathartic.

16. The Indus.

17. A root used as culinary spice and as perfume.

18. An aromatic gum.

19. A dye used as cosmetic and medicine.

20. A root of ginger grass, from which medicinal and cosmetic oils were derived.

21. Realgar and orpiment are sulfides of arsenic used as pigment.

22. Reference to the epoch-making discovery of the monsoons, made probably during Augustus' reign, possibly not until that of Claudius.

12

The Empire Idealized

AELIUS ARISTIDES of Smyrna (A.D. 117–ca. 185), a prominent Greek rhetorician, delivered his famous Roman Panegyric at the imperial capital in 143. A work of art rather than of history, it was designed primarily to entertain rather than to instruct and is typical of the increasingly popular panegyrical literature of the imperial period. In addition to illustrating the cultural tastes of the second century A.D., it also reveals the satisfaction with which the middle and upper classes viewed the serenity and stability of life under the good emperors. Unlike Tacitus, Aelius Aristides emphasized and idealized the positive aspects of imperial rule. As seen in the following excerpts, these included the development of urban life, protection by an effective yet disciplined army, freedom from fears of revolution and invasion, and a community of interest between Romans and Hellenes created by liberal bestowal of citizenship and by government that produced justice and peace.

Aelius Aristides, Roman Panegyric 1-2, 7-8, 10-13, 28, 31-34, 36-39, 59-60, 63-66, 70-82, 107-109

1] IT IS A time-honored custom of travellers setting forth by land or sea to make a prayer pledging the performance of some vow — whatever they have in mind — on safe arrival at their destination. I recall a poet who playfully parodied the custom by pledging "a grain of incense — with gilded horns!" As for me the vow that I made as I journeyed hither was not of the usual stupid and irrelevant kind, nor one unrelated to the art of my profession: merely that if I came through safely I would salute your city with a public address. 2] But since it was quite impossible to pledge words commensurate

From J. H. Oliver, "The Ruling Power: A Study of the Roman Empire in the Second Century after Christ through the Roman Oration of Aelius Aristides," TRANSACTIONS OF THE AMERICAN PHILOSOPHICAL SOCIETY (Philadelphia, 1953), vol. 43, part 4, pp. 895–899, 901–904, 907. Reprinted by permission of the American Philosophical Society and James H. Oliver.

with your city, it became evident that I had need of a second prayer. It is perhaps really presumptuous to dare undertake an oration to equal such majesty in a city. However, I have promised to address you, and I can speak only as I can. Yet even so it may not be unacceptable, for I could name others too who hold that if they do the very best they can, it will seem good enough even to the gods.

* * *

7] Homer says of snow that as it falls, it covers "the crest of the range and the mountain peaks and the flowering fields and the rich acres of men, and," he says, "it is poured out over the white sea, the harbors and the shores." So also of this city. Like the snow, she covers mountain peaks, she covers the land intervening, and she goes down to the sea, where the commerce of all mankind has its common exchange and all the produce of the earth has its common market. Wherever one may go in Rome, there is no vacancy to keep one from being, there also, in mid-city.

8] And indeed she is poured out, not just over the level ground, but in a manner with which the simile cannot begin to keep pace, she rises great distances into the air, so that her height is not to be compared to a covering of snow but rather to the peaks themselves. And as a man who far surpasses others in size and strength likes to show his strength by carrying others on his back, so this city, which is built over so much land, is not satisfied with her extent, but raising upon her shoulders others of equal size, one over the other, she carries them. It is from this that she gets her name, and strength (rômê) is the mark of all that is hers. Therefore, if one chose to unfold, as it were, and lay flat on the ground the cities which now she carries high in air, and place them side by side, all that part of Italy which intervenes would, I think, be filled and become one continuous city stretching to the Strait of Otranto.

* * *

10] Some chronicler, speaking of Asia, asserted that one man ruled as much land as the sun passed, and his statement was not true because he placed all Africa and Europe outside the limits where the sun rises in the East and sets in the West. It has now however turned out to be true. Your possession is equal to what the sun can pass, and the sun passes over your land. Promontories in the sea, even the Chelidonean and Cyanean Isles, do not limit your empire,[1] nor does the distance from which a horseman can reach the sea in one day, nor do you reign within fixed boundaries, nor does another dictate to what point your control reaches; but the sea like a girdle lies extended, at once in the middle of the civilized world and of your hegemony.

11] Around it lie the great continents greatly sloping, ever offering to you in full measure something of their own. Whatever the seasons make grow and whatever countries and rivers and lakes and arts of Hellenes and non-Hellenes produce are brought from every land and sea, so that if one would look at all these things, he must needs behold them either by visiting the entire civilized world or by coming to this city. For whatever is grown and made among each people cannot fail to be here at all times and in abundance. And here the merchant vessels come carrying these many products from all regions in every season and even at every equinox, so that the city appears a kind of common emporium of the world.

12] Cargoes from India and, if you will, even from Arabia the Blest one can see in such numbers as to surmise that in those lands the trees will have been stripped bare and that the inhabitants of these lands, if they need anything, must come here and beg for a share of their own. Again one can see Babylonian garments and ornaments from the barbarian country beyond arriving in greater quantity and with more ease than if shippers from Naxos or from Cythnos, bearing something from those islands, had but to enter the port of Athens. Your farms are Egypt, Sicily and the civilized part of Africa.

13] Arrivals and departures by sea never cease, so that the wonder is, not that the harbor has insufficient space for merchant vessels, but that even the sea has enough, [if] it really does.

And just as Hesiod said about the ends of the Ocean, that there is a common channel where all waters have one source and destination, so there is a common channel to Rome and all meet here, trade, shipping, agriculture, metallurgy, all the arts and crafts that are or ever have been, all the things that engendered or grow from the earth. And whatever one does not see here neither did nor does exist. And so it is not easy to decide which is greater, the superiority of this city in respect to the cities that now are or the superiority of this empire in respect to the empires that ever were.

* * *

28] Now, however, the present empire has been extended to boundaries of no mean distance, to such, in fact, that one cannot even measure the area within them. On the contrary, for one who begins a journey westward from the point where at that period the empire of the Persian found its limit, the rest is far more than the entirety of his domain, and there are no sections which you have omitted, neither city nor tribe nor harbor nor district, except possibly some that you condemned as worthless. The Red Sea and the Cataracts of the Nile and Lake Maeotis, which formerly were said to lie on the boundaries of the earth, are like the courtyard walls to the house which is this city of yours. On the other hand, you have explored Ocean. Some writers did not believe that Ocean existed at all, or did not believe that it flowed around the earth; they thought that poets had invented the name and had introduced it into literature for the sake of entertainment. But you have explored it so thoroughly that not even the island therein has escaped you.

*　　*　　*

31] All directions are carried out by the chorus of the civilized world at a word or gesture of guidance more easily than at some plucking of a chord; and if anything need be done, it suffices to decide and there it is already done.

The governors sent out to the city-states and ethnic groups[2] are each of them rulers of those under them, but in what concerns themselves and their relations to each other they are all equally among the ruled, and in particular they differ from those under their rule in that it is they — one might assert — who first show how to be the right kind of subject. So much respect has been instilled in all men for him who is the great governor, who obtains for them their all.

32] They think that he knows what they are doing better than they do themselves. Accordingly they fear his displeasure and stand in greater awe of him than one would of a despot, a master who was present and watching and uttering commands. No one is so proud that he can fail to be moved upon hearing even the mere mention of the Ruler's name, but, rising, he praises and worships him and breathes two prayers in a single breath, one to the gods on the Ruler's behalf, one for his own affairs to the Ruler himself. And if the governors should have even some slight doubt whether certain claims are valid in connection with either public or private lawsuits and petitions from the governed, they straightway send to him with a request for instructions what to do, and they wait until he renders a reply, like a chorus waiting for its trainer.

33] Therefore, he has no need to wear himself out traveling around the whole empire nor, by appearing personally, now among some, then among others, to make sure of each point when he has the time to tread their soil. It is very easy for him to stay where he is and manage the entire civilized world by letters, which arrive almost as soon as they are written, as if they were carried by winged messengers.

34] But that which deserves as much wonder and admiration as all the rest together, and constant expression of gratitude both in word and action, shall now be mentioned. You who hold so vast an empire and rule it with such a firm hand and with so much unlimited power have very decidedly won a great success, which is completely your own.

*   *   *

36] For all who have ever gained empire you alone rule over men who are free. Caria has not been given to Tissaphernes, nor Phrygia to Pharnabazus, nor Egypt to someone else; nor is the country said to be enslaved, as household of so-and-so, to whomsoever it has been turned over, a man himself not free. But just as those in states of one city appoint the magistrates to protect and care for the governed, so you, who conduct public business in the whole civilized world exactly as if it were one city state, appoint the governors, as is natural after elections, to protect and care for the governed, not to be slave masters over them. Therefore governor makes way for governor unobtrusively, when his time is up, and far from staying too long and disputing the land with his successor, he might easily not stay long enough even to meet him.

37] Appeals to a higher court are made with the ease of an appeal from deme to dicastery,[3] with no greater menace for those who make them than for those who have accepted the local verdict. Therefore one might say that the men of today are ruled by the governors who are sent out, only in so far as they are content to be ruled.

38] Are not these advantages beyond the old "Free Republic" of every people? For under Government by the People it is not possible to go outside after the verdict has been given in the city's court nor even to other jurors, but, except in a city so small that it has to have jurors from out of town, one must ever be content with the local verdict . . . [deprived] undeservedly, or, as plaintiff, not getting possession even after a favorable verdict.

But now in the last instance there is another judge, a mighty one, whose comprehension no just claim ever escapes.

39] There is an abundant and beautiful equality of the humble with the great and of the obscure with the illustrious, and, above all, of the poor man with the rich and of the commoner with the noble, and the word of Hesiod comes to pass, "For he easily exalts, and the exalted he easily checks," namely this judge and princeps as the justice of the claim may lead, like a breeze in the sails of a ship, favoring and accompanying, not the rich man more, the poor man less, but benefiting equally whomsoever it meets.

* * *

59] But there is that which very decidedly deserves as much attention and admiration now as all the rest together. I mean your magnificent citizenship with its grand conception, because there is nothing like it in the records of all mankind. Dividing into two groups all those in your empire — and with this word I have indicated the entire civilized world — you have everywhere appointed to your citizenship, or even to kinship with you, the better part of the world's talent, courage, and leadership, while the rest you recognized as a league under your hegemony.

60] Neither sea nor intervening continent are bars to citizenship, nor are Asia and Europe divided in their treatment here. In your empire all paths are open to all. No one worthy of rule or trust remains an alien, but a civil community of the World has been established as a Free Republic under one, the best, ruler and teacher of order; and all come together as into a common civic center, in order to receive each man his due.

* * *

63] Let this passing comment, which the subject suggested, suffice. As we were saying, you who are "great greatly" distributed your citizenship. It was not because you stood off and refused to give a share in it to any of the others that you made your citizenship an object of wonder. On the contrary, you sought its expansion as a worthy aim, and you have caused the word Roman to be the label, not of membership in a city, but of some common nationality, and this not just one among all, but one balancing all the rest. For the categories into which you now divide the world are not Hellenes and Barbarians, and it is not absurd, the distinction which you made, because you show them a citizenry more numerous, so to speak, than the entire Hellenic race. The division which you substituted is one into Romans and non-Romans. To such a degree have you expanded the name of your city.

64] Since these are the lines along which the distinction has been made, many in every city are fellow-citizens of yours no less than of their own kinsmen, though some of them have not yet seen this city. There is no need of garrisons to hold their citadels, but the men of greatest standing and influence in every city guard their own fatherlands for you. And you have a double hold upon the cities, both from here and from your fellow citizens in each.

65] No envy sets foot in the empire, for you yourselves were the first to disown envy, when you placed all opportunities in view of all and offered those who were able a chance to be not governed more than they governed in turn. Nor does hatred either steal in from those who are not chosen. For since the constitution is a universal one and, as it were, of one state, naturally your governors rule not as over the property of others but as over their own. Besides, [under] this constitution all the masses have permission to [take refuge with you]¹ from the power of the local magnates, [but there is] the indignation and punishment from you which will come upon them immediately, if they themselves dare to make any unlawful change.

66] Thus the present regime naturally suits and serves both rich and poor. No other way of life is left. There has developed in your constitution a single harmonious, all-embracing union; and what formerly seemed to be impossible has come to pass in your time: to treat imperial rule as an [occasion] for great generosity and at the same time to rule none [the less] with firmness.¹

*   *   *

70] Wars, even if they once occurred, no longer seem to have been real; on the contrary, stories about them are interpreted more as myths by the many who hear them. If anywhere an actual clash occurs along the border, as is only natural in the immensity of a great empire, because of the madness of Getae or the misfortune of Libyans or the wickedness of those around the Red Sea, who are unable to enjoy the blessings they have, then simply like myths they themselves quickly pass and the stories about them.

71a] So great is your peace, though war was traditional among you.

72a] In regard to the civil administration of the whole empire it has been stated in what way you thought of it and what kind you established. Now it is time to speak about the army and military affairs, how you contrived in this matter and what organization you gave it.

71b] Yes, for the shoemakers and masons of yesterday are not the hoplites and cavalry of today. On the stage a farmer appears as a soldier after a quick change of costume, and in poor homes the same person cooks the meal, keeps the house, makes the bed. But you were not so undiscriminating. You did not expect that those engaged in other occupations would be made into soldiers by the need, nor did you leave it to your enemies to call you together. 72b] Rather in this too it is amazing how wise you were, and there is no precedent to serve as a parallel all the way.

73] For the Egyptians also progressed to the point of segregating the military, and it was deemed a very clever invention of theirs to have those who defended their country settled in special areas away from the rest. As in so many other respects, when compared to others, they were, it seemed, "clever Egyptians," as the saying goes. But when you visualized the same thing, you did not execute it in the same way. Instead you made a more equitable and more skillful segregation. In the former system it was not possible for each of the two groups to have equality of citizenship; the soldiers, who alone and forever bore the hardships, were in an inferior status to those who did not fight. Therefore the system was neither fair, nor agreeable to them. With you, on the other hand, since all have equality, a separate establishment for the military is successful.

74] Thus a courage like that of Hellenes and Egyptians and any others one might mention is surpassed by yours, and all, far as they are behind you in actual arms, trail still further in the conception. On the one hand you deemed it unworthy of your rule for those from this city to be subject to the levy and to the hardships and to enjoy no advantage from the present felicity; on the other hand you did not put your faith in alien mercenaries. Still you needed soldiers before the hour of crisis. So what did you do? You found an army of your own for which the citizens were undisturbed. This possibility was provided for you by that plan for all the empire, according to which you count no one an alien when you accept him for any employment where he can do well and is then needed.

75] Who then have been assembled and how? Going over the entire league, you looked about carefully for those who could perform this liturgy, and when you found them, you released them from the fatherland and gave them your own city, so that they became reluctant henceforth to call themselves by their original ethnics. Having made them fellow-citizens, you made them also soldiers, so that the men from this city would not be subject to the levy, and those performing military service would none the less be citizens, who together with their enrollment in the army had lost their own cities but from that very day had become your fellow-citizens and defenders.

76] Under your hegemony this is the contribution which all make to the armed forces, and no city is disaffected. You asked from each only as many as would cause no inconvenience to the givers and would not be enough by themselves to provide the individual city with a full quota of an army of its own. Therefore all cities are well pleased with the dispatch of these men to be their own representatives in the union army, while locally each city has no militia of its own men whatsoever, and [for military protection] they look nowhere but to you, because it is for this sole purpose that those who went out from the cities have been marshalled in good order.

77] And again, after you selected from everywhere the most competent men, you had a very profitable idea. It was this. You thought that when even those picked out for their excellent physiques and bodily superiority train for the festivals and the prize contests, then those who would be the contenders in the greatest engagements of real war, and victors in as many victories as one might chance to win in behalf of such an empire, ought not to come together merely in a crisis. You thought that the latter, selected from all as the strongest and, especially, most competent, ought to train for a long while ahead of time so as to be superior the minute they took their stand.

78] So these men, once you eliminated the morally and the socially base, you [introduced into] the community of the ruling nation, not without the privileges I mentioned nor in such a way that they would envy those who stay in the city because they themselves were not of equal rights at the start, but in such a way that they would consider their share of citizenship as an honor. Having found and treated them thus, you led them to the boundaries of the empire. There you stationed them at intervals, and you assigned areas to guard, some to some, others to others.

79] They account also for the plan which you devised and evolved in regard to the walls, which is worth comment now. One would call this city neither unwalled in the reckless manner of the Lacedaemonians nor again fortified with the splendor of Babylon or of any other city which before or after may have been walled in a more impressive style. On the contrary, you have made the fortification of Babylon seem frivolity and a woman's work indeed.

80] To place the walls around the city itself as if you were hiding her or fleeing from your subjects you considered ignoble and inconsistent with the rest of your concept, as if a master were to show fear of his own slaves. Nevertheless, you did not forget walls, but these you placed around the empire, not the city. And you erected walls splendid and worthy of you, as far away as possible, visible to those within the circuit, but, for one starting from the city, an outward journey of months and years if he wished to see them.

81] Beyond the outermost ring of the civilized world, you drew a second line, quite as one does in walling a town, another circle, more widely curved and more easily guarded. Here you built the walls to defend you and then erected towns bordering upon them, some in some parts, others elsewhere, filling them with colonists, giving these the comfort of arts and crafts, and in general establishing beautiful order.

82] An encamped army like a rampart encloses the civilized world in a ring. The perimeter of this enclosure, if a survey were made, would not be ten parasangs, nor twenty, nor a little more, nor a distance that one could say offhand, but as far as from the settled area of Aethiopia to the Phasis and from the Euphrates in the interior to the great outermost island toward the West; all this one can call a ring and circuit of the walls.

* * *

107] Your ways and institutions, which were really introduced by you, are ever held in honor and have become ever more firmly established. The present great governor[4] like a champion in the games clearly excells to such an extent his own ancestors that it is not easy to declare by how much he excells men of a different stock. One would say that justice and law are in truth whatever he decrees. This too [one can see] clearly before all else, that the partners whom he has to help him rule, men [like] sons of his own, similar unto him, are more than had any of his predecessors.

108] But the trial which we undertook at the beginning of our speech is beyond any man's power, namely to compose the oration which would equal the majesty of your empire, for it would require just about as much time as time alloted to the empire, and that would be all eternity. Therefore it is best to do like those poets who compose dithyrambs and paeans, namely to add a prayer and so close the oration.

109] Let all the gods and the children of the gods be invoked to grant that this empire and this city flourish forever and never cease until stones [float] upon the sea and trees cease to put forth shoots in spring, and that the great governor and his sons be preserved and obtain blessings for all.

My bold attempt is finished. Now is the time to register your decision whether for better or for worse.

NOTES

1. Translator's emendation.
2. Areas not organized as municipalities or city-states.
3. I.e., appeal from a popular assembly to a court of law.
4. Antoninus Pius.

13

The Stoic Emperor

THE RAMBLING Meditations of Marcus Aurelius (A.D. 121–180) is not a work of formal philosophy but, rather, a collection of self-revelatory musings that show how Stoicism supported a ruler whose empire was faced with the direst calamities. Stoicism did not merely inspire Marcus with an unflinching determination to do his duty as emperor. It also taught him that a man could achieve virtue only by living in harmony with nature. This involved subjecting one's natural inclinations to a law of reason, since the Stoics believed that the essence of the cosmos, including both God and man, was rational. There was no place in such a system for uncontrolled emotions that might prevent the philosopher from attaining a virtuous state. The Meditations, which reveal a man of almost impossibly high principles and equanimity, make Marcus seem the sadder for his depreciation of warm — if baser — feelings that make the complete human being.

Marcus Aurelius, Meditations, I, 1-17; III, 5, 9, 11; V, 33-34; VI, 30, 47-49; VIII, 1-6, 8-10, 50; IX, 1, 22-23; X, 1-3, 11, 15, 25; XI, 1

i

1] FROM MY grandfather Verus: the lessons of noble character and even temper.

2] From my father's reputation and my memory of him: modesty and manliness.

3] From my mother: piety and bountifulness, to keep myself not only from doing evil but even from dwelling on evil thoughts, simplicity too in diet and to be far removed from the ways of the rich.

From A. S. L. Farquharson, trans., Marcus Aurelius, MEDITATIONS (New York and Oxford, 1961, Everyman's Library edition), pp. 1–5, 12, 13–14, 30–31, 35, 38–39, 48–50, 55, 57, 60, 64–65, 67–69, 72–73. Reprinted by permission of E. P. Dutton & Co., Inc. and The Clarendon Press.

4] From my mother's grandfather: not to have attended public schools but enjoyed good teachers at home, and to have learned the lesson that on things like these it is a duty to spend liberally.

5] From my tutor: not to become a partisan of the Green jacket or the Blue in the races, nor of Thracian or Samnite gladiators; to bear pain and be content with little; to work with my own hands, to mind my own business, and to be slow to listen to slander.

6] From Diognetus: to avoid idle enthusiasms; to disbelieve the professions of sorcerers and imposters about incantations and exorcism of spirits and the like; not to cock-fight or to be excited about such sports; to put up with plain speaking and to become familiar with philosophy; to hear the lectures first of Baccheius, then of Tandasis and Marcian, in boyhood to write essays and to aspire to the camp-bed and skin coverlet and the other things which are part of the Greek training.

7] From Rusticus: to get an impression of need for reform and treatment of character; not to run off into zeal for rhetoric, writing on speculative themes, discoursing on edifying texts, exhibiting in fanciful colours the ascetic or the philanthropist. To avoid oratory, poetry and preciosity; not to parade at home in ceremonial costume or to do things of that kind; to write letters in the simple style, like his own from Sinuessa to my mother. To be easily recalled to myself and easily reconciled with those who provoke and offend, as soon as they are willing to meet me. To read books accurately and not be satisfied with superficial thinking about things or agree hurriedly with those who talk round a subject. To have made the acquaintance of the *Discourses* of Epictetus, of which he allowed me to share a copy of his own.

8] From Apollonius: moral freedom, not to expose oneself to the insecurity of fortune; to look to nothing else, even for a little while, except to reason. To be always the same, in sharp attacks of pain, in the loss of a child, in long illnesses. To see clearly in a living example that a man can be at once very much in earnest and yet able to relax.

Not to be censorious in exposition; and to see a man who plainly considered technical knowledge and ease in communicating general truths as the least of his good gifts. The lesson how one ought to receive from friends what are esteemed favours, neither lowering oneself on their account, nor returning them tactlessly.

9] From Sextus: graciousness, and the pattern of a household governed by its head, and the notion of life according to Nature. Dignity without pretence, solicitous consideration for friends, tolerance of amateurs and of those whose opinions have no ground in science.

A happy accommodation to every man, so that not only was his conversation more agreeable than any flattery, but he excited the greatest reverence at that very time in the very persons about him. Certainty of grasp, and method in the discovery and arrangement of the principles necessary to human life.

Never to give the impression of anger or of any other passion, but to be at once entirely passionless and yet full of natural affection. To praise without noise, to be widely learned without display.

10] From Alexander the grammarian: to avoid fault-finding and not to censure in a carping spirit any who employ an exotic phrase, a solecism or harsh expression, but oneself to use, neatly and precisely, the correct phrase, by way of answer or confirmation or handling of the actual question — the thing, not its verbal expression — or by some other equally happy reminder.

11] From Fronto: to observe how vile a thing is the malice and caprice and hypocrisy of absolutism; and generally speaking that those whom we entitle 'Patricians' are somehow rather wanting in the natural affections.

12] From Alexander the Platonist: seldom and only when absolutely necessary to say to anyone or write in a letter: 'I am too busy'; nor by such a turn of phrase to evade continually the duties incident to our relations to those who live with us, on the plea of 'present circumstances.'

13] From Catulus: not to neglect a friend's remonstrance, even if he may be unreasonable in his remonstrance, but to endeavour to restore him to his usual temper. Hearty praise, too, of teachers, like what is recorded of Athenodotus and Domitius, and genuine love towards children.

14] From Severus: love of family, love of truth, and love of justice. To have got by his help to understand Thrasea, Helvidius, Cato, Dio, Brutus, and to conceive the idea of a commonwealth based on equity and freedom of speech, and of a monarchy cherishing above all the liberty of the subject. From him too consistency and uniformity in regard for philosophy; to do good, to communicate liberally, to be useful; to believe in the affection of friends and to use no concealment towards those who incurred his censure, and that his friends had no necessity to conjecture his wishes or the reverse, but he was open with them.

15] From Maximus: mastery of self and vacillation in nothing;

cheerfulness in all circumstances and especially in illness. A happy blend of character, mildness with dignity, readiness to do without complaining what is given to be done. To see how in his case everyone believed 'he really thinks what he says, and what he does he does without evil intent'; not to be surprised or alarmed; nowhere to be in a hurry or to procrastinate, not to lack resource or to be depressed or cringing or on the other hand angered or suspicious. To be generous, forgiving, void of deceit. To give the impression of inflexible rectitude rather than of one who is corrected. The fact too that no one would ever have dreamed that he was looked down on by him or would have endured to conceive himself to be his superior. To be agreeable also (in social life).

16] From my father (by adoption):[1] gentleness and unshaken resolution in judgments taken after full examination; no vain-glory about external honours; love of work and perseverance; readiness to hear those who had anything to contribute to the public advantage; the desire to award to every man according to desert without partiality; the experience that knew where to tighten the rein, where to relax. Prohibition of unnatural practices, social tact and permission to his suite not invariably to be present at his banquets nor to attend his progress from Rome, as a matter of obligation, and always to be found the same by those who had failed to attend him through engagements. Exact scrutiny in council and patience; not that he was avoiding investigation, satisfied with first impressions. An inclination to keep his friends, and nowhere fastidious or the victim of manias but his own master in everything, and his outward mien cheerful. His long foresight and ordering of the merest trifle without making scenes. The check in his reign put upon organized applause and every form of lip-service; his unceasing watch over the needs of the empire and his stewardship of its resources; his patience under criticism by individuals of such conduct. No superstitious fear of divine powers nor with man any courting of the public or obsequiousness or cultivation of popular favour, but temperance in all things and firmness; nowhere want of taste or search for novelty.

In the things which contribute to life's comfort, where Fortune was lavish to him, use without display and at the same time without apology, so as to take them when they were there quite simply and not to require them when they were absent. The fact that no one would have said that he was a sophist, an impostor or a pedant, but a ripe man, an entire man, above flattery, able to preside over his own and his subject's business.

Besides all this the inclination to respect genuine followers of philosophy, but towards the other sort no tendency to reproach nor on the other hand to be hoodwinked by them; affability too and humour, but not to excess. Care of his health in moderation, not as one in love with living nor with an eye to personal appearance nor on the other hand neglecting it, but so far as by attention to self to need doctoring or medicine and external applications for very few ailments.

A very strong point, to give way without jealousy to those who had some particular gift like literary expression or knowledge of the Civil Law or customs or other matters, even sharing their enthusiasm that each might get the reputation due to his individual excellence. Acting always according to the tradition of our forefathers, yet not endeavouring that this regard for tradition should be noticed. No tendency, moreover, to chop and change, but a settled course in the same places and the same practices. After acute attacks of headache, fresh and vigorous at once for his accustomed duties; and not to have many secrets, only very few and by way of exception, and those solely because of matters of State. Discretion and moderation alike in the provision of shows, in carrying out public works, in donations to the populace, and so on; the behaviour in fact of one who has an eye precisely to what it is his duty to do, not to the reputation which attends the doing.

He was not one who bathed at odd hours, not fond of building, no connoisseur of the table, of the stuff and colour of his dress, of the beauty of his slaves. His costume was brought to Rome from his country house at Lorium; his manner of life at Lanuvium; the way he treated the tax-collecter who apologized at Tusculum, and all his behaviour of that sort. Nowhere harsh, merciless or blustering, nor so that you might ever say 'to fever heat,' but everything nicely calculated and divided into its times, as by a leisured man; no bustle, complete order, strength, consistency. What is recorded of Socrates would exactly fit him: he could equally be abstinent from or enjoy what many are too weak to abstain from and too self-indulgent in enjoying. To be strong, to endure, and in either case to be sober belong to the man of perfect and invincible spirit, like the spirit of Maximus in his illness.

17] From the gods: to have had good grandparents, good parents, a good sister, good masters, good intimates, kinsfolk, friends, almost everything; and that in regard to not one of them did I stumble into offence, although I had the kind of disposition which might in some

circumstances have led me to behave thus; but it was the goodness of
the gods that no conjunction of events came about which was likely
to expose my weakness. That I was not brought up longer than I was
with my grandfather's second wife, that I preserved the flower of my
youth and did not play the man before my time, but even delayed a
little longer. That my station in life was under a governor and a
father who was to strip off all my pride and to lead me to see that it
is possible to live in a palace and yet not to need a bodyguard or
embroidered uniforms or candelabra and statues bearing lamps and
the like accompaniments of pomp, but that one is able to contract
very nearly to a private station and not on that account to lose dignity or to be more remiss in the duties that a prince must perform on
behalf of the public. That I met with so good a brother, able by his
character not only to rouse me to care of myself but at the same time
to hearten me by respect and natural affection; that my children were
not deficient in mind nor deformed in body; that I made no further
progress in eloquence and poetry and those other pursuits wherein,
had I seen myself progressing along an easy road, I should perhaps
have become absorbed. That I made haste to advance my masters to
the honours which they appeared to covet and did not put them off
with hopes that, as they were still young, I should do it later on. To
have got to know Apollonius, Rusticus, Maximus. To have pictured
to myself clearly and repeatedly what life in obedience to Nature
really is, so that, so far as concerns the gods and communications
from the other world, and aids and inspirations, nothing hinders my
living at once in obedience to Nature, though I still come somewhat
short of this by my own fault and by not observing the reminders
and almost the instructions of the gods. That my body has held out
so well in a life like mine; that I did not touch Benedicta or Theo-
dotus, but that even in later years when I experienced the passion of
love I was cured; that though I was often angry with Rusticus I
never went to extremes for which I should have been sorry; that
though my mother was fated to die young, she still spent her last
years with me. That whenever I wanted to help anyone in poverty or
some other necessity I was never told that I could not afford it, and
that I did not myself fall into the same necessity so as to take help
from another; that my wife is what she is, so obedient, so affectionate,
and so simple; that I was well provided with suitable tutors for my
children. That I was granted assistance in dreams, especially how to
avoid spitting blood and fits of giddiness, and the answer of the
oracle at Caieta: 'Even as thou shalt employ thyself'; and that, al-

though in love with philosophy, I did not meet with any sophist or retire to disentangle literary works or syllogisms or busy myself with problems 'in the clouds.' For all these things require 'the gods to help and Fortune's hand.'

iii

5] Do not act unwillingly nor selfishly nor without self-examination, nor with divergent motives. Let no affection veneer your thinking. Be neither a busy talker nor a busybody. Moreover, let the God within be the guardian of a real man, a man of ripe years, a statesman, a Roman, a magistrate, who has taken his post like one waiting for the Retreat to sound, ready to depart, needing no oath nor any man as witness. And see that you have gladness of face, no need of service from without nor the peace that other men bestow. You should stand upright, not be held upright.

* * *

9] Reverence your faculty of judgment. On this it entirely rests that your governing self no longer has a judgment disobedient to Nature and to the estate of a reasonable being. This judgment promises deliberateness, familiar friendship with men, and to follow in the train of the gods.

* * *

11] To the above supports let one more be added. Always make a figure or outline of the imagined object as it occurs, in order to see distinctly what it is in its essence, naked, as a whole and parts; and say to yourself its individual name and the names of the things of which it was compounded and into which it will be broken up. For nothing is so able to create greatness of mind as the power methodically and truthfully to test each thing that meets one in life, and always to look upon it so as to attend at the same time to the use which his particular thing contributes to a Universe of a certain definite kind, what value it has in reference to the Whole, and what to man, who is a citizen of the highest City, whereof all other cities are like households. What is this which now creates an image in me, what is its composition, how long will it naturally continue, what virtue is of use to meet it; for example, gentleness, fortitude, truth, good faith, simplicity, self-reliance and the rest? Therefore, in each case, we must say: this has come from God; this by the actual co-ordination of events, the complicated web and similar coincidence or chance;

this again from my fellow man, my kinsman, my comrade, yet one does not know what is natural for himself. But I do know; wherefore I use him kindly and justly, according to the natural law of fellow-ship, aiming, however, at the same time at his desert, where the question is morally indifferent.

v

33] In how short a time, ashes or a bare anatomy, and either a name or not even a name; and if a name, then a sound and an echo. And all that is prized in life empty, rotten and petty; puppies biting one another, little children quarrelling, laughing and then soon crying. And Faith, Self-respect, Right and Truth

> 'fled to Olympus from the spacious earth.'

What, then, still keeps one here, if the sensible is ever-changing, never in one stay, the senses blurred and subject to false impressions; the soul itself an exhalation from blood, and a good reputation in such conditions vanity? What shall we say? Wait in peace, whether for extinction or a change of state; and until its due time arrives, what is sufficient? What else than to worship and bless the gods, to do good to men, to bear them and to forbear; and, for all that lies within the limits of mere flesh and spirit, to remember that this is neither yours nor in your power?

34] You are able always to have a favourable tide, if you are able to take a right path, if, that is, you are able both to conceive and to act with rectitude. These two things are common to God's soul and to man's, that is, to the soul of every reasonable creature: not to be subject to another's hindrance, to find his good in righteous act and disposition, and to terminate his desire in what is right.

vi

30] Take heed not to be transformed into a Caesar, not to be dipped in the purple dye; for it does happen. Keep yourself therefore simple, good, pure, grave, unaffected, the friend of justice, religious, kind, affectionate, strong for your proper work. Wrestle to continue to be the man Philosophy wished to make you. Reverence the gods, save men. Life is brief; there is one harvest of earthly existence, a holy disposition and neighbourly acts. In all things like a pupil of Antoninus; his energy on behalf of what was done in accord with reason.

his equability everywhere, his serene expression, his sweetness, his disdain of glory, his ambition to grasp affairs. . . .

* * *

47] Watch and see the courses of the stars as if you ran with them, and continually dwell in mind upon the changes of the elements into one another; for these imaginations wash away the foulness of life on the ground.

48] Moreover, when discoursing about mankind, look upon earthly things below as if from some place above them — herds, armies, farms, weddings, divorces, births, deaths, noise of law courts, lonely places, divers foreign nations, festivals, mournings, market places, a mixture of everything and an order composed of contraries.

49] Behold the past, the many changes of dynasties; the future too you are able to foresee, for it will be of like fashion, and it is impossible for the future to escape from the rhythm of the present. Therefore to study the life of man for forty years is no different from studying it for a hundred centuries. For what more will you see?

viii

1] This also conduces to contempt of vainglory, that it is no longer in your power to have lived your whole life, or at any rate your life from manhood, in the pursuit of philosophy. To yourself as well as to many others it is plain that you fall far short of philosophy. And so you are tainted, and it is no longer easy for you to acquire the reputation of a philosopher. Your calling too in life has a rival claim. Therefore, if you have truly seen where the matter at issue lies, put away the question of what men will think of you and be satisfied if you live the rest of your life, be it more or less, as your nature wills. Consider accordingly what it does will, and let nothing besides distract you; for experience has taught you in how many paths you have strayed and nowhere found the good life: not in logical arguments, not in riches, not in glory, not in self-indulgence, nowhere. Where then is it to be found? In doing what man's nature requires. How then will he do this? If he hold fast doctrines upon which impulses and actions depend. What doctrines are these? They concern good and evil, how nothing is good for man which does not make him just, sober, brave and free; nothing evil which does not produce effects the opposite of these.

2] On the occasion of each act ask yourself: 'How is this related to me? Shall I repent of it? But a little while and I am dead and all

things are taken away. What more do I require, if my present work
is the work of an intelligent and social creature, subject to the same
law as God?'

3] Alexander, Julius Caesar and Pompeius, what are they by comparison with Diogenes, Heraclitus and Socrates? For these men saw
reality and its causal and material aspects, and their ruling selves
were self-determined; but as for the former, how much there was to
provide for, and of how many things they were the servants.

4] Even if you break your heart, none the less they will do just the
same.

5] In the first place, be not troubled; for all things are according to
Universal Nature, and in a little while you will be no one and nowhere, even as Hadrian and Augustus are no more. Next, looking
earnestly at the question, perceive its essence, and reminding yourself
that your duty is to be a good man, and what it is that man's nature
demands, do that without swerving, and speak the thing that appears
to you to be most just, provided only that it is with kindness and
modesty and without hypocrisy.

6] The work of Universal Nature is this: to transfer what is here to
there, to make changes, to take up from here and to carry there. All
things are alterations, but the assignments too are impartial: all
things are familiar, but not so that we need dread some new experience.

*   *   *

8] You are not able to read; but you are able to restrain your arro-
gance, you are able to rise above pleasures and pains, you are able to
be superior to fame, you are able not only not to be angry with the
unfeeling and graceless, but to care for them besides.

9] Let no one any longer hear you finding fault with your life in a
palace; nay, do not even hear yourself.

10] Regret is blame of oneself for having let something useful go
by; but the good must be something useful and worth the attention
of a really good man. Now no really good man would regret having
let a pleasure go by: no pleasure, therefore, is either useful or good.

*   *   *

50] The cucumber is bitter? Put it down. There are brambles in the
path? Step to one side. That is enough, without also asking: 'Why did
these things come into the world at all?' Because the student of Nature will ridicule the question, exactly as a carpenter or cobbler would
laugh at you if you found fault because you see shavings and clip-

pings from their work in their shops. Still, they do have a place to throw rubbish into, whereas Universal Nature has nothing outside herself, and yet the astonishing thing in *her* way of working is that, having fixed her own limits, she is ever changing into herself everything within those limits that looks as though it were going bad and getting old and useless, and out of these things creating again others that are young, in order that she may need no substance from outside nor require any place to throw away what begins to decay. Thus she is satisfied with her own room, her own material and her own way of working.

ix

1] Whosoever does injustice commits sin; for Universal Nature having made reasonable creatures for the sake of one another, to benefit each other according to desert but in no wise to do injury, manifestly he who transgresses her will sins against the most venerable of the gods, because Universal Nature is a nature of what is, and what is is related to all that exists.

And further, he who lies sins in regard to the same divine being, and she is named Truth and is the first cause of all truths. Now he who lies voluntarily commits sin in so far as by deceit he does injustice, and he who lies involuntarily sins, in so far as he is discordant with Universal Nature and creates disorder by fighting against the natural order of the Universe; for he who is carried of himself counter to truth does so fight, since he had before received from Nature aptitudes by neglecting which he is now not able to distinguish falsehood from truth.

Moreover, he who runs after pleasures as goods and away from pains as evils commits sin; for being such a man he must necessarily often blame Universal Nature for distributing to bad and good contrary to their desert, because the bad are often employed in pleasures and acquire what may produce these, while the good are involved in pain and in what may produce this.

And further, he who fears pains will sometimes fear what is to come to pass in the Universe, and this is at once sinful, while he who pursues pleasures will not abstain from doing injustice, and this is plainly sinful. But those who wish to follow Nature, being likeminded with her, must be indifferent towards the things to which she is indifferent, for she would not create both were she not indifferent to pain and pleasure, death and life, honour and dishonour, which Universal Nature employs indifferently, plainly commits sin.

And by 'Universal Nature employing these indifferently,' I mean
that in the natural order they happen indifferently to what comes to
pass and follows upon an original impulse of Providence, whereby
from an original cause it had an impulse to this world order, having
conceived certain principles of what should come to be, and appointed powers generative of substances and changes and successions
of the like kind.

*   *   *

22] Make haste to your own governing self, to that of the Whole,
and that of this man. To your own, to make it a righteous mind; to
that of the Whole, to remind yourself what it is of which you are a
part; to this man's that you may observe whether it is ignorance or
design, and may reflect at the same time that his self is of one kind
with your own.

23] As you are yourself a complement of a social system, so let every
act of yours be complementary of a social living principle. Every act
of yours, therefore, which is not referred directly or remotely to the
social end sunders your life, does not allow it to be a unity, and is a
partisan act, like a man in a republic who for his own part sunders
himself from the harmony of his fellows.

x

1] Wilt thou one day, my soul, be good, simple, single, naked,
plainer to see than the body surrounding thee? Wilt thou one day
taste a loving and devoted disposition? Wilt thou one day be filled
and without want, craving nothing and desiring nothing, animate or
inanimate, for indulgence in pleasures; not time wherein longer to
indulge thyself, nor happy situation of place or room or breezes nor
harmony of men? Wilt thou rather be satisfied with present circumstance and pleased with all the present, and convince thyself that all
is present for thee from the gods and all is well for thee and will be
well whatsoever is dear to them to give and whatsoever they purpose
to bestow for the sustenance of the perfect living creature, the good
and just and beautiful, which begets, sustains, includes and embraces
all things that are being resolved into the generation of others like
themselves? Wilt thou one day be such as to dwell in the society of
gods and men so as neither to find fault at all with them nor to be
condemned by them?

2] Observe what your nature requires in so far as you are governed
by mere physical nature; then do that and accept that, if only your

nature as part of the animal world will not be rendered worse. Next you are to observe what your nature as part of the animal world requires and to take it all, if only your nature as a reasonable being will not be rendered worse. But what is reasonable is consequently also social. Make use then of these rules and do not be troubled about anything besides.

3] Every event happens in such a way that your nature can either support it or cannot. If then it happens so that your nature can support it, do not complain but support it as it is your nature to do; but if so that your nature cannot support it, do not complain, for it will destroy you quickly. Remember, however, that your nature can support everything which it is in the power of your own judgment to make tolerable and endurable by representing to yourself that to do this is to your advantage or is your duty.

* * *

11] Acquire a methodical insight into the way all things change, one into another; attend continually to this part of Nature and exercise yourself in it, for nothing is so likely to promote an elevation of mind. He has put off the body and, reflecting that he will be bound almost at once to leave all these things behind and to depart from men, he has devoted his whole self to justice in what is being accomplished by himself, and to Universal Nature in what comes to pass otherwise. And he spends no thought about what someone may say or think about him or do against him, but is contented with these two things, if he is himself acting justly in what is done in the present, and he has put away every preoccupation and enthusiasm, and has no other will than to pursue a straight path according to the law and, pursuing it, to follow in God's train.

* * *

15] Small is this balance of life left to you. Live as on a height; for here or there matters nothing, if everywhere one lives in the Universe, as in a city. Let men see, let them study a true man, a man who lives in accord with Nature. If they cannot bear him, let them kill him, for it were better so than for him to live on those terms.

* * *

25] He who runs away from his master is a fugitive slave. But law is a master and therefore the transgressor of law is a fugitive slave. In the same way, also, he who gives way to sorrow or anger or fear, wishes that something had not been or were not now, or should not be hereafter, of what is appointed by that which ordains all things; and that is law, laying down for every man what falls to his lot. He therefore who yields to fear or pain or anger is a fugitive slave.

xi

1] The properties of the rational soul: it is conscious of itself, it moulds itself, makes of itself whatever it will, the fruit which it bears it gathers itself (whereas others gather the fruits of the field and what in animals corresponds to fruit), it achieves its proper end, wherever the close of life comes upon it; if any interruption occur, its whole action is not rendered incomplete as is the case in the dance or a play and similar arts, but in every scene of life and wherever it may be overtaken, it makes what it proposed to itself complete and entire, so that it can say: 'I have what is my own.'

Moreover, it goes over the whole Universe and the surrounding void and surveys its shape, reaches out into the boundless extent of time, embraces and ponders the periodic rebirth of the Whole and understands that those who come after us will behold nothing new nor did those who come before us behold anything greater, but in a way the man of forty years, if he have any understanding at all, has seen all that has been and that will be by reason of its uniformity. A property too of the rational soul is love of one's neighbour, truth, self-reverence and to honour nothing more than itself; and this last is a property of law also; accordingly right principle and the principle of justice differ not at all.

NOTE

1. Antoninus Pius.

14

Christianity and the Empire

TERTULLIAN of Carthage (ca. A.D. 150–220) renounced paganism for a particularly ascetic type of Christianity, which eventually caused him to be accused as a heretic. He is generally acknowledged as the most creative and eloquent Christian writer before St. Augustine. Extremely learned, fiery, and argumentative, he produced many metaphysical works defining his own Christian theology as well as treatises explaining Christianity to the pagans and defending it against false allegations. His Apology, written in 197, is the greatest of his works in defense of Christianity. Using language not unworthy of Cicero and drawing upon a profound first-hand knowledge of pagan society and culture, he brilliantly rebutted the charges commonly leveled at the Christians: that they practiced cannibalism and incest and that they were disloyal. Tertullian's defense against the charge of subversion, a selection from which is given below, is an important statement of Christian principles made on the eve of the great persecutions of the third century.

Tertullian, Apology, I, 4-7, 10-13; II, 1-3, 6-8; IV, 1-2; VII, 1-5, 13-14; IX, 1-4, 16-20; X, 1-2; XXV, 1-9, 15-17; XXVII, 1-3; XXVIII, 3-4; XXX, 1-7; XXXI, 1-3; XXXII, 1; XXXIII, 1-4; XXXV, 5-10

i

4] THIS THEN, is the first grievance we lodge against you, the injustice of the hatred you have for the name of Christian. The motive which appears to excuse this injustice is precisely that which both aggravates and convicts it; namely, ignorance. For, what is more unjust than that men should hate what they do not know, even though the matter itself deserves hatred? Only when one knows whether a thing deserves hatred does it deserve it.

From Sister Emily Joseph Daly, C.S.J., trans., APOLOGETICAL WORKS OF TERTULLIAN AND MINUCIUS FELIX OCTAVIUS (Washington, 1950), FATHERS OF THE CHURCH, vol. 10, pp. 8–12, 17–18, 25–26, 28, 30–31, 34–35, 77–82, 84–89, 91–93. Reprinted by permission of The Catholic University of America Press.

5] But, when there is no knowledge of what is deserved, how is the justice of hatred defensible? Justice must be proved not by the fact of a thing's existence, but by knowledge of it. When men hate because they are in ignorance of the nature of the object in their hatred, what is to prevent that object from being such that they ought not to hate it? Thus we counterbalance each attitude by its opposite: men remain in ignorance as long as they hate, and they hate unjustly as long as they remain in ignorance.

6] The proof of their ignorance, which condemns while it excuses their injustice, is this: In the case of all who formerly indulged in hatred [of Christianity] because of their ignorance of the nature of what they hated, their hatred comes to an end as soon as their ignorance ceases. From this group come the Christians, as a result, assuredly, of their personal experience. They begin now to hate what once they were and to profess what once they hated; and the Christians are really as numerous as you allege us to be.

7] Men cry that the city is filled with Christians; they are in the country, in the villages, on the islands; men and women, of every age, of every state and rank of life, are transferring to this group, and this they lament as if it were some personal injury.

* * *

10] 'But,' says one, 'a thing is not considered good simply because it wins many converts: How great a number of men are given thorough training for evil! How many go astray into ways of perversity!' Who denies that? Yet, if a thing is really evil, not even those whom it attracts dare to defend it as good. All evil is drenched with fear or shame by nature.

11] For example, evil-doers are anxious to remain in hiding. They shun the light. They tremble when caught; they deny when accused. Even under torture they do not easily or always confess. When condemned beyond all hope, they lament. They tell of the attacks upon themselves of an evil spirit; their moral weaknesses they impute to fate or to the stars. What they recognize as evil they do not want to acknowledge as their own.

12] In what respect is the Christian like this? No one of them is ashamed, no one has any regrets, except that he was not a Christian earlier. If a charge is brought against him, he glories in it. If he is accused, he offers no defense. When questioned, he confesses of his own accord. For the word of condemnation he gives thanks.

13] What kind of evil is this that has none of the natural signs of evil — fear, shame, subterfuge, repentance, lament? What crime is this for which the accused rejoices, when the accusation is the object of his prayer and the condemnation his joy? *You* cannot call this madness, you who stand convicted of knowing nothing about it.

ii

1] If, then, it is decided that we are the most wicked of men, why do you treat us so differently from those who are on a par with us, that is, from all other criminals? The same treatment ought to be meted out for the same crime.

2] When others are charged with the same crimes as we, they use their own lips and the hired eloquence of others to prove their innocence. There is full liberty given to answer the charge and to cross-question, since it is unlawful for men to be condemned without defense or without a hearing.

3] Christians alone are permitted to say nothing that would clear their name, vindicate the truth, and aid the judge to come to a fair decision. One thing only is what they wait for; this is the only thing necessary to arouse public hatred: the confession of the name of Christian, not an investigation of the charge.

* * *

6] On the other hand, we find that it has been forbidden to search us out. For when Pliny the Younger was in charge of his province and had condemned certain Christians and had driven others from their established position, he was so disturbed because of the numbers involved that he consulted Trajan, emperor at the time, as to what he should do thereafter. He explained that, except for their obstinate refusal to offer sacrifice, he had learned nothing else about their religious rites except that they met before daybreak to sing to Christ and to God and to bind themselves by oath to a way of life which forbade murder, adultery, dishonesty, treachery, and all other crimes.

7] Trajan wrote back that men of this kind should not be sought out, but, when brought to court, they should be punished.

8] Oh, how unavoidably ambiguous was that decision! He says that they should not be sought — as though they were innocent; then prescribes that they should be punished — as though they were guilty! He spares them, yet vents his anger upon them; he pretends to close his eyes, yet directs attention toward them! Judgment, why do you thus ensnare yourself? If you condemn them, why not also search for them? If you do not search for them, why not also acquit them?

iv

1] Now that I have set down these remarks as a preface, as it were, to stigmatize the injustice of the public hatred against us, I shall refute the charges which are brought against us, but I shall even hurl them back upon those who make them, so that men may thereby know that among the Christians those crimes do not exist which they are not unaware exist among themselves; and that, at the same time, they may blush when, as utter reprobates, they accuse — I do not say the most righteous of men — but, as they themselves would have it, their equals.

2] We shall reply to each charge individually: to those which we are said to commit in secret, and to those which we are found to be committing before the eyes of all — charges on the basis of which we are held to be criminals, deceivers, reprobates, and objects of ridicule.

vii

1] We are spoken of as utter reprobates and are accused of having sworn to murder babies and to eat them and of committing adulterous acts after the repast. Dogs, you say, the pimps of darkness, overturn candles and procure license for our impious lusts.

2] We are always spoken of in this way, yet you take no pains to bring into the light the charges which for so long a time have been made against us. Now, either bring them into the light, if you believe them, or stop believing them, inasmuch as you have not brought them to light! Because of your hypocrisy, the objection is made against you that the evil does not exist which you yourselves dare not bring to light. Far different is the duty you enjoin upon the executioner against the Christians, not to make them state what they do, but to make them deny what they are.

3] The origin of this religion, as we have already said, dates from the time of Tiberius. Truth and hatred came into existence simultaneously. As soon as the former appeared, the latter began its enmity. It has as many foes as there are outsiders, particularly among Jews because of their jealousy, among soldiers because of their blackmailing, and even among the very members of our own household because of corrupt human nature.

4] Day by day we are besieged; day by day we are betrayed; oftentimes, in the very midst of our meetings and gatherings, we are surprised by an assault.

5] Who has ever come upon a baby wailing, as the accusation has it? Who has ever kept for the judge's inspection the jaws of Cyclopes and Sirens, bloodstained as he had found them? Who has ever found any traces of impurity upon [Christian] wives? Who has discovered such crimes, yet concealed them or been bribed to keep them secret when dragging these men off to court? If we always keep under cover, whence the betrayal of our crimes?

* * *

13] It is well that time brings all things to light, as even your own proverbs and sayings testify, in accordance with the design of nature which has so ordained things that nothing remains a secret for long, even though rumor has not spread it abroad.

14] Rightly, then, is rumor alone for so long a time aware of the crimes of Christians; this is the witness you bring forth against us. What it has sometime or other spread abroad and over such an interval of time hardened into a matter of opinion, it has not yet been able to prove, so that I call upon the steadfastness of nature itself against those who assume that such accusations are credible.

ix

1] To refute these points at greater length, I will point out that you yourselves commit these very crimes — sometimes openly, sometimes secretly — and that, perhaps, is the reason why you have believed them also of us.

2] In Africa, babies used to be sacrificed publicly to Saturn even down to the pro-consulate of Tiberius. He impaled the priests themselves on the very trees overshadowing their temple. The crosses were votive offerings to expiate their crimes. As witness of this there is the army of my own country, which performed this task for this very proconsul.

3] Even now this holy crime is continued in secret. Christians are not alone in despising you; no crime is wiped out forever, or else some god is changing his ways.

4] Since Saturn did not spare his own sons, surely he did not insist on sparing the children of others, who, for example, were offered to him by their very own parents. They gladly complied and they fondled their babies so that they would not be crying when they were sacrificed. Yet, there is considerable difference between murder and parricide!

* * *

16] Another point — Who are more expert at practising incest than those whom Jupiter himself has instructed? Ctesias relates that the Persians have intercourse with their own mothers. The Macedonians, too, were suspected of it because, the first time they attended the tragedy of *Oedipus,* they mocked the grief of the incestuous son, saying: 'He lay with his mother!'

17] Well, now! Consider how great chance there is for incestuous unions occasioned by mistaken identity. The promiscuousness of your wanton living affords the opportunity. In the first place, you expose your children to be taken up by some passerby out of the pity of a stranger's heart; or you release them from your authority to be adopted by better parents. Sooner or later, the memory of the alienated family necessarily fades away. As soon as a mistake has occurred, the transmission of incest goes on, the stock spreading together with its crime.

18] Finally, then, wherever you are, at home, abroad, across the sea, your lust travels as your companion, and its outbursts everywhere — or even some slight indulgence — can easily beget children for you any place at all, though you may not know it. The result is that a brood thus scattered through illicit human intercourse may fall in with its own kindred and in blind ignorance fail to recognize it as begotten of incestuous blood.

19] As for us, an ever-watchful and steadfast chastity shields us from such an occurrence and, in so far as we refrain from adultery and every excess after marriage, we are safe, too, from the danger of incest. Some are even more secure, since they ward off the entire violence of this error by virginal continence, and as old men are still [as pure as] boys.

20] If you would realize that these sins exist among yourselves, then you would perceive clearly that they do not exist among Christians. The same eyes would tell you the facts in both cases. But, a two-fold blindness easily imposes itself, so that those who do not see what

does exist seem to see what does not. I will point out that this is true
in everything. Now I will speak of the more manifest crimes.

x

1] 'You do not worship the gods,' you say, 'and you do not offer
sacrifice for the emperors.' It follows that we do not offer sacrifices
for others for the same reason that we do not do it even for ourselves
— it follows immediately from our not worshipping the gods. Consequently, we are considered guilty of sacrilege and treason. This is
the chief accusation against us — in fact, it is the whole case — and
it certainly deserves investigation, unless presumption and injustice
dictate the decision, the one despairing of the truth, the other refusing
it.

2] We cease worshipping your gods when we find out that they are
non-existent. This, then, is what you ought to demand, that we prove
that those gods are non-existent and for that reason should not be
worshipped, because they ought to be worshipped only if they were
actually gods. Then, too, the Christians ought to be punished if the
fact were established that those gods do exist whom they will not
worship because they consider them non-existent.

xxv

1] It seems to me that I certainly have given sufficient proof of [the
difference between] false and true divinity, now that I have pointed
out how the proof depends not merely on discussion and argument,
but also on the spoken testimony of those very ones whom you believe to be gods; so that there is no necessity of adding anything
further to this topic.

2] However, since we made particular mention of the name of
Rome, I will not avoid the issue which is provoked by that presumption on the part of those who say that the Romans, as a result of their
painstaking, scrupulous, religious observance, have been exalted to
such sublime heights that they have become masters of the world;
and that, in consequence, their gods have brought it about that
those surpass all others in prosperity who surpass all others in
devotion to their deity.

3] You may be sure that the price was paid by the Roman gods to
the name of Rome for the favor: Sterculus, Mutunus, and Larentina
have exalted the Roman Empire. For, I would not expect gods from
abroad to have been willing to do more for a race of foreigners than

for their own, or to have surrendered to a race from across the sea their native soil where they were born, grew up, gained renown, and were buried.

4] Let Cybele account for it if she so ardently loved the city of Rome as the memorial of the race of Trojans who were, as you know, born and bred in her service, and whom she protected against the arms of the Greeks — if she looked forward to the prospect of going over to the avengers of Troy, knowing as she did that they would one day subdue Greece, the conqueror of Phrygia!

5] Why, even in our own day she has offered strong proof of the exalted dignity she conferred on our city. On March 17, near Sirmium, Marcus Aurelius was lost to the state. On the 24th of the same month, the most devoted archigallus, after slashing his arms, offered his own impure blood in sacrifice and then proceeded to issue the usual recommendation to pray for the welfare of the Emperor Marcus — though death had already carried him off!

6] O tardy messengers, O sleepy dispatches! It was your fault that Cybele did not learn earlier of the demise of the emperor. Indeed, the Christians might well laugh at such a goddess!

7] Jupiter, too, should not have allowed his Crete to be immediately shattered by the Roman fasces, forgetting the familiar Idaean cave and the bronze cymbals of the Corybantes and the highly delightful odor of his nurse there! Would he not have preferred that grave of his there to the entire Capitol, so that that land which covered the ashes of Jupiter might rather be pre-eminent in the world?

8] And would Juno want her beloved Punic city, 'preferred to Samos,' wiped out, particularly by the race of Aeneas? As far as I know, 'Here were her arms, here her chariot; that this should be the realm of all peoples was the plan which the goddess was even then cherishing and fostering, should the fates allow.' This poor soul, 'spouse and sister of Jupiter,' had no power against the Fates! It is certainly true that 'On Fate depends Jupiter himself.'

9] Yet, the Romans did not surrender so much of their honor to the Fates which yielded Carthage to them, contrary to the design and prayer of Juno, as they did to that most wanton of prostitutes, Larentina.

*　　*　　*

15] The sacrileges of the Romans are as numerous as their trophies; their triumphs over the gods as many as those over nations; there is as much plunder as there are statues of the captured gods still on hand.

16] The gods, therefore, endure being adored by their enemies and decree 'empire without end' to those whose offences they should have requited, rather than their servile fawning. However, the injury of those who are devoid of feeling is as free from punishment as the worship of them is devoid of significance.

17] Certainly, the assumption cannot harmonize with truth that those people seem to have attained greatness on the merits of their religious service who, as we have pointed out, have either grown by giving offence to religion or have given offence by their growth. Even those whose realms were melted into the sum total of the Roman Empire were not devoid of religious attitudes when they lost their power.

xxvii

1] Enough has been said to refute the charge of intending to offend divinity, since it cannot seem that we are offending that which we have shown does not exist. Therefore, when called upon to sacrifice, we take a firm stand against it because of the conviction of our knowledge, whereby we are certain whose services they are which reach us under the shameful misuse of images and the consecration of human names.

2] Some think it madness that, when we could offer sacrifice here and now and then go away unpunished, preserving the same attitude of mind as before, we prefer to be obstinate rather than safe.

3] You are, of course, offering advice whereby we may take advantage of you; but we realize the origin of such suggestions, who it is that prompts all this, and how at one time clever persuasion and then again harsh severity is employed to break down our perseverance.

xxviii

3] We have come, then, to the second charge alleged against us, that of offending a more august majesty. You pay your obeisance to Caesar with greater fear and craftier timidity than to Olympian Jupiter himself. And rightly so, if you but knew it! For, what living man — whoever he may be — is not more powerful than any of your dead ones?

4] But you do this, not for any logical reason, but out of regard for his manifest and perceptible power. In this point, too, it will be seen that you are lacking in religious feeling toward your gods, since you show more fear to a human lord. Finally, one is more ready among you to take a false oath by all the gods together than by the lone genius of Caesar.

xxx

1] For, in our case, we pray for the welfare of the emperors to the eternal God, the true God, the living God, whom even the emperors themselves prefer to have propitious to them before all other gods. They know who has given them power; they know — for they are men — who has given them life; they feel that He is the only God in whose power alone they are, commencing with whom they are second, after whom they stand first, who is before all and above all gods. Why not? — since they are above all men; since, as living being, they surpass, at any rate, the dead.

2] They consider to what extent power of empire avails and thus they come to understand God; against Him they cannot avail, through Him they do avail. Let the emperor [have a mind to] war against heaven, lead heaven in chains in his triumph, send his sentries to heaven, and on heaven impose his tax! He cannot do it.

3] So he is mighty, because he is less than heaven, for he is himself the property of Him to whom heaven and every creature belong. From Him comes the emperor, from whom came the man, also, before he became the emperor; from Him comes the emperor's power and his spirit as well.

4] Looking up to Him, we Christians — with hands extended, because they are harmless, with head bare because we are not ashamed, without a prayer leader because we pray from the heart — constantly beseech Him on behalf of all emperors. We ask for them long life, undisturbed power, security at home, brave armies, a faithful Senate, an upright people, a peaceful world, and everything for which a man or a Caesar prays.

5] Such petitions I cannot ask from any other save from Him, and I know that I shall obtain them from Him, since He is the only One who supplies them and I am one who ought to obtain my request. For, I am His servant; I alone worship Him; for His teaching I am put to death; I offer Him the rich — and better — sacrifice which He Himself has commanded, the prayer sent up from a chaste body, an innocent heart, and a spirit that is holy;

6] not grains of incense worth a mere penny, or tears of the

Arabic tree, or two drops of wine, or the blood of a worthless ox that is longing for death, and, in addition to all this filth, a polluted conscience — so that I wonder when, among you, victims are examined by the most vicious of priests, why it is the hearts of the slain animals are examined rather than those of the priests themselves.

7] So, then, as we kneel with arms extended to God, let the hooks dig into us, let the crosses suspend us, the fires lick up, the swords cut our throats, and wild beasts leap upon us: the very posture of a Christian in prayer makes him ready for every punishment. Carry on, good officials, torture the soul which is beseeching God on behalf of the emperor! Here will lie the crime, where there reigns truth and devotion to God!

xxxi

1] Well, now, we have been flattering the emperor and have lied about the prayers we said just to escape rough treatment! That ingenious idea of yours is certainly of advantage to us, for you permit us to prove whatever we allege in our defense. If you think that we have no interest in the emperor's welfare, look into our literature, the Word of God. We ourselves do not keep it concealed; in fact, many a chance hands it over to outsiders.

2] Learn from this literature that it has been enjoined upon us, that our charity may more and more abound, to pray to God even for our enemies, and to beg for blessings for our persecutors. Now, who are any greater enemies and persecutors of Christians than those on whose account we are charged with the crime of treason?

3] But it is clearly and expressly said: 'Pray for kings, for princes and for rulers, that all may be peaceful for you!' For, when the empire is shaken, and its other members are shaken, we, too, although we are considered outsiders by the crowd, are naturally involved in some part of the disaster.

xxxii

1] There is also another, even greater, obligation for us to pray for the emperors; yes, even for the continuance of the empire in general and for Roman interests. We realize that the tremendous force which is hanging over the whole world, and the very end of

the world with its threat of dreadful afflictions, is arrested for a time
by the continued existence of the Roman Empire. This event we have
no desire to experience, and, in praying that it may be deferred, we
favor the continuance of Rome.

xxxiii

1] Why should I say more about the respect and the loyalty of
Christians toward the emperor? We are under obligation to look up
to him as one whom our Lord has chosen. So, I might well say:
'Caesar belongs more to us, since he has been appointed by our
God.'

2] And so, as he is mine, I do more for his welfare, not only
because I pray for it to Him who can really grant it, or because I
am such that I deserve to be heard, but also because, as I set the dignity of Caesar below that of God, I commend him the more to God
to whom alone I subordinate him. However, I do subordinate him to
God; I do not make him His equal.

3] I will not call the emperor God, either because I do not know
how to lie, or because I dare not make fun of him, or because
even he himself does not want to be called God. If he is a man, it
is to his interest as a man to yield precedence to God. Let him consider it enough to be called emperor. That, indeed, is a title of
dignity which God has given him. One who says he is God says he
is not the emperor; unless he were a man he could not be emperor.

4] Why, even during his triumph, right in his lofty chariot, he is
reminded that he is a man. For, someone behind him whispers: 'Look
behind you! Remember you are a man!' And certainly, he rejoices
all the more in this, that he shines forth in such great glory that
he needs a reminder of his condition. He would be of less importance
were he then called 'God,' because it would not be true. He is of
greater importance who is called to look back, lest he think that
he is God.

xxxv

5] Now, on this question of religious worship rendered to a less
august majesty, the point on which action is brought against us
Christians as a second charge of sacrilege, inasmuch as we do not
celebrate with you the festivals of the emperors in a manner which
neither modesty, self-respect, nor virtue permits, a manner urged by

the opportunity for self-indulgence rather than any worthy motive — in this regard I would like to point out your loyalty and sincerity, in case here, too, those who want us to be considered not Romans, but enemies of the Roman emperors, may prove, perchance, to be worse than Christians.

6] It is the Romans themselves, the very people born and bred on the Seven Hills, that I arraign: does that Roman tongue spare any emperor of its own? As witness, there is the Tiber, and the training schools for wild beasts.

7] If only nature had enclosed our breasts with some kind of glass-like material to make them transparent, whose heart would not appear engraved with the scene of one new Ceasar after another presiding over the distribution of the dole, even in that hour when they shout in applause: 'From our years may Jupiter multiply for thee thine own!' A Christian can no more make such remarks than he can hope for a new emperor.

8] 'But, that's the rabble,' you say. Perhaps it is the rabble; still, they are Romans, and none is more clamorous in their demands for punishment of the Christians than the rabble. Yes, of course, the other classes of society are conscientiously loyal, as their position of authority requires. There is never a hostile whisper from the Senate, the knights, the camp, or the palace itself.

9] Whence come men like Cassius and Niger and Albinus? Whence, those who between the two laurels lay hands on Caesar? Whence, those who practise the art of wrestling in order to choke him to death? Whence, those who burst into the palace in arms, bolder than any Sigerius or Parthenius? From the ranks of the Romans, unless I am mistaken — that is, from among non-Christians.

10] And so, all of them, right until the very outbreak of their disloyalty, offered sacrifices for the well-being of the emperor and swore by his *genius,* some publicly, others privately; naturally, they gave Christians the name of public enemies.

15

Regimentation and Oppression

THE FOLLOWING documents are chosen to illustrate aspects of the great social and economic crisis that transformed the empire in the third century A.D. In section a the excerpts from Justinian's Digest, drawn largely from third-century edicts, describe the compulsory nature of services performed by municipal councilors, while a papyrus from the Egyptian town of Oxyrhynchus records a complaint to the bureaucracy by two privileged councilors who had illegally been nominated to the onerous posts of tax collectors. The first two inscriptions in section b are protests by peasants on imperial estates in Asia Minor against unlawful exactions and outrageous treatment they suffered at the hands of military and fiscal agents, while a third with similar complaints comes from villagers in Thrace. As the records show, the emperors, although well-meaning, were powerless to enforce regulations prohibiting corruption and oppression. The series of documents ends with section c, Diocletian's famous Edict on Maximum Prices of A.D. 301, a measure designed to control runaway inflation.

a Control of the Decurions

Justinian, Digest, *l, ii, 1 and 2, 8; iv, 1, 2; iv, 3, 15–16; iv, 4]*

THE GOVERNOR of the province shall see to it that decurions who are proved to have left the area of the municipality to which they belong and to have moved to other places are recalled to their native soil and perform the appropriate public services. . . .

Persons over fifty-five are forbidden by imperial enactments to be called to the position of decurion against their will, but if they do consent to this they ought to perform the duties, although if they are over seventy they are not compelled to assume compulsory municipal services. . . .

Municipal duties of a personal character are: representation of a

From N. Lewis and M. Reinhold, ROMAN CIVILIZATION (New York, 1955), vol. ii, pp. 446–447. Reprinted by permission of the Columbia University Press.

municipality, that is, becoming a public advocate, assignment to taking the census or registering property; secretaryships; camel transport; commissioner of food supply and the like, of public lands, of grain procurement, of water supply; horse races in the circus; paving of public streets; grain storehouses, heating of public baths; distribution of food supply; and other duties similar to these. From the above-mentioned, other duties can be deduced in accordance with the laws and long-established custom of each municipality. . . .

The governor of the province shall see to it that the compulsory public services and offices in the municipalities are imposed fairly and in rotation according to age and rank, in accordance with the gradation of public services and offices long ago established, so that the men and resources of municipalities are not inconsiderately ruined by frequent oppression of the same persons. If two sons are under parental power, the father is not compelled to support their public services at the same time. . . .

The care of constructing or rebuilding a public work in a municipality is a compulsory public service from which a father of five living children is excused; and if this service is forcibly imposed, this fact does not deprive him of the exemption that he has from other public services. The excusing of those with insufficient resources who are nominated to public services or offices is not permanent but temporary. For if a hoped-for increase comes to one's property by honorable means, when his turn comes an evaluation is to be made to determine whether he is suitable for the services for which he was chosen. . . . A person who is responsible for public services to his municipality and submits his name for military service for the purpose of avoiding the municipal burden cannot make the condition of his community worse.

Oxyrhynchus Papyrus]

To . . . , strategus of the Oxyrhynchite name,[1] from Aurelius Theon and Aurelius Arsinoüs, sons of Theon, Antinoïtes of the Sebasteian tribe and Dioscureian deme. In the previous cycle of the persons about to serve in the quarters of this city, the amphodogrammateus[2] then in office, Aurelius Sarapion, [ignoring our rights,]

From A. S. Hunt, trans. and ed., OXYRHYNCHUS PAPYRI (London, 1911), viii, no. 1119, pp. 207–209. Reprinted by permission of The Egyptian Exploration Society.

in the list of burdens submitted by him returned us for the collection
of money-taxes in the metropolis, and we immediately on receiving
information of it . . . did not acquiesce but applied to the most high
senate,[3] recounting the audacity and illegality of the said amphodogrammateus. The senate was indignant and sent to the most high
epistrategus[4] Antonius Alexander, who, heedful of the rights especially accorded to our native city, sent to the then strategus Aurelius
Dius also called Pertinax directing that the amphodogrammateus
should be compelled either to present some other persons instead
of us for the office, or [to pay the penalty for] his illegality. The
strategus sent the whole correspondence to the amphodogrammateus,
and he, being aware of the danger hanging over him in consequence
of his illegal action . . . , himself promised in amends for his error,
for which he pleaded the excuse of ignorance, to undertake the
burden for the future. Now, therefore, in order that the present
phylarch[5] may not appear to be ignorant of these facts . . . because
one of us, Aurelius Theon, is there in our native city attending to
the duties to which we have been assigned, since the turn has come
to our senate in the present year to . . . , we submit to you the following copies, begging that they may be communicated for his information by means of one of your assistants to Aurelius Heras, phylarch
of the quarters about to serve. The third year of the Emperors and
Caesars Gaius Vibius Trebonianus Gallus and Gaius Vibius Afinius
Gallus Veldumianus Volusianus Pii Felices Augusti, Mesore.[6] The
copies are as follows: —

The officials and senate of the illustrious city of the Antinoïtes,[7]
new Hellenes, to Antonius Alexander the most high epistrategus,
greeting. You are aware, highest of procurators, you who during
your procuratorship have been especially concerned with the exceptional rights claimed by our native city, that originally the deified
Hadrian . . . [distinguishing] it from the other cities in Egypt clearly
established the law that we should bear office and burdens nowhere
but at home, and we were relieved of all offices and burdens elsewhere; and next . . . his successors on the throne often confirmed
our immunity in this respect, and they have been scrupulously followed by the praefects[8] appointed from time to time and by you
the most high epistrategi, who not only release us from all external
offices and burdens but also punish the lawlessness of those who
attempt to offend against the Imperial legislation and the judgements of praefects. Whereas, then, Aurelius Theon and Aurelius

Arsinoüs . . . our fellow-citizens have approached us in a petition accusing Sarapion, amphodogrammateus of the city of Oxyrhynchus, of having illegally nominated them both for the collection of money-taxes in the metropolis, . . . we apply to your heedfulness in order that you may direct the strategus of the said nome to have one of two things done, namely that the amphodogrammateus, if he gives way, should nominate to the office other persons in their stead, or else [be compelled to] appear before you at your coming auspicious visit, in order that in accordance with the ancestral usages of our constitution he may render an account for his outrage upon the Imperial laws and the judgements of praefects . . . We pray for your health. The second year of the Marci Julii, Hathur 30th.[9]

Copy of the letter. Antonius Alexander to the strategus of the Oxyrhynchite nome, greeting. I have ordered the document sent me by the officials and senate of the illustrious city of the Antinoïtes, now Hellenes, to be appended for your information to this letter. See that the amphodogrammateus whom they accuse of having nominated to the office of collector members of their polity appear . . . to give an account for his defiance of the law, if he still attempts to subject them to the office as persons within his province. I pray for your health. The second year of the Marci Julii, Mecheir 3.[9]

Copy of the report. To Aurelius Dius also called Pertinax, strategus of the Oxyrhynchite nome, from Aurelius Sarapion, amphodogrammateus of the city of Oxyrhynchus. I received from you on Phamenoth the 1st a missive to which was appended a copy of a letter written to you by Antonius Alexander, the most high epistrategus, with an enclosure in the latter of the appeal made to him by the most high senate of the Antinoïtes on behalf of Aurelius Theon and Aurelius Arsinoüs, twins . . . , who were nominated by me for the collection of money-taxes in the metropolis, one of whom, Arsinoüs, . . . , directing that I should go down to appear before the most high epistrategus, if I still attempt to subject them to the burden as persons within our province. I have accordingly investigated the matter and found that they possess hereditary Antinoïte rights, and I immediately on learning this undertook the burden on their behalf; I accordingly make this report. The second year of the Marci Julii, Pharmouthi 13.[9]

Presented by us, Aurelius Theon and Aurelius Arsinoüs, sons of Theon.

Delivered by me, . . . 3rd year, Mesore 29 . . . pages 25–27.

b *Complaints of the Lower Classes*

In Asia Minor]

... THAT SOME defense of their impudence may seem left them,[1] they arrested nine, put them in bonds, and claimed that they were sending them to your most eminent procurators,[2] since the eminent Aelius Aglaus is performing the duties of the proconsulate too.[3] They exacted from one of the nine more than 1,000 Attic drachmae as a ransom for his safety and let him go, but they held the rest in bonds, and we do not know, most divine of emperors, whether they will bring them alive to the most eminent Aglaus or dispose of them too as they did the previous ones. And so we have done the one thing possible for unfortunates thus cruelly deprived of life and kin, and the one thing possible for us: we have informed your procurator in charge of the police,[4] Aurelius Marcianus, and your most eminent procurators in Asia. We are suppliants, most divine of emperors that have ever been, of your divine and unsurpassable kingship; we beg you to attend to the trials of the estates since we are hindered by the threats of the *colletiones*[5] and their representatives to put us too, who are left, in danger of our lives, and because of their obstruction cannot work the land or meet payments and obligations to our lords in the immediate future. We petition you to favor our request and command the governor of our people and your most eminent procurators to exact justice for this wrong, and to forbid entrance to the imperial estates and the resulting annoyance to us by both the *colletiones* and those, who under pretext of public offices and liturgies, annoy and vex your farmers, since the first right to accounting on all that we have inherited from our ancestors belongs to the most sacred imperial treasury by the law of the estates. For, to tell your divinity the truth, unless your heavenly right hand exact some justice for these wrongs and bring aid for the future, we who are left, unable to endure the greed of the *colletiones* and the ... on the pretexts aforesaid, must desert our ancestral homes and family tombs and move to private property to preserve ourselves (for wrongdoers are more inclined to spare the dwellers there than they are your farmers), and become exiles from the imperial estates where we have been engendered and

From T. S. Broughton, trans., and Tenney Frank, ed., AN ECONOMIC SURVEY OF ANCIENT ROME (Baltimore, 1938), vol. 4, pp. 657–658, 660–661. Reprinted by permission of The Johns Hopkins Press.

reared, where we have abode for generations, and as farmers fulfill our obligations to our lord's account.

* * *

With Good Fortune. The Emperor Caesar M. Julius Philippus Augustus and M. Julius Philippus, most noble Caesar,[6] to M. Aurelius Eglectus by Didymus, a centenary soldier of the secret police.[7] The most illustrious proconsul will look into the truth of what you charge and make it his care if any injurious practices are going on.

A petition to the Emperor Philip and the most noble Caesar Philip from Aurelius Eglectus concerning the commune of the Aragueni, your residents and farmers, who belong to the people and commune in the district of Appia of the Totteani Soeni, places in Phrygia, presented through the soldier, T. Ulpius Didymus. While all men in your most blessed times, most pious and blameless among rulers that have ever been, live calm and peaceful lives and all evildoing and oppression have ceased, we alone suffer things alien to these most fortunate times and address this petition to you. Our petition is contained in the following:

We are your estate, most sacred emperors, a people entire who flee for refuge and become suppliants of your divinity. We are being unreasonably oppressed and are suffering exactions at the hands of those who ought to preserve the public welfare. For although we happen to live inland and are not under military commanders, we suffer things alien to your most blessed times. Those who pass through the Appian region desert the travelled roads; the military commanders and the soldiers, the leaders among those eminent in the city, and your Caesarians[8] come in, deserting the travelled roads, take us away from our work, press our plough oxen into service, and exact what we do not owe them. As a result we are oppressed and suffer more than ordinary injustice. Once before we have had recourse, Augustus, to your majesty, when you administered the praetorian prefectship, informing you of what had happened. How your divine soul was disturbed about it the attached letter makes clear: 'We have sent the content of your petition to the proconsul who will see that you have no longer cause for complaint.' The result was that when our petition brought us no aid, we suffered exactions of things not due throughout the countryside, people coming upon us and trampling upon us unjustly; and likewise we have suffered more than ordinary oppression at the hands of the Caesarians, our goods have been expended upon them, and the states desolated and laid waste, for we live in the interior and do not dwell by the main road. . . .

In Thrace]

1] With Good Fortune.

December 15, in the consulship of Fulvius Pius and Pontius Proculus.[9]

This was copied and certified from the record of petitions and rescripts made by our Lord Emperor Caesar Marcus Antonius Gordian Pius Felix Augustus, which were posted at Rome in the portico of Trajan's Baths in the words that are recorded below. Given through Aurelius Pyrrhus, soldier of the tenth praetorian cohort Pia Felix Gordiana, who is a fellow villager and fellow landholder of Proculus.

2] To Emperor Caesar Marcus Antonius Gordian Pius Felix Augustus.

A petition from the villagers of Scaptopara, also known as Gresa.[10]

In your most prosperous and everlasting times you often have written that the villages should be settled and should thrive rather than that the inhabitants should be unsettled. For that contributes to the security of mankind and is an advantage to the most sacred fisc. Therefore, we convey to your Divinity a petition that is just when we pray you to assent graciously to our request, which follows.

We have our homes and our possessions in the aforesaid village, which is a desirable resort, because it has the advantage of hot springs and is accessible from the two army stations in Thrace. And while its inhabitants remained for years without being disturbed or troubled, they paid their taxes without fail and fulfilled their other obligations. But when from time to time some persons began to act insolently and to treat us with violence, the village began at once to decline. A well-known festival is celebrated within two miles of our village; and those persons who come to the festival, which lasts fifteen days, do not lodge there, but, leaving that place, come to our village and compel us to provide billets and much else besides for their entertainment without any recompense. In addition to these persons, soldiers also, although being dispatched to other places,

From A. C. Johnson, F. C. Bourne, and P. Coleman-Norton, ANCIENT ROMAN STATUTES, no. 287 (Austin, Tex., 1961). Reprinted by permission of the University of Texas Press and A. C. Johnson, F. C. Bourne, and P. Coleman-Norton.

leave their proper routes and, coming to us, in like manner compel us to provide billets and other necessities without paying for them. Not only the provincial governors, but also your procurators sojourn here, primarily for the enjoyment of the baths.

Now we entertain the higher magistrates almost continuously of necessity, but, since we cannot endure the others, we have appealed again and again to the governors of Thrace, and they in accordance with imperial orders have commanded that we shall be unmolested, for we have made it clear that we cannot endure it any longer, but we have it in mind even to abandon our ancestral hearths because of the violence of these invaders. And, as a matter of fact, we have been reduced from many householders to a very few. And the orders of the governors hold good for a little while and no one molests us either for demands for billets or for provision of food, but, as time passes, again they get the courage to fasten themselves on us in great numbers, as many as despise our simple civilian status.

Therefore, since we cannot longer bear these burdens and we who remain are really on the point of abandoning the homes of our forefathers, as the others have done, we beg this favor of you, unconquered Augustus, that by your godlike rescript you will compel every person to keep to the route prescribed for him and not, by leaving other villages, to invade our village nor to compel us to supply him with necessities gratuitously nor to provide billets for those persons who are not entitled to them, for the governors again and again have issued orders not to furnish billets except to those persons dispatched to us for official business by governors and procurators; and, if we continue to suffer these burdens, we shall flee from our homes and a very heavy loss will be inflicted upon the fisc; and we also entreat you that we may receive your pity and godlike consideration, so that we may be able to remain in our homes and to contribute to the sacred taxes and other levies. That will be our lot in this most felicitous age, if you give instructions that your godlike letter be engraved on stone and displayed in a public place, so that we who have received this boon by your good fortune will be able to acknowledge its receipt, just as we now do, though . . .

3] Diogenes of Tyre, the official agent, has come from the godlike benevolence for this petition. In my judgment some god foreordained this present request. It seems to me a stroke of good fortune that the most godlike emperor has granted that we refer the judicial investigation of these matters personally to you, a man who, he knew, had taken previous action about this problem by means of proclamation and edicts.

This is the petition. The village of the soldier who is being helped lies in the fairest part of our territory of Pataulia, well endowed with mountans and plains. Besides these, it has baths of hot waters, most suitable not only for luxurious living but also for health and healing of bodily ills. Nearby is a festival, where people gather frequently during the year, and around October 1 it enjoys freedom from taxes for a period of fifteen days. Accordingly, it has so happened that the seeming assets of this village have turned to liabilities. For the reasons that have just been cited, it frequently happens that many soldiers sojourn here and oppress the village with the exaction of living quarters and oppressive requisitions. As a result, the village, once prosperous and populous, has sunk now to extreme poverty. Although they have entreated the governors again and again, the governors' orders have held good for a little while, but afterward fell into utter neglect, because the soldiery had made a habit of such extortion. They, therefore, necessarily appealed to the most godlike emperor . . .

4] Emperor Caesar Marcus Antonius Gordian Pius Felix Augustus to the villagers through Pyrrhus, their fellow landowner.

This kind of complaint, offered with requests, you ought to bring before the governor's courts and to seek there a settlement about these matters that are alleged rather than a definite authorized regulation by an imperial rescript.

I have written it. I have certified it. Seals.

c   Control of Inflation

THAT THE fortune of our state — to which, after the immortal gods, as we recall the wars which we have successfully fought, we must be grateful for a world that is tranquil and reclining in the embrace of the most profound calm, and for the blessings of a peace that was won with great effort — be faithfully disposed and suitably adorned, is the demand of public opinion and the dignity and majesty of Rome; therefore, we, who by the gracious favor of the gods have repressed the former tide of ravages of barbarian nations by destroying them, must guard by the due defences of justice a

From Tenney Frank, trans. and ed., AN ECONOMIC SURVEY OF ANCIENT ROME (Baltimore, 1940), vol. 5, pp. 310–317. Reprinted by permission of The Johns Hopkins Press.

peace which was established for eternity. If, indeed, any self-restraint might check the excesses with which limitless and furious avarice rages — avarice which with no thought for mankind hastens to its own gain and increase, not by years or months or days but by hours and even minutes — ; or, if the general welfare could endure undisturbed the riotous license by which it, in its misfortune, is from day to day most grievously injured, there would perhaps be left some room for dissimulation and silence, since human forbearance might alleviate the detestable cruelty of a pitiable situation. Since, however, it is the sole desire of unrestrained madness to have no thought for the common need and since it is considered among the unscrupulous and immoderate almost the creed of avarice, swelling and rising with fiery passions, to desist from ravaging the wealth of all through necessity rather than its own wish; and since those whom extremes of need have brought to an appreciation of their most unfortunate situation can no longer close their eyes to it, we — the protectors of the human race — viewing the situation, have agreed that justice should intervene as arbiter, so that the long-hoped-for solution which mankind itself could not supply might, by the remedies of our foresight, be applied to the general betterment of all. Common knowledge recognizes and the facts themselves proclaim how nearly too late our provision for this situation is, while we were laying plans or reserving remedies already devised, in the hope that as was to be expected through the laws of nature — mankind, apprehended in the most serious offenses, might reform itself, for we think it far better that the stains of intolerable depredation be removed from men's minds by the feeling and decision of the same men whom, as they daily plunged into more and more serious offenses and turned, in their blindness, to crimes against the state, their grievous iniquity had charged with most cruel inhumanity, the enemies of individual and state. We, therefore, hasten to apply the remedies long demanded by the situation, satisfied that there can be no complaints that the intervention of our remedy may be considered untimely or unnecessary, or trivial or unimportant among the unscrupulous who, in spite of perceiving in our silence of so many years a lesson in restraint, have been unwilling to copy it. For who is so insensitive and so devoid of human feeling that he cannot know, or rather, has not perceived, that in the commerce carried on in the markets or involved in the daily life of cities immoderate prices are so widespread that the uncurbed passion for gain is lessened neither by abundant supplies nor by fruitful years; so that without a doubt men who are busied in these affairs constantly plan actually to control the very winds and weather from the movements of the stars, and, evil as they are, they cannot endure the watering of the fertile fields by the rains from above which bring the hope of future harvests, since they reckon it their own loss if abundance comes through the moderation of the weather. And the men whose aim it always is to profit even from the generosity of the gods, to restrain general prosperity, and furthermore to use a poor year to traffic in harvest (?) losses and agents' services — men who, individually abounding in great riches which could completely satisfy whole nations, try to capture smaller fortunes and strive after ruinous percentages — concern for humanity in general persuades us to set a limit, our subjects, to the avarice of such men. But even now we must detail the facts whose urgency after long delay has finally driven our tolerance to action, in order that — although it is difficult for the avarice which rages throughout the whole world to be described by a specific illustration or, rather, fact — nevertheless, the establishment of a remedy may be considered more just when utterly unrestrained men are forced by some sign and token to recognize the untamed desires of their own minds. Who, therefore, does not know that insolence, covertly attacking the public welfare — wherever the public safety demands that our armies be directed, not in villages or towns only, but on every road — comes to the mind of the profiteer to extort prices for merchandise, not fourfold or eightfold, but such that human speech is incapable of describing either the price or the act; and finally that sometimes in a single purchase a soldier is deprived of his bonus and salary, and that the contribution of the whole world to support the armies falls to the abominable profits of thieves, so that our soldiers seem with their own hands to offer the hopes of their service and their completed labors to the profiteers, with the result that the pillagers of the nation constantly seize more than they know how to hold. Aroused justly and rightfully by all the facts which are detailed above, and with mankind itself now appearing to be praying for release, we have decreed that there be established, not the prices of articles for sale — for such an act would be unjust when many provinces occasionally rejoice in the good fortune of wished-for low prices and, so to speak, the privilege of prosperity —, but a maximum, so that when the violence of high prices appears anywhere — may the gods avert such a calamity! — avarice which, as if in immense open areas, could not be restrained, might be checked by the limits of our statute or by the boundaries of a regulatory law. It is our pleasure, therefore, that the prices listed in the subjoined summary be observed in the whole of our empire in such fashion that every man may know that while permission to exceed them has been forbidden him, the blessing of low prices has in no case been restricted in those places where supplies are seen to abound, since special provision is made for these when avarice is definitely quieted. Moreover, among buyers and sellers who customarily visit ports and foreign provinces this universal decree should be a check so that, when they too know that in the time of high prices there is no possibility of transcending the determined prices for commodities, such a reckoning of places, transportation, and the whole business may be made at the time of sale that the justice of our decree forbidding those who transport merchandise to sell anywhere at higher prices may be evident. Since, therefore, it is agreed that even in the time of our ancestors it was customary in passing laws to restrain insolence by attaching a prescribed penalty — since it is indeed rare for a situation tending to the good of humanity to be embraced spontaneously, and since, as a guide, fear is always found the most influential preceptor in the performance of duty — it is our pleasure that anyone who shall have resisted the form of this statute shall for his daring be subject to a capital penalty. And let no one consider the penalty harsh since there is at hand a means of avoiding the danger by the observance of moderation. To the same penalty, moreover, is he subject who in the desire to buy shall have conspired against the statute with the greed of the seller. Nor is he exempt from the same penalty who, although possessing necessities of life and business, believes that subsequent to this regulation he must withdraw them from the general market, since a penalty should be even more severe for him who introduces poverty than for him who harasses it against the law. We, therefore, urge upon the loyalty of all our people that a law constituted for the public good may be observed with willing obedience and due care; especially since in such a statute provision has been made, not for single states and peoples and provinces, but for the whole world, to whose ruin very few are known to have raged excessively, whose avarice neither fullness of time nor the riches for which they strive could lessen or satisfy.[2]

NOTES

a, 1. Governor of a district in the Fayum, of which Oxyrhynchus was the capital.

2. Municipal scribe whose responsibility it was to publish nominations to local office.

3. I.e., municipal council.

4. An official administering several nomes.

5. Municipal decurion charged with the liturgy of nominating other decurions to offices.

6. A.D. 254.

7. Antinoöpolis, a city founded by Hadrian, whose citizens enjoyed special privileges.

8. Governors-general of all Egypt.

9. A.D. 244.

b, 1. Imperial officials, soldiers, and tax collectors. The date is early third century.

2. Managers of imperial estates.

3. I.e., the provincial governor *pro tempore.*

4. Better translation: "procurator in charge of the staff administering the estate."

5. "Revenuers," tax collectors.

6. A.D. 244–247.

7. The reading is uncertain.

8. Financial officials.

9. A.D. 238.

10. In Thrace.

c, 1. The introduction, listing the many imperial honors and titles, is omitted.

2. A list follows, enumerating the maximum prices for twenty-two general categories of commodities.

16

Constantine and Christianity

THE AUTHORSHIP of this Life of Constantine, long attributed to Eusebius of Caesarea (A.D. 265–ca. 339), a bishop at the imperial court, has only recently been seriously questioned. Some deny that Eusebius wrote any part of the work and attribute it to an anonymous author of the late fourth century. Others discern a Eusebian core to which ecclesiastical writers immediately after Constantine may have added their own embellishments. The burden of proof rests with those who deny its traditional attribution. The following selections show how the work combines basically factual information with much tendentious and fanciful material. This use of imagination expressed the understandable desire of a grateful Church to glorify an emperor epochal in its history. The sincerity of Constantine's Christian convictions, although occasionally denied, is by no means disproved by the assertion in the Life that he was initially attracted to the Christian God because of his power over human affairs.

Eusebius, Life of Constantine, I, 13, 18, 22, 24, 26-31, 37-39; II, 61, 63; III, 4-7, 10-11, 13-14

i

13] OF CONSTANTIUS *his Father, who refused to imitate Diocletian, Maximian, and Maxentius, in their Persecution of the Christians.* At a time when four emperors[1] shared the administration of the Roman empire, Constantius alone, following a course of conduct different from that pursued by his colleagues, entered into the friendship of the Supreme God.

For while they besieged and wasted the churches of God, leveling them to the ground, and obliterating the very foundations of the

From E. C. Richardson, trans., and P. Schaff and Henry Wace, ed., EUSEBIUS, THE LIFE OF CONSTANTINE (New York, Oxford and London, 1890), in A Select Library of Nicene and Post-Nicene Fathers of the Christian Church, second series, vol. i, pp. 485, 487–493, 515, 520–523.

houses of prayer, he kept his hands pure from their abominable impiety, and never in any respect resembled them. They polluted their provinces by the indiscriminate slaughter of godly men and women; but he kept his soul free from the stain of this crime. They, involved in the mazes of impious idolatry, enthralled first themselves, and then all under their authority, in bondage to the errors of evil demons, while he at the same time originated the profoundest peace throughout his dominions, and secured to his subjects the privilege of celebrating without hindrance the worship of God. In short, while his colleagues oppressed all men by the most grievous exactions, and rendered their lives intolerable, and even worse than death, Constantius alone governed his people with a mild and tranquil sway, and exhibited towards them a truly parental and fostering care. . . .[2]

* * *

18] *That after the Abdication of Diocletian and Maximian, Constantius became Chief Augustus, and was blessed with a Numerous Offspring.* The immediate consequence of this conduct was a recompense from the hand of God, insomuch that he came into the supreme authority of the empire. For the older emperors, for some unknown reason, resigned their power; and this sudden change took place in the first year after their persecution of the churches.[3]

From that time Constantius alone received the honors of chief Augustus, having been previously, indeed, distinguished by the diadem of the imperial Cæsars, among whom he held the first rank; but after his worth had been proved in this capacity, he was invested with the highest dignity of the Roman empire, being named chief Augustus of the four who were afterwards elected to that honor. Moreover, he surpassed most of the emperors in regard to the number of his family, having gathered around him a very large circle of children both male and female. And, lastly, when he had attained to a happy old age, and was about to pay the common debt of nature, and exchange this life for another, God once more manifested His power in a special manner on his behalf, by providing that his eldest son Constantine should be present during his last moments, and ready to receive the imperial power from his hands.[4]

* * *

22] *How, after the Burial of Constantius, Constantine was proclaimed Augustus by the Army.* Nor did the imperial throne remain long unoccupied: for Constantine invested himself with his father's purple, and proceeded from his father's palace, presenting to all a renewal, as it were, in his own person, of his father's life and reign. He then conducted the funeral procession in company with his father's friends, some preceding, others following the train, and performed the last offices for the pious deceased with an extraordinary degree of magnificence, and all united in honoring this thrice blessed prince with acclamations and praises, and while with one mind and voice, they glorified the rule of the son as a living again of him who was dead, and hastened at once to hail their new sovereign by the titles of Imperial and Worshipful Augustus, with joyful shouts. . . .

* * *

24] *It was by the Will of God that Constantine became possessed of the Empire.* Thus then the God of all, the Supreme Governor of the whole universe, by his own will appointed Constantine, the descendant of so renowned a parent, to be prince and sovereign: so that, while others have been raised to this distinction by the election of their fellow-men, he is the only one to whose elevation no mortal may boast of having contributed.

* * *

26] *How he resolved to deliver Rome from Maxentius.* While, therefore, he regarded the entire world as one immense body, and perceived that the head of it all, the royal city of the Roman empire, was bowed down by the weight of a tyrannous oppression;[5] at first he had left the task of liberation to those who governed the other divisions of the empire, as being his superiors in point of age. But when none of these proved able to afford relief, and those who had attempted it had experienced a disastrous termination of their enterprise, he said that life was without enjoyment to him as long as he saw the imperial city thus afflicted, and prepared himself for the overthrowal of the tyranny.

27] *That after reflecting on the Downfall of those who had worshiped Idols, he made Choice of Christianity.* Being convinced, however, that he needed some more powerful aid than his military forces could afford him, on account of the wicked and magical enchantments which were so diligently practiced by the tyrant, he sought Divine assistance, deeming the possession of arms and a numerous soldiery of secondary importance, but believing the co-operating power of Deity invincible and not to be shaken. He considered, therefore, on what God he might rely for protection and assistance. While engaged in this enquiry, the thought occurred to him, that, of the many emperors who had preceded him, those who had rested their hopes in a multitude of gods, and served them with sacrifices and offerings, had in the first place been deceived by flattering predictions, and oracles which promised them all prosperity, and at last had met with an unhappy end, while not one of their gods had stood by to warn them of the impending wrath of heaven; while one alone who had pursued an entirely opposite course, who had condemned the error, and honored the one Supreme God during his whole life, had found him to be the Saviour and Protector of his empire, and the Giver of every good thing. Reflecting on this, and well weighing the fact that they who had trusted in many gods had also fallen by manifold forms of death, without leaving behind them either family or offspring, stock, name, or memorial among men: while the God of his father had given to him, on the other hand, manifestations of his power and very many tokens: and considering farther that those who had already taken arms against the tyrant, and had marched to the battle-field under the protection of a multitude of gods, had met with a dishonorable end (for one of them had shamefully retreated from the contest without a blow, and the other, being slain in the midst of his own troops, became, as it were, the mere sport of death);[6] reviewing, I say, all these considerations, he judged it to be folly indeed to join in the idle worship of those who were no gods, and, after such convincing evidence, to err from the truth; and therefore felt it incumbent on him to honor his father's God alone.

28] *How, while he was praying, God sent him a Vision of a Cross of Light in the Heavens at Mid-day, with an Inscription admonishing him to conquer by that.* Accordingly he called on him with earnest prayer and supplications that he would reveal to him who he was, and stretch forth his right hand to help him in his present difficulties. And while he was thus praying with fervent entreaty, a most marvelous sign appeared to him from heaven, the account of which it might have been hard to believe had it been related by any other person. But since the victorious emperor himself long afterwards declared it to the writer of this history, when he was honored with his acquaintance and society, and confirmed his statement by an oath, who could hesitate to accredit the relation, especially since the testimony of after-time has established its truth? He said that about noon, when the day was already beginning to decline, he saw with his own eyes the trophy of a cross of light in the heavens, above the sun, and bearing the inscription, CONQUER BY THIS. At this sight he himself was struck with amazement, and his whole army also, which followed him on this expedition, and witnessed the miracle.

29] *How the Christ of God appeared to him in his Sleep, and commanded him to use in his Wars a Standard made in the Form of the Cross.* He said, moreover, that he doubted within himself what the import of this apparition could be. And while he continued to ponder and reason on its meaning, night suddenly came on; then in his sleep the Christ of God appeared to him with the same sign which he had seen in the heavens, and commanded him to make a likeness of that sign which he had seen in the heavens, and to use it as a safeguard in all engagements with his enemies.

30] *The Making of the Standard of the Cross.* At dawn of day he arose, and communicated the marvel to his friends: and then, calling together the workers in gold and precious stones, he sat in the midst of them, and described to them the figure of the sign he had seen, bidding them represent it in gold and precious stones. And this representation I myself have had an opportunity of seeing.

31] *A Description of the Standard of the Cross, which the Romans now call the Labarum.* Now it was made in the following manner. A long spear, overlaid with gold, formed the figure of the cross by means of a transverse bar laid over it. On the top of the whole was fixed a wreath of gold and precious stones; and within this, the symbol of the Saviour's name, two letters indicating the name of Christ by means of its initial characters, the letter P being intersected by X in its centre: and these letters the emperor was in the habit of wearing on his helmet at a later period. From the cross-bar of the spear was suspended a cloth, a royal piece, covered with a profuse embroidery of most brilliant precious stones; and which, being also richly interlaced with gold, presented an indescribable degree of beauty to the beholder. This banner was of a square form, and the upright staff, whose lower section was of great length, bore a golden half-length portrait of the pious emperor and his children on its upper part, beneath the trophy of the cross, and immediately above the embroidered banner.

The emperor constantly made use of this sign of salvation as a safeguard against every adverse and hostile power, and commanded that others similar to it should be carried at the head of all his armies.

* * *

37] *Defeat of Maxentius's Armies in Italy.* Constantine, however, filled with compassion on account of all these miseries, began to arm himself with all warlike preparation against the tyranny. Assuming therefore the Supreme God as his patron, and invoking his Christ to be his preserver and aid, and setting the victorious trophy, the salutary symbol, in front of his soldiers and body-guard, he marched with his whole forces, trying to obtain again for the Romans the freedom they had inherited from their ancestors.

And whereas, Maxentius, trusting more in his magic arts than in the affection of his subjects, dared not even advance outside the city gates, but had guarded every place and district and city subject to his tyranny, with large bodies of soldiers, the emperor, confiding in the help of God, advanced against the first and second and third divisions of the tyrant's forces, defeated them all with ease at the first assault, and made his way into the very interior of Italy.

38] *Death of Maxentius on the Bridge of the Tiber.* And already he was approaching very near Rome itself, when, to save him from the necessity of fighting with all the Romans for the tyrant's sake, God himself drew the tyrant, as it were by secret cords, a long way outside the gates. And now those miracles recorded in Holy Writ, which God of old wrought against the ungodly (discredited by most as fables, yet believed by the faithful), did he in every deed confirm to all alike, believers and unbelievers, who were eye-witnesses of the wonders. For as once in the days of Moses and the Hebrew nation, who were worshipers of God, "Pharaoh's chariots and his host hath he cast into the sea, and his chosen chariot-captains are drowned in the Red Sea," — so at this time Maxentius, and the soldiers and guards with him, "went down into the depths like stone," when, in his flight before the divinely-aided forces of Constantine, he essayed to cross the river which lay in his way, over which, making a strong bridge of boats, he had framed an engine of destruction, really against himself, but in the hope of ensnaring thereby him who was beloved by God.[7] For his God stood by the one to protect him, while the other, godless, proved to be the miserable contriver of these secret devices to his own ruin. So that one might well say, "He hath made a pit, and digged it, and is fallen into the ditch which he made. His mischief shall return upon his own head, and his violence shall come down upon his own pate." Thus, in the present instance, under divine direction, the machine erected on the bridge, with the ambuscade concealed therein, giving way unexpectedly before the appointed time, the bridge began to sink, and the boats with the men in them went bodily to the bottom. And first the wretch himself, then his armed attendants and guards, even as the sacred oracles had before described, "sank as lead in the mighty waters." So that they who thus obtained victory from God might well, if not in the same words, yet in fact in the same spirit as the people of his great servant Moses, sing and speak as they did concerning the impious tyrant of old: "Let us sing unto the Lord, for he hath been glorified exceedingly: the horse and his rider hath he thrown into the sea. He is become my helper and my shield unto salvation." And again, "Who is like unto thee, O Lord, among the gods? who is like thee, glorious in holiness, marvelous in praises, doing wonders?"

39] *Constantine's Entry into Rome.* Having then at this time sung these and suchlike praises to God, the Ruler of all and the Author of victory, after the example of his great servant Moses, Constantine entered the imperial city in triumph. And here the whole body of the senate, and others of rank and distinction in the city, freed as it were from the restraint of a prison, along with the whole Roman populace, their countenances expressive of the gladness of their hearts, received him with acclamations and abounding joy; men, women, and children, with countless multitudes of servants, greeting him as deliverer, preserver, and benefactor, with incessant shouts. But he, being possessed of inward piety toward God, was neither rendered arrogant by these plaudits, nor uplifted by the praises he heard: but, being sensible that he had received help from God, he immediately rendered a thanksgiving to him as the Author of his victory.

ii

61] *How Controversies originated at Alexandria through Matters relating to Arius.* In this manner the emperor, like a powerful herald of God, addressed himself by his own letter to all the provinces, at the same time warning his subjects against superstitious error, and encouraging them in the pursuit of true godliness. But in the midst of his joyful anticipations of the success of this measure, he received tidings of a most serious disturbance which had invaded the peace of the Church. This intelligence he heard with deep concern, and at once endeavored to devise a remedy for the evil. The origin of this disturbance may be thus described. The people of God were in a truly flourishing state and abounding in the practice of good works. No terror from without assailed them, but a bright and most profound peace, through the favor of God, encompassed his Church on every side. Meantime, however, the spirit of envy was watching to destroy our blessings, which at first crept in unperceived, but soon revelled in the midst of the assemblies of the saints. At length it reached the bishops themselves, and arrayed them in angry hostility against each other, on pretense of a jealous regard for the doctrines of Divine truth. Hence it was that a mighty fire was kindled as it were from a little spark, and which, originating in the first instance in the Alexandrian church,[8] overspread the whole of Egypt and Libya, and the further Thebaid. Eventually it extended its ravages to the other provinces and cities of the empire; so that not only the prelates of the churches might be seen encountering each other in the strife of words, but the people themselves were completely divided, some adhering to one faction and others to another. Nay, so notorious did the scandal of these proceedings become, that the sacred matters of inspired teaching were exposed to the most shameful ridicule in the very theaters of the unbelievers.

*   *   *

63] *How Constantine sent a Messenger and a Letter concerning Peace.* As soon as the emperor was informed of these facts, which he heard with much sorrow of heart, considering them in the light of a calamity personally affecting himself, he forthwith selected from the Christians in his train one whom he well knew to be approved for the sobriety and genuineness of his faith,[9] and who had before this time distinguished himself by the boldness of his religious profession, and sent him to negotiate peace between the dissentient parties at Alexandria.

iii

4] *A Farther Notice of the Controversies raised in Egypt by Arius.* In such occupations as these he employed himself with pleasure: but the effects of that envious spirit which so troubled the peace of the churches of God in Alexandria, together with the Theban and Egyptian schism, continued to cause him no little disturbance of mind. For in fact, in every city bishops were engaged in obstinate conflict with bishops, and people rising against people; and almost like the fabled Symplegades,[10] coming into violent collision with each other. Nay, some were so far transported beyond the bounds of reason as to be guilty of reckless and outrageous conduct, and even to insult the statues of the emperor. This state of things had little power to excite his anger, but rather caused in him sorrow of spirit; for he deeply deplored the folly thus exhibited by deranged men. 5] *Of the Disagreement respecting the Celebration of Easter.* But before this time another most virulent disorder had existed, and long afflicted the Church; I mean the difference respecting the salutary feast of Easter. For while one party asserted that the Jewish custom should be adhered to, the other affirmed that the exact recurrence of the period should be observed, without following the authority of those who were in error, and strangers to gospel grace.

Accordingly, the people being thus in every place divided in respect of this, and the sacred observances of religion confounded for a long period (insomuch that the diversity of judgment in regard to the time for celebrating one and the same feast caused the greatest disagreement between those who kept it, some afflicting themselves with fastings and austerities, while others devoted their time to festive relaxation), no one appeared who was capable of devising a remedy for the evil, because the controversy continued equally balanced between both parties. To God alone, the Almighty, was the healing of these differences an easy task; and Constantine appeared to be the only one on earth capable of being his minister for this good end. For as soon as he was made acquainted with the facts which I have described, and perceived that his letter to the Alexandrian Christians had failed to produce its due effect, he at once aroused the energies of his mind, and declared that he must prosecute to the utmost this war also against the secret adversary who was disturbing the peace of the Church.

6] *How he ordered a Council to be held at Nicæa.* Then as if to bring a divine array against this enemy, he convoked a general council, and invited the speedy attendance of bishops from all quarters, in letters expressive of the honorable estimation in which he held them. Nor was this merely the issuing of a bare command, but the emperor's good will contributed much to its being carried into effect: for he allowed some the use of the public means of conveyance, while he afforded to others an ample supply of horses for their transport. The place, too, selected for the synod, the city Nicæa in Bithynia (named from *"Victory"*), was appropriate to the occasion.[11] As soon then as the imperial injunction was generally made known, all with the utmost willingness hastened thither, as though they would outstrip one another in a race; for they were impelled by the anticipation of a happy result to the conference, by the hope of enjoying present peace, and the desire of beholding something new and strange in the person of so admirable an emperor. Now when they were all assembled, it appeared evident that the proceeding was the work of God, inasmuch as men who had been most widely separated, not merely in sentiment, but also personally, and by difference of country, place, and nation, were here brought together, and comprised within the walls of a single city, forming as it were a vast garland of priests, composed of a variety of the choicest flowers.

7] *Of the General Council, at which Bishops from all Nations were Present.* In effect, the most distinguished of God's ministers from all the churches which abounded in Europe, Lybia, and Asia were here assembled. And a single house of prayer, as though divinely enlarged, sufficed to contain at once Syrians and Cilicians, Phœnicians and Arabians, delegates from Palestine, and others from Egypt; Thebans and Libyans, with those who came from the region of Mesopotamia. A Persian bishop too was present at this conference, nor was even a Scythian found wanting to the number. Pontus, Galatia, and Pamphylia, Cappadocia, Asia, and Phrygia, furnished their most distinguished prelates; while those who dwelt in the remotest districts of Thrace and Macedonia, of Achaia and Epirus, were notwithstanding in attendance. Even from Spain itself, one whose fame was widely spread took his seat as an individual in the great assembly.[9] The prelate of the imperial city was prevented from attending by extreme old age; but his presbyters were present, and supplied his place. Constantine is the first prince of any age who bound together such a garland as this with the bond of peace, and presented it to his Saviour as a thank-offering for the victories he had obtained over every foe, thus exhibiting in our own times a similitude of the apostolic company.

*   *   *

10] *Council in the Palace. Constantine, entering, took his Seat in the Assembly.* Now when the appointed day arrived on which the council met for the final solution of the questions in dispute,[12] each member was present for this in the central building of the palace, which appeared to exceed the rest in magnitude. On each side of the interior of this were many seats disposed in order, which were occupied by those who had been invited to attend, according to their rank. As soon, then, as the whole assembly had seated themselves with becoming orderliness, a general silence prevailed, in expectation of the emperor's arrival. And first of all, three of his immediate family entered in succession, then others also preceded his approach, not of the soldiers or guards who usually accompanied him, but only friends in the faith. And now, all rising at the signal which indicated the emperor's entrance, at last he himself proceeded through the midst of the assembly, like some heavenly messenger of God, clothed in raiment which glittered as it were with rays of light, reflecting the glowing radiance of a purple robe, and adorned with the brilliant splendor of gold and precious stones. Such was the external appearance of his person; and with regard to his mind, it was evident that he was distinguished by piety and godly fear. This was indicated by his downcast eyes, the blush on his countenance, and his gait. For the rest of his personal excellencies, he surpassed all present in height of stature and beauty of form, as well as in majestic dignity of mien, and invincible strength and vigor. All these graces, united to a suavity of manner, and a serenity becoming his imperial station, declared the excellence of his mental qualities to be above the praise. As soon as he had advanced to the upper end of the seats, at first he remained standing, and when a low chair of wrought gold had been set for him, he waited until the bishops had beckoned to him, and then sat down, and after him the whole assembly did the same.

11] *Silence of the Council, after Some Words by the Bishop Eusebius.* The bishop who occupied the chief place in the right division of the assembly then rose, and, addressing the emperor, delivered a concise speech, in a strain of thanksgiving to Almighty God on his behalf. When he had resumed his seat, silence ensued, and all regarded the emperor with fixed attention; on which he looked serenely round on the assembly with a cheerful aspect, and, having collected his thoughts, in a calm and gentle tone gave utterance to the following words....[13]

*   *   *

13] *How he led the Dissentient Bishops to Harmony of Sentiment.* As soon as the emperor had spoken these words in the Latin tongue, which another interpreted, he gave permission to those who presided in the council to deliver their opinions. On this some began to accuse their neighbors, who defended themselves, and recriminated in their turn. In this manner numberless assertions were put forth by each party, and a violent controversy arose at the very commencement. Notwithstanding this, the emperor gave patient audience to all alike, and received every proposition with steadfast attention, and by occasionally assisting the argument of each party in turn, he gradually disposed even the most vehement disputants to a reconciliation.[14] At the same time, by the affability of his address to all, and his use of the Greek language, with which he was not altogether unacquainted, he appeared in a truly attractive and amiable light, persuading some, convincing others by his reasonings, praising those who spoke well, and urging all to unity of sentiment, until at last he succeeded in bringing them to one mind and judgment respecting every disputed question.

14] *Unanimous Declaration of the Council concerning Faith, and the Celebration of Easter.* The result was that they were not only united as concerning the faith, but that the time for the celebration of the salutary feast of Easter was agreed on by all. Those points also which were sanctioned by the resolution of the whole body were committed to writing, and received the signature of each several member. Then the emperor, believing that he had thus obtained a second victory over the adversary of the Church, proceeded to solemnize a triumphal festival in honor of God.

NOTES

1. The Tetrarchy, with Diocletian and Maximian as Augusti and Galerius and Constantius Chlorus as their respective Caesars, was established in A.D. 293.

2. This paragraph is inaccurate. Although Constantius was not an eager persecutor, he probably enforced the first edict of A.D. 303 that decreed destruction of churches.

3. A.D. 305.

4. Constantius died at York, July 306.

5. By Maxentius, Maximian's son, who claimed the imperial title for himself.

6. Galerius and Severus, other Augusti.

7. The Battle of the Milvian Bridge, October 28, 312.

8. These oblique references to Arianism are explicable if we assume that Eusebius was the author of this work, since he himself tended towards Arianism.

9. Hosius, Bishop of Cordova.

10. Legendary rocks in the Black Sea that crushed passing ships.

11. The first Ecumenical Council was convoked May 20, 325.

12. June 19, 325.

13. The speech that follows is eliminated here; it is probably apocryphal.

14. The assertion that Constantine assisted the theologians is undoubtedly erroneous. He probably neither understood nor cared about the subtle differences of church opinion.

17

Rome and the Provinces in the Fourth Century

AMMIANUS MARCELLINUS (ca. A.D. 330–400), a pagan Greek of the decurion class of Antioch, ranks with Livy and Tacitus as one of the greatest historians writing in Latin. He pursued a military career, knew most of the empire at first hand, and was well informed regarding many of the events described in the surviving portions of his history, which cover the years A.D. 353 to 378. In spite of his bombastic style, he was surprisingly accurate and impartial. The two selections following illustrate his interests and his approach to history. The first, the famous "Roman satire," portrays decadent society in Rome; although certainly highly rhetorical and exaggerated, it is probably essentially true. The second selection recounts a cause célèbre of the fourth century, the "Romanus affair," which clearly shows the extent to which official corruption at court and in the provinces defied reform and contributed materially to imperial collapse.

Ammianus Marcellinus, XXVIII, 4, 1-35; 6, 1-30

The Roman satire]

4, 1] After long lasting and serious dispersion from affairs in Rome, constrained by the great mass of foreign events, I shall return to a brief account of these, beginning with the prefecture of Olybrius,[1] which was exceedingly peaceful and mild; for he never allowed himself to be turned from humane conduct, but was careful and anxious that no word or act of his should ever be found harsh. He severely punished calumny, cut down the profits of the privy-purse wherever it was possible, fully and impartially distinguished justice from injustice, and showed himself most lenient towards those whom he governed.

From John C. Rolfe, trans., AMMIANUS MARCELLINUS (Cambridge, Mass., 1939), vol. iii, pp. 137–161, 169–187. Reprinted by permission of Harvard University Press and The Loeb Classical Library.

2] But a cloud was thrown over all these merits by a fault which indeed was not harmful to the community, but yet was a stain on a high official; for almost his whole private life, since he was inclined to luxury, he spent in playhouses and love affairs, though the latter were neither unlawful nor incestuous.

3] After him Ampelius² governed the city, a man who himself also lusted after pleasures. Born at Antioch, he had been formerly marshal of the court, was twice raised to the rank of proconsul, and then, long afterwards, to the high honour of the prefecture. Although admirable in other respects and well suited to gaining the favour of the people, he was nevertheless sometimes hard, and I wish he had been steadfast of purpose; for he could have corrected in part, even though to a small extent, the incitements of appetite and gross gluttony, if he had not let himself be turned to laxity and thus lost enduring fame.

4] For he gave orders that no wine-shop should be opened before the fourth hour, that no one of the common people should heat water, that up to a fixed hour of the day no victualler should offer cooked meat for sale, and that no respectable man should be seen chewing anything in public.

5] These shameful acts, and others worse than these, had, by being constantly overlooked, blazed up to such unbridled heights that not even that celebrated Cretan Epimenides,³ if, after the manner of myth, he had been called up from the lower world and returned to our times, would have been able single-handed to purify Rome; such was the stain of incurable sins that had overwhelmed most people.

6] And first, as often, according to the quantity of topics, I shall give an account of the delinquencies of the nobles and then of the common people, condensing the events in a rapid disgression.

7] Some men, distinguished (as they think) by famous fore-names, pride themselves beyond measure in being called Reburri, Flavonii, Pagonii, Gereones, and Dalii, along with Tarracii and Pherrasii, and many other equally fine-sounding indications of eminent ancestry.⁴

8] Others, resplendent in silken garments, as though they were to be led to death, or as if (to speak without any evil omen) they were bringing up the rear preceded by an army, are followed by a throng of slaves drawn up in troops, amid noise and confusion.

9] When such men, each attended by fifty servants, have entered the vaulted rooms of a bath, they shout in threatening tones: "Where on earth are our attendants?" If they have learned that an unknown courtesan has suddenly appeared, some woman who has been a common prostitute of the crowd of our city, some old strumpet, they all strive to be the first to reach her, and caressing the new-comer, extol her with such disgraceful flattery as the Parthians do Samiramis, the Egyptians their Cleopatras, the Carians Artemisia, or the people of Palmyra Zenobia. And those who stoop to do such things are men in the time of whose forefathers a senator was punished with the censor's brand of infamy, if he had dared, while this was still considered unseemly, to kiss his wife in the presence of their own daughter.

10] Some of these men, when one begins to salute them breast to breast, like menacing bulls turn to one side their heads, where they should be kissed, and offer their flatterers their knees to kiss or their hands, thinking that quite enough to ensure them a happy life; and they believe that a stranger is given an abundance of all the duties of courtesy, even though the great men may perhaps be under obligation to him, if he is asked what hot baths or waters he uses, or at what house he has been put up.

11] And although they are so important and, in their own opinion, such cultivators of the virtues, if they learn that someone has announced that horses or chariots are coming from anywhere whatever, they hover over this same man and ask him questions as anxiously as their ancestors looked up to the two sons of Tyndareus,[5] when they filled everything with joy by announcing those famous victories of olden days.

12] Their houses are frequented by idle chatterboxes, who with various pretences of approval applaud every word of the man of loftier fortune, emulating the witty flatteries of the parasites in the comedies. For just as the parasites puff up boastful soldiers by attributing to them the sieges and battles against thousands of enemies, comparing them with the heroes of old, so these also, admiring the rows of columns hanging in the air with lofty façade, and the walls gleaming with the remarkable colours of precious stones, raise these noble men to the gods.

13] Sometimes at their banquets the scales are even called for, in order to weigh the fish, birds, and dormice that are served, whose great size they commend again and again, as hitherto unexampled, often repeating it to the weariness of those present, especially when thirty secretaries stand near by, with pen-cases and small tablets, recording these same items, so that the only thing lacking seems to be a schoolmaster.

14] Some of them hate learning as they do poison, and read with

attentive care only Juvenal and Marius Maximus,[6] in their boundless idleness handling no other books than these, for what reason it
is not for my humble mind to judge.

15] Whereas, considering the greatness of their fame and of their
parentage, they ought to pore over many and varied works; they
ought to learn that Socrates, when condemned to death and thrown
into prison, asked a musician, who was skilfully rendering a song
of the lyric poet Stesichorus, that he might be taught to do this
while there was still time. And when the musician asked of what use
that could be to him, since he was to die on the following day,
Socrates replied: "In order that I may know something more before
I depart from life."

16] But a few among them are so strict in punishing offences, that
if a slave is slow in bringing the hot water, they condemn him to
suffer three hundred lashes; if he has intentionally killed a man, although many people insist that he be condemned to death, his
master will merely cry out: "What should a worthless fellow do,
notorious for wicked deeds? But if he dares to do anything else like
that hereafter, he shall be punished."

17] But the height of refinement with these men at present is, that
it is better for a stranger to kill any man's brother than to decline
his invitation to dinner. For a senator thinks that he is suffering the
loss of a rich property, if the man whom he has, after considerable
weighing of pros and cons, invited once, fails to appear at his table.

18] Some of them, if they make a longish journey to visit their
estates, or to hunt by the labours of others, think that they have
equalled the marches of Alexander the Great or of Caesar; or if
they have sailed in their gaily-painted boats from the Lake of Aver-
nus to Puteoli, it is the adventure of the golden fleece, especially if
they should dare it in the hot season. And if amid the gilded fans
flies have lighted on the silken fringes, or through a rent in the
hanging curtain a little ray of sun has broken in, they lament that
they were not born in the land of the Cimmerians.

19] Then when they come from the bath of Silvanus or from the
healing waters of Mamaea, as any one of them emerges he has himself dried with the finest linens, opens the presses and carefully
searches amongst garments shimmering with shifting light, of which
he brings enough with him to clothe eleven men. At length, some
are chosen and he puts them on; then he takes back his rings, which,
in order that the dampness may not injure them, he has handed to a
servant, and after his fingers have been as good as measured to receive them, he departs.

20] And, indeed, if any veteran has recently retired because of his years from service with the emperor, such a company of admirers attend him that . . . is considered to be the leader of the old song; the others quietly listen to what he says. He alone, like the father of a family, tells irrelevant stories and entertaining tales, and in most of them cleverly deceiving his hearers.

21] Some of these, though few in number, shrink from the name of gamblers, and therefore desire to be called rather *tesserarii*,[7] persons who differ from each other only as much as thieves do from brigands. But this must be admitted, that while all friendships at Rome are lukewarm, those alone which are formed at the gambling table, as if they were gained by glorious toil, have a bond of union and are united by complete firmness of exceeding affection; whence some members of these companies are found to be so harmonious that you would take them for the brothers Quintilius. And so you may see a man of low station, who is skilled in the secrets of dice-playing, walking abroad like Porcius Cato after his unexpected and unlooked-for defeat for the praetorship, with a set expression of dignity and sorrow because at some great banquet or assemblage a former proconsul was given a higher place of honour.

22] Some lie in wait for men of wealth, old or young, childless or unmarried, or even for those who have wives or children — for no distinction is observed in this respect — enticing them by wonderful trickeries to make their wills; and when they have set their last decisions in order and left some things to these men, to humour whom they have made their wills in their favour, they forthwith die; so that you would not think that the death was brought about by the working of the allotment of destiny, nor could an illness easily be proved by the testimony of witnesses; nor is the funeral of these men attended by any mourners.

23] Another, who attained some rank, moderate though it be, walking with neck puffed up, looks askance at his former acquaintances, so that you might think that a Marcellus was returning after the taking of Syracuse.

24] Many of them, who deny that there are higher powers in heaven, neither appear in public nor eat a meal nor think they can with due caution take a bath, until they have critically examined the calendar and learned where, for example, the planet Mercury is, or what degree of the constellation of the Crab the moon occupies in its course through the heavens.

25] Another, if he finds a creditor of his demanding his due with too great urgency, resorts to a charioteer who is all too ready to dare any enterprise, and causes the creditor to be charged with being a poisoner; and he is not let off until he has surrendered the bill of indebtedness and paid heavy costs. And besides, the accuser has the voluntary debtor put in prison as if he were his property, and does not set him free until he acknowledges the debt.

26] In another place a wife by hammering day and night on the same anvil — as the old proverb has it — drives her husband to make a will, and the husband insistently urges his wife to do the same. Skilled jurists are brought in on both sides, one in a bedroom, the other, his rival, in the dining-room to discuss disputed points. These are joined by opposing interpreters of horoscopes, on the one side making profuse promises of prefectures and the burial of rich matrons, on the other telling women that for their husbands' funerals now quietly approaching they must make the necessary preparations. And a maid-servant bears witness, by nature somewhat pale, . . . As Cicero says: "They know of nothing on earth that is good unless it brings gain. Of their friends, as of their cattle, they love those best from whom they hope to get the greatest profit."

27] When these people seek any loan, you will see them in slippers like a Micon or a Laches;[8] when they are urged to pay, they wear such lofty buskins and are so arrogant that you would think them Cresphontes and Temenus, the famous Heraclidae. So much for the senate.

28] Let us now turn to the idle and slothful commons. Among them some who have no shoes are conspicuous as though they had cultured names, such as the Messores, Statarii, Semicupae and Serapini, and Cicymbricus, with Gluturinus and Trulla, and Lucanicus with Porclaca and Salsula, and countless others.[4]

29] These spend all their life with wine and dice, in low haunts, pleasures, and the games. Their temple, their dwelling, their assembly, and the height of all their hopes is the Circus Maximus. You may see many groups of them gathered in the fora, the cross-roads, the streets, and their other meeting-places, engaged in quarrelsome arguments with one another, some (as usual) defending this, others that.

30] Among them those who have enjoyed a surfeit of life, influential through long experience, often swear by their hoary hair and wrinkles that the state cannot exist if in the coming race the charioteer whom each favours is not first to rush forth from the barriers, and fails to round the turning-point closely with his ill-omened horses.

31] And when there is such a dry rot of thoughtlessness, as soon as the longed-for day of the chariot-race begins to dawn, before the sun is yet shining clearly they all hasten in crowds to the spot at top speed, as if they would outstrip the very chariots that are to take part in the contest; and torn by their conflicting hopes about the result of the race, the greater number of them in their anxiety pass sleepless nights.

32] If from there they come to worthless theatrical pieces, any actor is hissed off the boards who has not won the favour of the low rabble with money. And if this noisy form of demonstration is lacking, they cry in imitation of the Tauric race that all strangers — on whose aid they have always depended and stood upright — ought to be driven from the city. All this in foul and absurd terms, very different from the expressions of their interests and desires made by your commons of old, of whose many witty and happy sayings tradition tells us.

33] And it has now come to this, that in place of the lively sound of approval from men appointed to applaud, at every public show an actor of afterpieces, a beast-baiter, a charioteer, every kind of player, and the magistrates of higher and lower rank, nay even matrons, are constantly greeted with the shout "You should be these fellows' teachers!"; but what they ought to learn no one is able to explain.

34] The greater number of these gentry, given over to over-stuffing themselves with food, led by the charm of the odour of cooking and by the shrill voices of the women, like a flock of peacocks screaming with hunger, stand even from cockcrow beside the pots on tip-toe and gnaw the ends of their fingers as they wait for the dishes to cool. Others hang over the nauseous mass of half-raw meat, while it is cooking, watching it so intently that one would think that Democritus with other dissectors was examining the internal organs of dismembered animals and showing by what means future generations might be cured of internal pains.

35] But enough for the present of this account of affairs in the city. Now let us return to the other events which were caused by various incidents in the provinces.

The Romanus affair]

6, 1] From here, as if moving to another part of the world, let us come to the sorrows of the African province of Tripolis, over which (I think) even Justice herself has wept; and from what cause these blazed out like flames will appear when my narrative is completed. 2] The Austoriani, who are neighbours to those regions, are savages, always ready for sudden raids and accustomed to live by murder and robbery. These were subdued for a time, but then returned to their natural turbulence, for which they seriously alleged this reason: — 3] A certain man of their country, Stachao by name, when he was wandering freely in our territory, it being a time of peace, committed some violations of the laws, among which the most conspicuous was, that he tried by every kind of deceit to betray the province, as was proved by most trustworthy testimony. Accordingly he was burned to death.

4] To avenge his execution, under the pretext that he was a country-man of theirs and had been unjustly condemned, like beasts aroused by madness, they sallied forth from their homes while Jovian[9] was still ruling, and, fearing to come near Lepcis, a city strong in its walls and population, they encamped for three days in the fertile districts near the city. There they slaughtered the peasants, whom sudden fear had paralysed or had compelled to take refuge in caves, burned a great deal of furniture which could not be carried off, and returned laden with immense spoils, taking with them also as prisoner one Silva, the most eminent of the local magistrates, who chanced to be found in the country with his wife and children.

5] The people of Lepcis, greatly alarmed by this sudden calamity, before the evils which the insolence of the barbarians threatened should increase, implored the protection of Romanus, the newly-promoted commanding-general for Africa. As soon as he arrived, leading his military forces, and was asked to lend his aid in these troubles, he declared that he would not move his camp unless provisions in abundance should first be brought and 4000 camels equipped.

6] The unhappy citizens were stupefied by this answer, and declared that after suffering from fires and pillage they could not procure a remedy for their tremendous losses by providing such enormous supplies. Whereupon the general, after deluding them by spending forty days there, marched away without actually attempting anything.

7] The people of Tripolis, disappointed in this hope and fearing the worst, when the lawful day for the popular assembly (which with them comes once a year) had arrived, appointed Severus and Flaccianus as envoys, who were to take to Valentinian golden statues of Victory because of his accession to power, and to tell him fearlessly of the lamentable ruin of the province.

8] As soon as Romanus heard of this, he sent a swift horseman to Remigius, the chief-marshal of the court, a relative of his by marriage and a partner in his robberies, asking him to see to it that the investigation of this affair should be assigned by the emperor's authority to the deputy governor Vincentius and himself.

9] The envoys came to the court, and being given audience with the emperor, stated orally what they had suffered; and they presented decrees, containing a full account of the whole affair. Since the emperor, after reading these, neither believed the communication of the marshal, who countenanced the misdeeds of Romanus, nor the envoys, who gave contrary testimony, a full investigation was promised, but it was put off, in the way which supreme powers are usually deceived among the distractions to which the powerful are liable.

10] While the people of Tripolis were long in a state of anxiety and suspense, looking for some aid from the emperor's military support, the hordes of barbarians again came up, given confidence by what had happened before; and after overrunning the territory of Lepcis and Oea[10] with death and devastation, went away again, laden with vast heaps of booty; a number of decurions were put to death, among whom the former high-priest Rusticianus and the aedile Nicasius were conspicuous.

11] But the reason why this inroad could not be prevented was that, although at the request of the envoys the charge of military affairs also had been entrusted to the governor Ruricius, it was soon afterwards transferred to Romanus.

12] When now the news of this newly inflicted catastrophe was sent to Gaul, it greatly angered the emperor. Accordingly, Palladius, a tribune and secretary, was sent to pay the wages that were due the soldiers in various parts of Africa, and to investigate and give a fully trustworthy report of what had happened at Tripolis.[11]

13] However, during such delays caused by consultations and waiting for replies, the Austoriani, made insolent by two successful raids, flew to the spot like birds of prey made more savage by the incitement of blood, and after slaying all those who did not escape danger by flight, carried off the booty which they had previously left behind, besides cutting down the trees and vines.

14] Then one Mychon, a high-born and powerful townsman, was caught in the suburbs but gave them the slip before he was bound; and because he was lame and it was wholly impossible for him to make good his escape, he threw himself into an empty well; but the barbarians pulled him out with his rib broken, and placed him near

the city gates; there, at the pitiful entreaties of his wife, he was ran-
somed but was drawn up by a rope to the battlements, and died after
two days.

15] Then the savage marauders, roused to greater persistence,
assailed the very walls of Lepcis, which re-echoed with the
mournful wailing of the women, who had never before been besieged by an enemy, and were half-dead with a terror to which they
were unused. But after blockading the city for eight days together,
during which some of the besiegers were wounded without accomplishing anything, they returned in saddened mood to their own
abodes.

16] Because of this the citizens, despairing of being saved and
resorting to the last hope, although the envoys they had already sent
had not yet returned, dispatched Jovinus and Pancratius to give the
emperor a trustworthy account of what they had seen and had
personally suffered. These envoys, by inquiring of those mentioned
above (Severus, whom they met at Carthage, and Flaccianus), what
they had done, learned that they had been ordered to make their
report to the deputy and the general. Of these Severus was at once
attacked by a painful illness and died; but the aforementioned
envoys nevertheless hastened by long marches to the court.

17] After this, Palladius had entered Africa, and Romanus, intending to block in advance the purpose for which he had come, in order
to secure his own safety, had ordered the officers of the companies
through certain confidants of his secrets, that they should hand over
to Palladius the greater part of the pay which he had brought, since
he was an influential man and in close relations with the highest
officials of the palace; and so it was done.

18] Palladius immediately, being thus enriched, proceeded to Lepcis,
and in order to succeed in ferreting out the truth, he took with him to
the devastated regions two eloquent and distinguished townsmen,
Erechthius and Aristomenes, who freely told him of their own
troubles and those of their fellow-citizens and neighbours.

19] They openly showed him everything, and after he had seen the
lamentable ashes of the province, he returned, and reproaching Romanus for his inactivity, threatened to give the emperor a true report
of everything that he had seen. Then Romanus, filled with anger and
resentment, assured him that he also would then at once report
that Palladius, sent as an incorruptible notary, had diverted to his
own profit all the money intended for the soldiers.

20] Therefore, since his conscience was witness to disgraceful acts,

Palladius then came to an understanding with Romanus, and on his return to the palace, he misled Valentinian by the atrocious art of lying, declaring that the people of Tripolis had no cause for complaint. Accordingly, he was sent again to Africa with Jovinus, the last of all the envoys (for Pancratius had died at Treves), in order with the deputy to examine in person the value of the work of the second deputation also. Besides this, the emperor gave orders that the tongues of Erechthius and Aristomenes should be cut out, since the aforesaid Palladius had intimated that they had made some offensive statements.

21] The secretary, following the deputy, as had been arranged, came to Tripolis. As soon as Romanus learned of this, with all speed he sent his attendant thither, and with him an adviser of his, Caecilius by name, a native of that province. Through these all the towns-people were induced — whether by bribes or deceit is uncertain — to make grave charges against Jovinus, positively declaring that they had given him no commission to report what he had reported to the emperor. In fact, their dishonesty went so far that even Jovinus himself was forced to endanger his own life by confessing that he had lied to the emperor.

22] When this was known through Palladius, who had now returned,[12] Valentinian, being rather inclined to severity, gave orders that Jovinus, as the originator of the false statement, with Caelestinus, Concordius, and Lucius as accomplices and participants, should suffer capital punishment; further, that Ruricius, the governor, should suffer death as the author of a false report, the following also being counted against him — that there were read in his report certain expressions of his which seemed immoderate.

23] Ruricius was executed at Sitifis, the rest were punished at Utica through sentence of the deputy-governor Crescens. Flaccianus, however, before the death of the other envoys, was heard by the deputy and the general; and when he stoutly defended his life, he was all but killed by the angry soldiers, who rushed upon him with shouts and abusive language; for they declared against him that the Tripolitani could not possibly be defended for the reason that they themselves had declined to furnish what was necessary for the campaign.

24] And for this reason Flaccianus was imprisoned, until the emperor, who had been consulted about him, should make up his mind what ought to be done. But he bribed his guards — so it was permissible to believe — and made his escape to the city of Rome, where he kept in hiding until he passed away by a natural death.

25] In consequence of this remarkable end of the affair, Tripolis, though harassed by disasters from without and from within, remained silent, but not without defence; for the eternal eye of Justice watched over her, as well as the last curses of the envoys and the governor. For long afterwards[13] the following event came to pass: Palladius was dismissed from service, and stript of the haughtiness with which he swelled and retired to a life of inaction.

26] And when Theodosius, that famous leader of armies, had come into Africa to put an end to the dangerous attempts of Firmus, and, as he had been ordered, examined the moveable property of the outlawed Romanus, there was found also among his papers the letter of one Meterius, containing the words, "Meterius to Romanus his Lord and patron," and at the end, after much matter that would here be irrelevant: "The disgraced Palladius salutes you, and says that he was deposed for no other reason than that in the cause of the people of Tripolis he spoke to the sacred ears what was not true."

27] When this letter had been sent to the Palace and read, Meterius, on being seized by order of Valentinian, admitted that the letter was his. Therefore Palladius was ordered to be produced, but thinking of the mass of crimes that he had concocted, at a halting-station, as darkness was coming on, noticing the absence of the guards, who on a festal day of the Christian religion were spending the whole night in church, he knotted a noose about his neck and strangled himself.

28] When this favourable turn of fortune was fully known and the instigator of the awful troubles put to death, Erechthius and Aristomenes, who, when they learned that it had been ordered that their tongues should be cut out, as over-lavishly used, had withdrawn to far remote and hidden places, now hastened from concealment; and when the emperor Gratian — for Valentinian had died — was given trustworthy information of the abominable deception, they were sent for trial to the proconsul Hesperius and the deputy Flavianus. These officials, being men of impartial justice combined with most rightful authority, having put Caecilius to the torture, learned from his open confession that he himself had persuaded his citizens to make trouble for the envoys by false statements. This investigation was followed by a report, which disclosed the fullest confirmation of the acts which had been committed; to this no reply was made.

29] And that these dramas should leave no awful tragic effect untried, this also was added after the curtain had dropped. Romanus, setting out to the Palace, brought with him Caecilius, who intended to accuse the judges of having been biased in favour of the province;

and being received with favour by Merobaudes, he had sought that some more witnesses whom he needed should be produced.

30] When these had come to Milan, and had shown by credible evidence that they had been brought there under false pretences to satisfy a grudge, they were discharged and returned to their homes. Nevertheless, in Valentinianus' lifetime, in consequence of what we have stated above, Remigius also after retiring into private life strangled himself, as I shall show in the proper place.[14]

NOTES

1. A.D. 368–370.
2. A.D. 370–372.
3. A Greek hermit who purified Athens in 596 B.C.
4. These proper names betray the base origin of their holders even though they are high-sounding.
5. Castor and Pollux.
6. A verbose imperial biographer writing in the early third century.
7. Perhaps a pun, since *tesserarii* means both "dice players" and "officers of the day."
8. Stock comedy characters proverbial for their humility and obsequiousness.
9. A.D. 363–364.
10. Modern Tripoli.
11. A.D. 365.
12. A.D. 370.
13. A.D. 376.
14. Romanus escaped punishment.